101 Longeing & Long Lining Exercises:

English & Western

Cherry Hill

Illustrations by Richard Klimesh

Howell Book House
New York

Also by Cherry Hill

Longeing and Long Lining the English and Western Horse

Advanced English Exercises

Advanced Western Exercises

101 Arena Exercises

The Formative Years

Horseowner's Guide to Lameness (with Dr. Ted S. Stashak)

Maximum Hoof Power (with Richard Klimesh)

Beginning English Exercises

Beginning Western Exercises

Horse for Sale

Horsekeeping on a Small Acreage

Making Not Breaking

Horse Handling and Grooming

Intermediate English Exercises

Intermediate Western Exercises

Becoming an Effective Rider

From the Center of the Ring

Horse Health Care

Your Pony, Your Horse

To Richard, my book buddy

Howell Book House
A Simon & Schuster Macmillan Company
1633 Broadway
New York, NY 10019

MACMILLAN is a registered trademark of Macmillan, Inc.

Book design Nick Anderson
Cover design Michele Laseau

Library of Congress Cataloging-in-Publication data available on request.

Manufactured in the United States of America

10 9 8 7

Contents

Introduction

Ground training exercises are a blend of discipline, gymnastics, mental development, and dancing. They are essential links to all future training and riding.

The exercises in this book are organized by groups and presented in their approximate order of difficulty. Depending on your horse's level and style of training and his natural abilities and inherent problems, however, you might find some of the elementary exercises challenging and some of the advanced exercises easy.

Remember, the quality of the performance is much more important than just getting through the exercise!

I cannot stress this enough. Take your time and do the simple things well before you tackle more complex maneuvers and patterns. First, study the exercises in your favorite chair and walk through them in your mind until they are going smoothly before you head out to the arena. That way you will reap the great benefits of pre-performance visualization.

Even if you don't plan to perform the exercises in a particular section, due to tack or facility restrictions, be sure to read all the material in this book. It is presented in a progressive fashion and you will need to absorb it all in order to design your own personal training program.

Please read *Longeing and Long Lining the English and Western Horse* for a thorough understanding of horse behavior and learning, training principles, tack, and the ground training progression. That book provides the theory and explanation for the exercises in this one, and contains over 250 photos of horses learning many of the exercises described here. Its Recommended Reading section lists other books you might want to consult.

As you set goals for yourself and your horse, remember that expression and attitude are more important than mechanics. When you work your horse on the longe line, aim to develop his gaits so that they are pure and unhurried but have plenty of energy from the hindquarters. If you allow a horse to rush or work with an uneven or impure rhythm, it will carry over to his saddle work. Influencing the tempo of a horse's gaits on the longe line is one of the most difficult aspects of longeing. You must encourage energy and action from the horse by

---

The Successful Training Session

For a successful training session, follow these guidelines:

- Turn the horse out for free exercise before the lesson.
- Warm up the horse with grooming and in-hand work.
- Start the lesson with something that the horse knows well.
- Be sure he is mentally and physically warmed up when you introduce the new work.
- Allow time for rest breaks, review periods, and a good cool down.
- Always try to end on a good note to preserve your horse's self-esteem.

6

using your body language and the whip, while at the same time containing him with the action of your body and the longe line.

Obedience and the impulsion and purity of the gaits are the most important aspects of early longeing. Only after the horse has learned to be cooperative and move forward with energy and a consistent rhythm would you attempt to introduce the bridle and side reins.

How can you tell whether the work is progressing correctly?

1. Watch your horse from the center of your longe ring. Note rhythm, carriage, balance, frame, and relaxation.
2. Evaluate your own stance and movement and delivery of the aids.
3. Work regularly with a qualified instructor or trainer and ask for periodic evaluations. (See the Recommended Reading list, mentioned-above, for books on how to select and work with an instructor.)
4. Solicit the observational skills of a person experienced in ground training who can objectively report to you what he or she sees happening.
5. Have someone record your training sessions on videotape. Then watch the tape carefully with slow motion and freeze frame.

Develop a feel and a sense for when things are going right and when they are going wrong by answering the following questions:

- Is there appropriate left to right balance in my horse? Or is he overbent to the inside or counterflexed to the outside of the circle?
- Do I feel a mental connection with the horse

Ground Training Commands

Here's my repertoire of ground training commands:

"Walk on!" Higher pitch on "Walk" and great inflection variation—used to start a horse from a standstill.

"Ta-rot!" Higher pitch on "Ta," great inflection variation—used to trot a horse from a walk. When a horse is trotting, don't use the "Ta-rot" command; instead, adjust the trot with "Easy" or "Trot on" (described later in this list).

"Waaaaaaalk" Drawling, soothing tone—used to bring a horse down to a walk from a trot or canter.

"Trrrrahhhht" Low pitch with little inflection variation—used to bring a horse down to a trot from a canter/lope.

"Whoa" An abrupt "wo" with low pitch and punctuated end—used to stop a horse from any gait. Not to be used in a soothing, drawling manner (that would be "Easy"), as you want a prompt stop.

"Eeeee-asy" A soothing, drawn-out, middle-tone command—used for slowing a horse down within a gait or generally just calming a horse.

"Let's Go!" An energetic, brisk command with accent and rising inflection on the "Go!"—used for getting the horse to canter or lope. Many people use "Can-ter!"

"Trot On" Very similar in sound to "Ta-rot," except spoken with more even inflection and in a more medium tone—designed to get a horse who is trotting in a lazy manner to trot forward with more energy.

"Baaaack" Another soothing, drawn-out word in low, even tones—used during in-hand and long lining work to back a horse.

"Tuuuurrrrrrn" A melodic, circular command that starts out on a relatively high pitch and has a round, falling inflection—used to change the horse's direction when free longeing or longeing on a line with a cavesson or halter.

"OK" spoken just like you would if someone asked you, "Would you hand me that bridle?" and you say, "OK, I will." I use it with canter, "OK, Let's Go!" and whoa, "OK, Whoa." This way the transitions are not so abrupt, the horse has a bit of time to prepare.

"Uh!" A warning/reprimand noise that lets the horse know that you can see he is about to make a mistake, such as when he's rushing at the trot, almost ready to break into a canter. This just gets the horse's attention focused more on you.

"Goooood," "Good Boy," "Good Girl" Spoken with all the pleasure and pride you feel when your horse has done something particularly well. Use praise but don't overuse it.

through the longe line? Or is his attention elsewhere?

- Is the front to rear balance acceptable or is the horse heavy on the forehand, croup up, back hollow?
- Is the horse's rhythm regular or does he speed up, slow down, or break gait?
- Is the horse relaxed or is he tense?
- If using a bit, is he on the bit, or above it or behind it?
- Is the horse cantering/loping on the correct lead?
- Is he performing a four-beat lope or canter?
- Is he trotting so slowly as to be walking in front and trotting behind?
- Is he rushing at the walk and performing a pacey walk?

In most of the exercises in this book, the illustration indicates work in one direction only. Be sure to perform every exercise in *both* directions until the performance is equal. This will help prevent one-sidedness in your horse and allow you to become more ambidextrous.

When your horse is ready to move out of a small training pen, conduct the sessions in a large area so the horse is not being held in position by round pen or arena rails. The true test of the training will come when you correctly perform these exercises in an unenclosed flat spot in your pasture!

Although it might seem that some exercises are more appropriate for a Western horse and others for an English horse, all horses can benefit from all the exercises. The "bound up" dressage horse can be loosened up by some of the traditionally Western-style exercises. And the Western horse that is a little heavy on the forehand can benefit from the proper form and collection inherent in the English exercises. So, I invite you to experiment and improvise.

How many times should you repeat an exercise? This can vary from once or twice to infinity. With lead changes and backing, repetition often causes boredom and dullness and invites anticipation problems. Such maneuvers are best saved for the portion of the training session when the horse is thoroughly warmed up and prepared. Then you can ask for a few of these more advanced maneuvers. Transitions and circles, however, are the mainstay of your horse's training program and should be repeated often.

What to do when things go wrong?

1. Review each component of an exercise. Refer to *Longeing and Long Lining* for tack and training theory.
2. It may be necessary for you to return to some in-hand exercises to establish forward movement, acceptance of contact, or response to positioning aids. You will often find that returning to simple work will give a horse confidence and improve his ability to understand the more complex exercises.
3. Perform an exercise that the horse does very well, such as the walk-trot-walk transition. Work on purity and form. Don't think you are wasting your time because it would surprise you to know how few horse owners can perform this simple exercise perfectly.
4. Perform a simpler version of the exercise. If it is a canter pattern, try it at a walk or trot first.
5. Perform the exercise in the opposite direction. Sometimes, because of an inherent stiffness or crookedness in a horse, you will have difficulty with an exercise to the left but no problems to the right. Capitalize on this by refining your skills and the application of your aids in the "good direction" and then return to the "hard direction" with a renewed sense of what needs to be done. I often find that when I do work to the right, it improves work to the left.
6. By all means, if something is not working, do not repeat it over and over. Try something different!

VOICE COMMANDS

Along with body language (see Free Longeing), voice commands help you communicate with your horse. Carry-overs from a horse's in-hand work to longeing and long lining are the voice commands for "Walk," "Trot," "Whoa," and "Back."

Voice commands will be your link between longeing and riding. Since the body language you use during longeing won't carry over when you are in the saddle, it's nice to have a well-established set of voice commands to use during a horse's first lessons under saddle. Particularly useful for first rides are "Whoa," "Easy," and "Walk on," so be sure to make a strong connection with these helpful commands.

To be effective, a particular voice command should be consistent each time it is used. It should be consistent in tone, inflection, volume, and of course, the word used.

Tone refers to the pitch of your voice, high and shrill or low and deep. It makes sense to use a higher pitched voice to encourage a horse to move faster and a lower voice to slow him down or command him to stop.

Inflection is the way your voice modulates as you speak a word or phrase. It is the rise and fall or singsong quality of your voice. The emphasis given to a command can be crisp or drawling. A drawn-out command is soothing; a sharp command is a reprimand.

By using a high pitch and a great variation in inflection in "Ta-rot!" you sound as though you want the horse to move crisply forward.

Using a low pitch, a falling inflection with very little modulation variation works well for "Whoa."

As for volume, it is not necessary or productive to shout commands at your horse. Horses have quite a good sense of hearing. They can hear commands in quite low volumes. In fact, the "breaking patter" of experienced trainers is often just a muttering under the breath that human bystanders might not even be able to decipher but the horse understands clearly.

The word you choose to use for each voice command is really more significant for you than it is for the horse since you know what a word means but to the horse it is just a particular sound. It is okay if you choose to use nontraditional words for your voice commands, but try to choose words that are very different from each other and that "sound" like what you want the horse to do. Decide ahead of time which words you will use as longeing commands, and practice on a tape recorder until you perfect them.

Terms Used in Ground Training Exercises

Track right Working along the rail clockwise, making right turns. Sometimes it's confusing because when you come in the gate, you have to turn left to track right.

Track left Working along the rail counterclockwise, making left turns.

Stride One complete revolution of the horse's legs in the footfall pattern of the gait in which he is performing.

Step One beat in a gait. There are several steps in each stride. A step may involve more than one leg.

Inside Inside refers to the inside of the bend of the horse's body, which usually is also the inside of the round pen, circle, or arena. For example, when tracking to the right with normal bend, the inside is the right, which is the side toward the inside of the circle and the trainer. Outside is left.

Outside Outside generally refers to the outside of the bend of the horse's body, which usually is also the outside of the circle.

Metric Equivalents

Meters	Feet
6	20
8	26.5
10	33
20	66
40	132
60	198

Average Length of Stride at Various Gaits

Gait	Length of Stride in Feet
Working Walk	5.5
Collected Walk	5.0
Extended Walk	6.0
Working Trot	8.0 +
Collected Trot	7.0
Extended Trot	10.0
Working Canter	10.0
Collected Canter	8.0
Extended Canter	12.0

Horses vary greatly in their stride lengths, so the preceding and following information is average, approximate. It takes:

26 strides to trot a 20-meter (66-foot) diameter circle. (207-foot circumference)
13 strides to trot a 10-meter (33-foot) diameter circle. (103-foot circumference)

To work 50 feet down the long side, it takes:

9 strides at a working walk.
6 to 7 strides at a working trot.
5 strides at an extended trot.
5 to 6 strides at a working canter.

The horses and trainers in these exercise illustrations are not drawn to the scale of the arena or round pen. They are larger, for clarity of detail. It is suggested that all exercises be conducted in a 66-foot (20-meter) round pen and a 100-foot × 200-foot arena.

Start	➡
Trainer Path	· · · · · · · · · · · · · · · ·
Horse—Walk	— — — — — —
Horse—Trot (Jog)	— · — · — · —
Horse—Canter (Lope)	⌢⌢⌢⌢⌢⌢⌢
Halt	|

PART ONE

In-Hand Work

In-hand work is much more than getting a horse from point A to point B. It requires the development of physical skills by both horse and trainer. There must also be a mental connection between the horse and trainer for the lessons to progress well. In-hand work includes approaching, catching, haltering, handling the head, leading, turning, stopping, standing, backing, and much more.

There are certain exercises you should practice without your horse so that you become proficient with the ground training equipment and necessary body language.

As you progress through these exercises, choose movements that are natural and easy for you. Tailor the aids you will use to your own physique and personal training style.

When you begin the in-hand work with the horse, take the time to get really solid responses. It is much better to do simple things well than to bumble through advanced exercises in poor form. Take the time here. It will pay off.

In-hand work is suitable for any horse two months of age and older. (For more information refer to *Longeing and Long Lining*.)

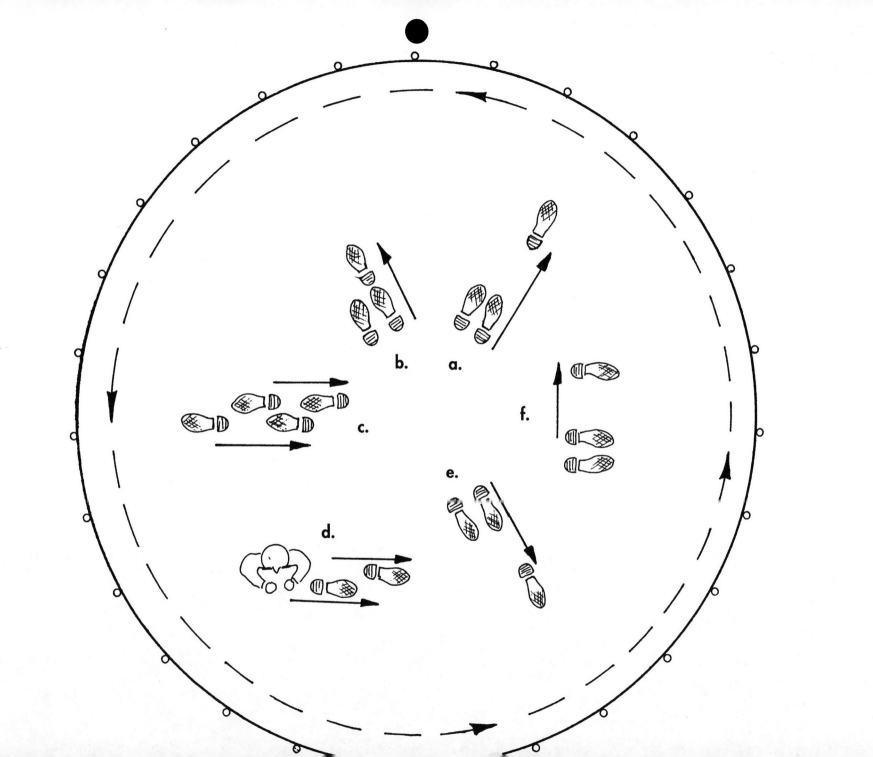

Fancy Footwork

If you practice the footwork necessary for ground training ahead of time, you will have a better chance of reacting appropriately when you have an untrained horse in front of you.

You generally have a driving foot and a restraining foot. The driving foot is the one nearest to the horse's hindquarters. When a horse tracks left, it would be your right foot. Your restraining foot is nearest the head. When a horse tracks left, it would be your left foot. Either foot can be used to push the horse sideways or out onto a larger circle.

a. When you want to cause a horse to move forward, at first you might have to step assertively toward the horse with your driving foot. I call this the "lunge" step because you are lunging forward as you would if you were fencing. Such a large step gets the horse's attention and scoots him forward. The size of your movement should always be tailored to the desired reaction and the nature of the horse you are training.

b. Later in the horse's training, your steps become subtler because the horse has learned what the larger steps ask for. These normal steps are the size steps you take unconsciously.

c. You will need to learn how to adeptly and safely back up while working your horse. In some cases, a horse will feel crowded and the only way you will be able to get the response you want from him is by giving him more room. Because you will be backing up while facing the horse, you must be sure to never leave tack or equipment where you could trip on it.

d. In the early stages of longeing, especially with a longe line, you might need to work in a concentric circle with the horse's working circle. (See Exercise 31.) This means you will need to face the horse to maintain contact and communication but your feet will, in effect, be walking at a 90-degree angle to your body. This takes a bit of twisting and physical coordination. You are essentially looking one way and walking another. Again, it's essential that you work on safe footing, with no tack or equipment to tangle your feet.

e. When you stop a horse, you usually will take a step toward the horse's shoulder with your restraining foot. This can be a "lunge" or it can be a normal step, depending on the stage of the horse's training.

f. When a horse is really scooting forward, you may have to precede your forward step with a sideways lunge so that you can in effect "get a little ahead of the horse." In extreme circumstances, when a horse is really racing around a pen and a sideways lunge won't "catch" him in time, you will need to turn around 180 degrees and "head him off at the pass."

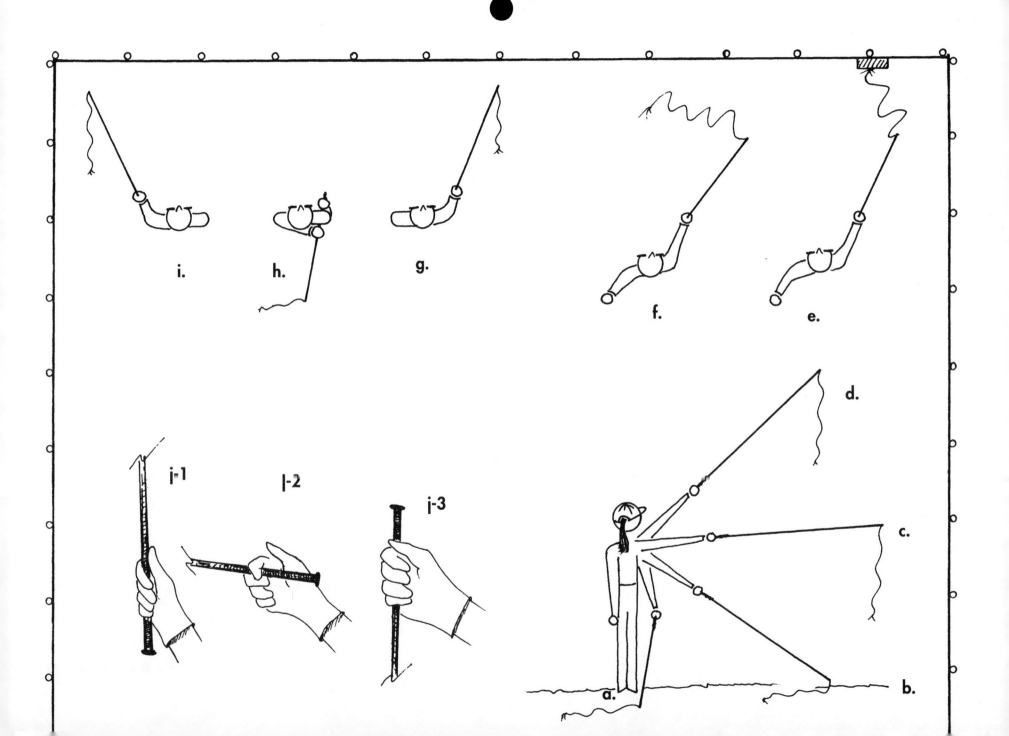

Whip Works

You should always know where your whip is and what it is saying because your horse will be watching it closely. A voice command should always precede a whip aid. A whip should not be a threat or instrument of abuse but rather a communication aid. Sometimes your signals might need to be "more vocal": large movements—even some cracking—and possibly contact with a horse who does not move forward. But as with all aids, you constantly refine and hone the use of the whip until your movements are quite small. In fact, many horses perform their complete longeing repertoire from subtle body language and a few quiet voice commands.

a. We are looking at the trainer's back. When a whip is held behind your back with the tip facing 180 degrees away from the horse, it is in a very neutral position. The whip is not telling the horse to do anything. You can also tuck the whip under your arm (as in Exercise **5-f**), tail facing behind you, for a neutral whip.

b. When the whip is held out to your side at about 45 degrees below the horizontal, the horse is aware of the whip but the signal is mild. This is what I use for the walk. In this case, since the whip is in the right hand, the horse would be traveling to the left.

c. When held out to the side approximately on the horizontal, the presence of the whip is more noticeable to the horse. This is the position I use for an active trot.

d. When held above the horizontal, the whip appears to be "over" the horse and just that fact makes it a stronger driving aid. This is the position I use for canter or lope. To initiate a prompt canter or lope, you might need to use a crack (**f**). To maintain a canter, you might move the whip in a rolling, circular way that makes an eerie wind sound.

e. Inevitably, there will be an occasion when you will want to actually contact the horse with the end of the whip's lash. If you pop the horse right over the tail head/croup, it often causes the horse to drop the croup (squat), which drives the hind legs under the horse and makes him move forward. If you pop the horse on his legs, it could cause him to kick backward. If you pop the horse on the belly, it usually drives him out and forward. The croup/tail head area is the most appropriate place to apply the whip to get a horse to move forward. Ahead of time, make sure that you can hit a 3-inch target. Tack the plastic lid from a large yogurt container on your training pen rail and practice hitting it.

f. The popping or cracking of a whip should be saved as your "ace in the hole." When you need to move a horse forward but he is too far away to actually reach with the whip, usually a snap of the whip will cause the horse to move forward more energetically. Like anything else, it takes practice to get a nice, sharp, clean crack! If you overuse the noise aspect of a whip, it will not only drive your friends to distraction but also make your horse immune to it and you will have lost an effective aid.

g. When you change the direction in which a horse is working, you will need to change the whip from one hand to another. If you do this haphazardly, you will be giving the horse all kinds of signals that neither of you wants or needs. Here's a method that keeps things organized and low key. To begin with, the horse is traveling to the left because you have the whip in your right hand.

h. Rotate the whip in your hand (see the **j** series) so that it is facing behind you. Tuck the whip under your right arm. With your left arm, reach behind your back and take the whip from your right side.

i. Rotate the whip in your left hand so that it is facing forward. (See **i** series in reverse.) Practice this until it comes smoothly and quickly because you will need it in upcoming exercises that contain a reverse.

j-1 This is a close-up of the whip in your right hand. The whip is facing forward, pointed toward the horse.

j-2 Let the tip of the whip drop down; the butt of the whip will rotate upward. Let it turn between your index and middle fingers. (If you are short and/or your whip is long, you will have to rotate your hand sideways when doing this so that the tip of the whip will clear the ground.)

j-3 Now the butt of the whip is facing backward, away from the horse.

See exercises 5, 8, and 33 for more on using the whip.

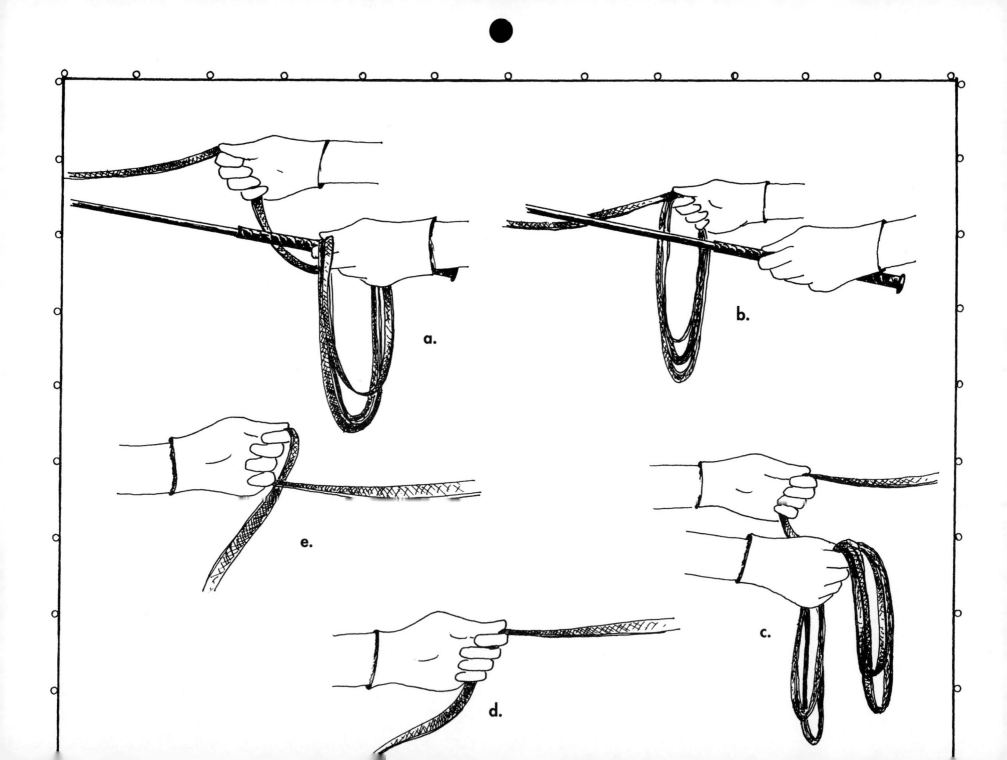

a.

b.

c.

d.

e.

Getting a Grip

Your longe line provides you with the means to control the gait, speed, and form of your horse's movement. Depending on how you hold it and use it, you can send your horse quite a variety of messages.

a. The most common way to hold a longe line and whip is to hold the line that is attached to the horse in one hand (right, when the horse is tracking right) and the balance of the line and the whip in the other hand (left). In this drawing, although the balance of the line is coiled neatly, it is coiled, which means that if the horse suddenly pulled the line it could zip through the fingers and trap the hand in a tightened loop. This possibility is complicated by the presence of the whip in the same hand as the loop.

b. Here is an alternative for a more experienced trainer. The line is held in one hand and the whip in the other. Although it is still dangerous because of the loops, it would be a little easier to drop the line here than in the previous example. The horse is tracking right.

c. The safest way to hold the excess line is to make a neat figure-8. Then if the line were suddenly pulled, provided the figure-8 was organized, you could let each layer out, one at a time, and (theoretically) have no fingers in the loops. The best way to decide which method is safest for you is to practice.

d. How the hand holds the line that is directly attached to the horse determines the type of conversation you will have. With the "feeling" hold, the line enters the hand between the thumb and index finger and exits at the bottom of the hand near the little finger. The communication here is a sensitive feel but not a very secure hold. If the horse pulled, you'd have little chance of holding onto the line.

e. With the "power" hold, the line enters the bottom of the hand and exits the top. This is a control grip because the right angle the line makes in your hand gives you much more leverage than the straight-line configuration in **d.**

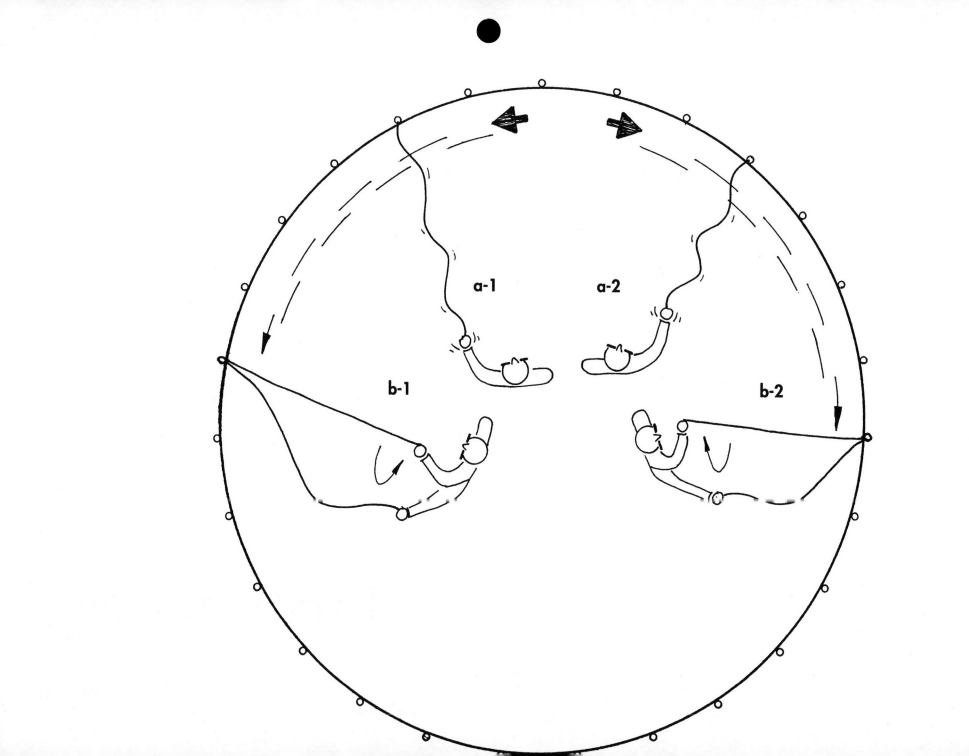

Slow Wave and Tidal Wave

Y ou will need to develop a vocabulary with the longe line so that you can indicate to your horse when he should slow down, change gaits, or stop.

a. **Slow Wave**   When you want to slow a horse down, calm him, or quietly change gait from a trot to a walk, for example, you would use a slow wave. A slow wave can range from a vibration to a tremor to a jiggle to a wiggle. You will need to choose the intensity that is necessary to get the results required. In **a-1**, the horse is tracking left and a gentle wave is cast in the line held in the trainer's left hand. An appropriate voice command should also be used. In **a-2**, the horse is tracking right.

b. **Tidal Wave**   A more assertive use of the line is the tidal wave. This is appropriate when the horse is racing or bolting and not listening. The tidal wave is most effective if you first pitch some slack forward in the line and then pop the line backward with a snap. You are in effect letting the line get ahead of the horse, "leading him on." Then your backward pull on the line will have an even greater effect. In **b-1**, the horse is tracking left. The trainer puts slack in the line, getting a bit ahead of the horse if possible, and then swiftly pulls back on the line with a sharp jerk. This will either get the horse to shift gears downward a notch or two or could stop the horse dead in his tracks. In **b-2**, the horse is tracking right. There are many variations of line use between the slow wave and the tidal wave.

Refer to Exercise 68, Long Line Lingo, to learn more line talk.

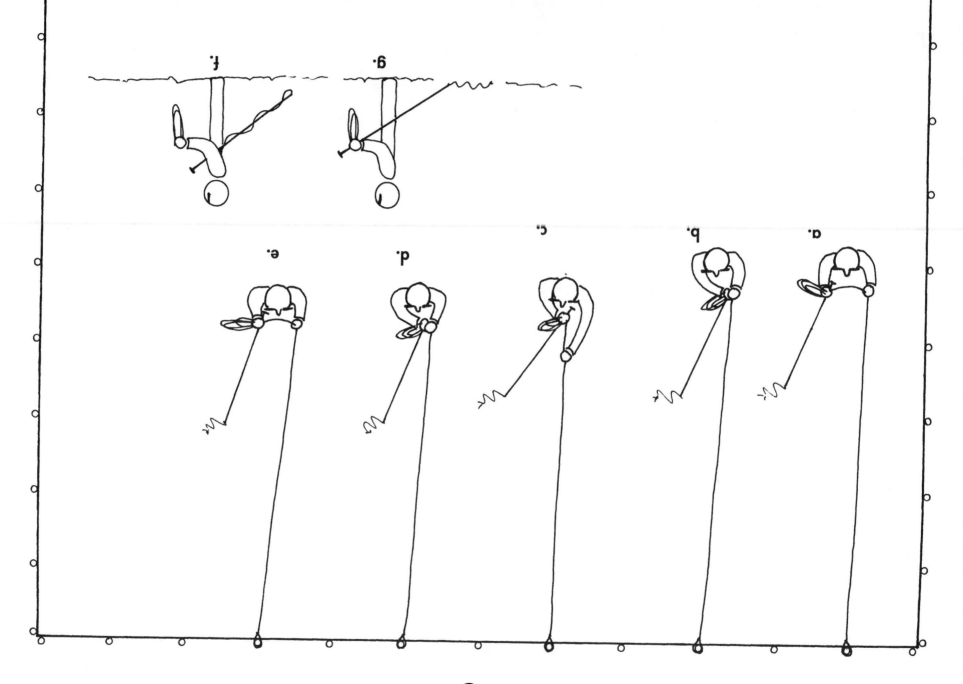

Exercise 5

Becoming Well Adjusted

As you work your horse on longe and long lines, you will constantly be changing the length of the lines. You do this to retain a steady contact with the horse. As you work on circles and spirals of various sizes, you will need to draw in the lines and let them out. Develop a method that is systematic, effective, and safe. Practice by attaching your longe line to the fence, using some elastic cord so that you can develop a "feel."

When you make a line adjustment, if you leave the whip pointing forward you can make the adjustment quickly, and the whip presents a visual driving aid to the horse. There is a lot to keep track of in your hands, however.

a. If you are holding the line in your left hand (horse tracking left) and you have the balance of the line and the whip in your right hand, this is how to proceed.

b. Bring your right hand over to your left hand and momentarily hold the line, the loop, and the whip in your right hand. This requires some coordination and practice. Be sure to maintain contact with the horse.

c. Reach forward with your left arm as far as it will comfortably extend on the line.

d. Bring the slack back toward your right hand. Give the extra new loop to your right hand.

e. Move your right hand back to its normal position.

f. If your horse has good impulsion, and you don't need the whip for a visual cue, you can tuck the whip under your arm, with the tip facing backward while you make the line adjustments.

g. If you feel a forward pointing whip would flop around and confuse the horse or give him unwanted signals, hold the whip in your right hand but pointing backward as you adjust your lines.

Exercise 6

Head Down

If you can't control a horse's head, you can't control the horse. You should be able to handle the horse's head all over without him raising his head, tossing it, or trying to pull away.

First assess your horse's tolerance for head handling. Handle his ears, mouth, and forelock and note his reaction. If he doesn't just stand there and love it, you have some work to do.

You can start this whole procedure by using a halter and lead rope with a chain over the horse's nose, and progress to just a halter and lead rope and then to no tack. Or you can start with no tack right from the beginning. The choice will depend on your experience and the level of the horse's handling.

Standing on the near side, place your left hand on the bridge of his nose and your right hand on his poll. You are going to do several things simultaneously. With the index and middle fingers of your right hand, you are going to press the bony prominence at his poll. With your left hand you are going to exert some intermittent pressure on the bridge of his nose.

In both instances, the application of pressure should not turn into a wrestling match. You won't win. What you need to do is apply pressure and release; pressure and release. You don't want to apply heavy, steady pressure because the horse will push *into* the pressure. Instead, you want to apply intermittent pressure, which is much more effective at breaking up resistance and softening a horse.

Another technique that helps soften is to gently wag the horse's head back and forth from left to right, just about 1/2 inch in each direction. This is more effective than just pressing down on the horse's nose with your left hand.

Try to coordinate your aids. Poll pressure, a little nose wag, release. As you feel your horse respond, increase the sideways wag toward you so that eventually the horse lowers his head and brings it slightly to the left, toward you when you are on the near side.

As with all exercises, be sure to do this one from the off side as well. You might be surprised at how inept you feel working on a horse's off side. It is best if you work on becoming ambidextrous right from the beginning; otherwise your lack of smoothness will show up in more advanced ground training and riding.

a.

b.

Exercise 7

Soft Neck

Almost all the work in this book consists of circling. You can imagine how impossible it would be to attempt these exercises if your horse were stiff and wouldn't bend. You can go a long way toward success in bending with this exercise and exercises 29, *Turn on the Long Line,* and 52, *Introducing the Bridle.* These preliminary exercises show the horse that he *can* bend, and in a relaxed manner.

Once you have taught your horse to put his head down (Exercise 6), *Soft Neck* should come easily. It is actually a softening of the poll, throatlatch, and neck that is the goal here.

As with the head down lesson, I prefer to hold this lesson in a box stall or small pen with the horse wearing no tack. Standing on the near side, lower the horse's head as described in Exercise 6. Remove your right hand from the horse's poll but keep your left hand on the bridge of his nose. The horse should not raise his head as long as you have a hand on the bridge of his nose.

As you work on this lesson, your horse's tendency will be to move his hindquarters away from the direction of bend. If you have not taught the horse an absolute whoa yet, you might want to position his body along a stall wall or the rail of your training pen to discourage him from moving his hindquarters away from the bend.

a. For the exercise, you will need to apply aids in a simultaneous and coordinated fashion. Tell the horse whoa. Move the fingers of your left hand slightly more over to the right side of the horse's face. Now, apply light intermittent pressure on the right side of his face, again, in a wagging sort of movement. If you do this and nothing more, your horse will likely bend his head toward you with the movement occurring at the throatlatch. This is good.

Now place your right hand in the middle of the horse's neck and repeat the exercise to ask the horse to bend at his throatlatch and neck without moving his legs or body. You might get better results if you alternate the pressure of your fingertips on the middle of his neck with the pressure of your fingers on the right side of his face.

b. Repeat the exercise from the off side.

If you encounter resistance, you should review the head down lesson. Your horse should have a peaceful expression during these head-handling exercises.

This is designed to be a relaxed, enjoyable exercise that should calm your horse and create a good feeling for both of you.

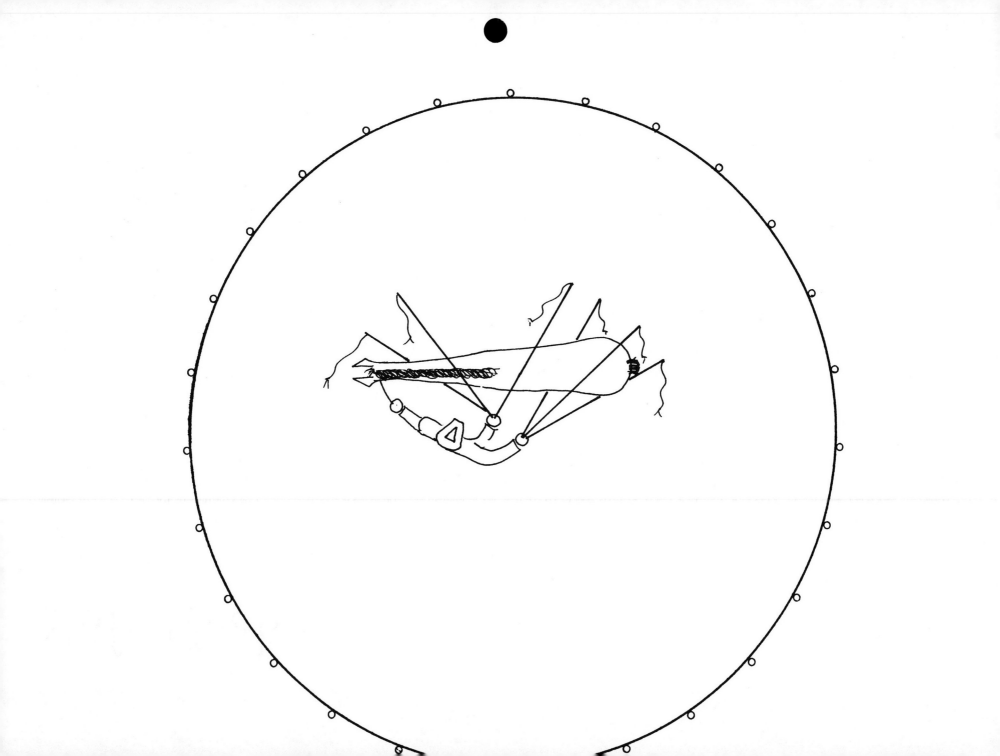

Exercise 8

Whip Sacking

The whip is an aid, not something the horse should fear. Although a horse needs a healthy respect for a whip, he should not be afraid of it or his work will always contain excess, unproductive tension.

You might want to use an assistant for this lesson if you don't feel you will be able to control the horse.

When you "sack out" a horse to an object, you want to gradually desensitize him to it. You want him to eventually be unconcerned about it. To achieve the goal, you don't want to overload the horse's senses. You wouldn't want to snap and pop the whip all over the horse thinking that eventually he will get used to it. What that will do is make him have a life-long association with the whip as monster.

Self-preservation has taught the horse to be wary of unusual motions, sounds, sights, smells, and unfamiliar objects touching him. Setting up a specific group of lessons to help a horse overcome his natural fears will pay off in the long run. When working specifically on building confidence in the horse, never trigger active *resistance*. In other words, do not stimulate him beyond his ability to cope. If you see the horse ready to blow up or flee, ease up and gradually work back up to his current tolerance level. Add more stress on another day.

I feel that it is best never to trigger active resistance from the horse during "sacking out." When a horse actively resists, you have two problems to solve: One is to remove the active resistance and the other is to convince the horse that the whip is not bad. By "active resistance," I mean that the horse moves, tries to leave the county.

Passive resistance is natural and okay at first. It includes raising the head, tensing, opening the eyes wide, and maybe taking a few steps sideways. Eventually, you want passive resistance to disappear too.

To begin, the horse needs to be haltered and on a 10-foot lead line held close to the halter. If necessary, hold the horse along a wall or rail to discourage him from moving sideways away from you and the whip.

Let the horse look at and smell the whip. Then begin rubbing the horse all over with the whip. If you choose to begin on the tip of his nose, his sheath, or his hocks, you will probably get a reaction that you are not looking for. So start instead on the thick muscle masses, such as the neck, shoulder, hindquarters, and then work up to the back. Before you finish, you should be able to stroke any part of the horse's body with the whip from either side.

Show your horse that the whip is nothing to fear. If you skip this step, then the first time the horse sees a long longeing whip behind him he may panic. Once a whip has scared a horse, it is often more difficult to convince him that it is merely a training aid and nothing to fear.

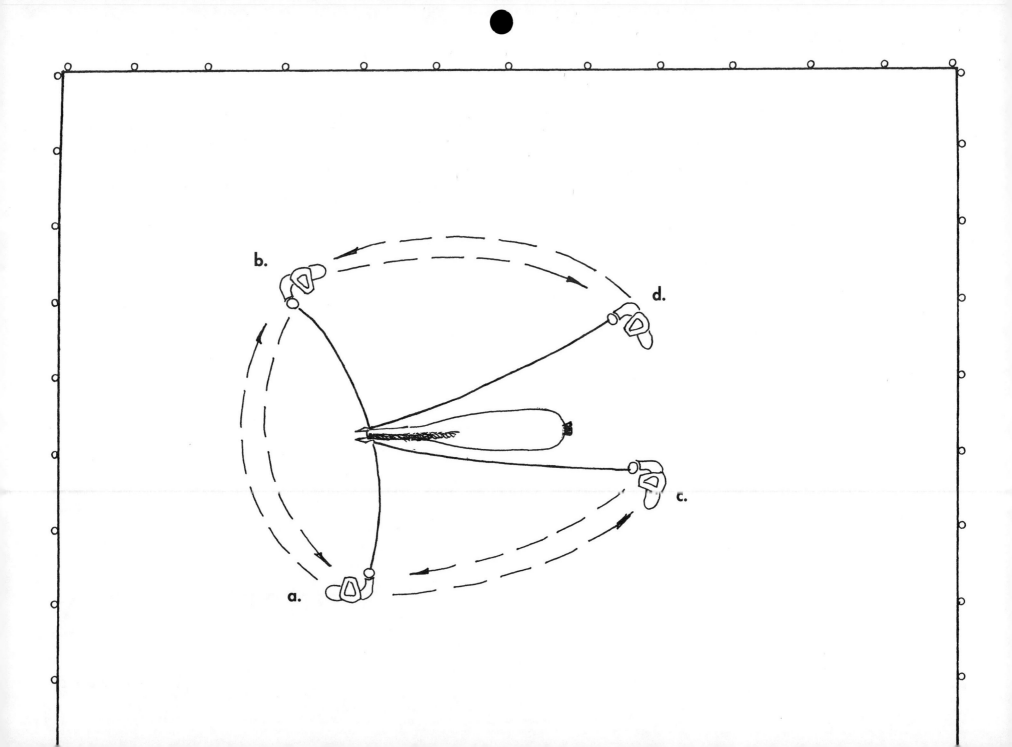

Exercise 9

Whoa on a Long Line

You practice "Whoa" in-hand every time you stop your horse and require him to stand still. But that is with you at his side. You need to teach him that he can stand still even though you are 10 feet away from him in any direction. This will prevent him from moving off prematurely when you are getting set up to longe or long line. It is a good patience and discipline exercise. You might have to perform this lesson over several days, gradually building up the length of time you require the horse to stand.

Start from your normal in-hand position by his shoulder on the near side. Give the voice command, "Whoa," and then step a foot or so away from the horse, but still in the same basic in-hand position.

a. Work your way out on the line until you are about 10 feet from the horse's head. At first you should only expect your horse to stand for a few seconds. If he moves, it will probably be a turn toward you, asking "Are you sure this is what you want me to do?" If that happens, go back to your normal in-hand position, place him back exactly where he was before he moved, tell him "Whoa," and leave him again. This should be a relaxing type of lesson, not forceful or confrontational. If your horse acts as though he is full of jumping beans, perhaps you did not turn him out for free exercise prior to work.

b. Once the horse accepts the idea of standing still without you close, begin to challenge him. Step across his field of vision in the front, and cross from the near side to the off side. You might want to do this at 4 to 6 feet before you try it full out at the 10-foot goal. You might have better luck starting from the in-hand position on the off side, as you did in step a. Return to position a. after the horse has accepted you on the off side.

c. Next you will go to the horse's blind spot at his hindquarters. This is to prepare him for the possibility of the two of you getting in this position during longeing and the certainty that you will be in this position during long lining. Again, start from the in-hand position, say "Whoa," and move to the hindquarters. When you are in the horse's blind spot, you can talk quietly to him so he can "hear" where you are even if he can't see you. The confident horse will accept you back there. The nervous horse will want to turn around and face you. This takes time and patience on your part but there is no better way to spend your time in preparation for long lining. The first time you return to the horse's head, do so by walking out to the side and then walking to his head. Later, you can challenge him by walking straight up to his head from behind, but realize when you do this that you are in a blind alley and all he will sense is motion.

d. Repeat on the off side.

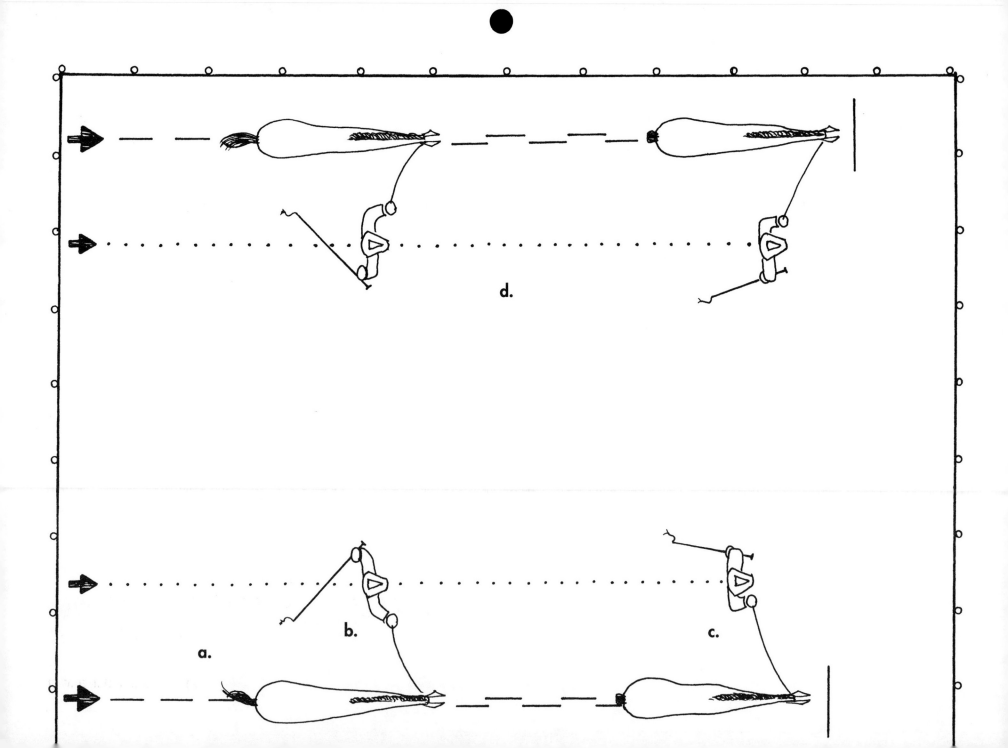

a.

b.

c.

d.

Exercise 10

Walk-Trot-Whoa

To get your horse ready for the sensation of forward motion on a long line, practice regular in-hand maneuvers on a long line. If you can perform this *Walk-Trot-Whoa* exercise with the horse 4 to 6 feet away from you, the first longeing lessons will go more smoothly. First practice on a normal-length lead until the horse is perfect. Then go to 4 to 6 feet.

Hold the lessons in an arena so that you can work the horse along the rail of the long side at first. This will help you keep his body straight. Be sure you are wearing safe, comfortable shoes or boots and are not wearing spurs. Carry a 30- to 40-inch in-hand whip, which usually has only a 2-inch lash. If you do not have an in-hand whip, wrap the long lash of your longeing whip around the shaft of the whip and tie it near the handle.

a. Starting on the near side, walk a few strides along the rail. If you need to, you can push the horse sideways, away from you, with the butt end of the whip.

b. To trot, use your voice command and simultaneously give a little flick of the whip toward the horse's hindquarters and take one or two jog steps in place. This body language is easy for the horse to read and he will respond in kind. When you've trotted several strides, prepare for the halt.

c. Use a preparatory command such as "OK" or "and" while you are lowering the whip and moving it away from the horse. Your body should start to assume the "crouch" position. When you say "Whoa", be sure there is no question in your voice. At the same time you use the final voice command, plant both feet, hinge your knees and crouch a bit. If necessary you will give a tug on the lead rope. Too large a tug will turn the horse toward you, which you do not want. If you have trouble stopping your horse, perform the exercise as Walk-Trot-Walk-Whoa until you feel you can cut out the walk steps before the whoa. Although you can use a chain over his nose for a few lessons to gain control, another way you can

slow down or stop a pushy horse is to get ahead of him and let your body or the whip butt serve as a visual cue to push him into the rail.

d. Repeat the exercise, working from the off side. Unless you work regularly from the off side, you will be surprised at how foreign this feels. Practice off side maneuvers with a trained horse. Many horses and many handlers become "one sided" from lack of work on the off side.

Forward Movement To encourage forward movement, *never* pull on the lead rope to try and urge the horse forward. When leading him at the walk, move forward energetically, as though you have somewhere to go. Look ahead. If the horse lags, encouragement should come from behind in the form of a light tap on the rump from a whip; strive to stay in proper position at the horse's shoulder. When the horse is moving ahead calmly, there should be no pressure on the halter or any contact from the whip.

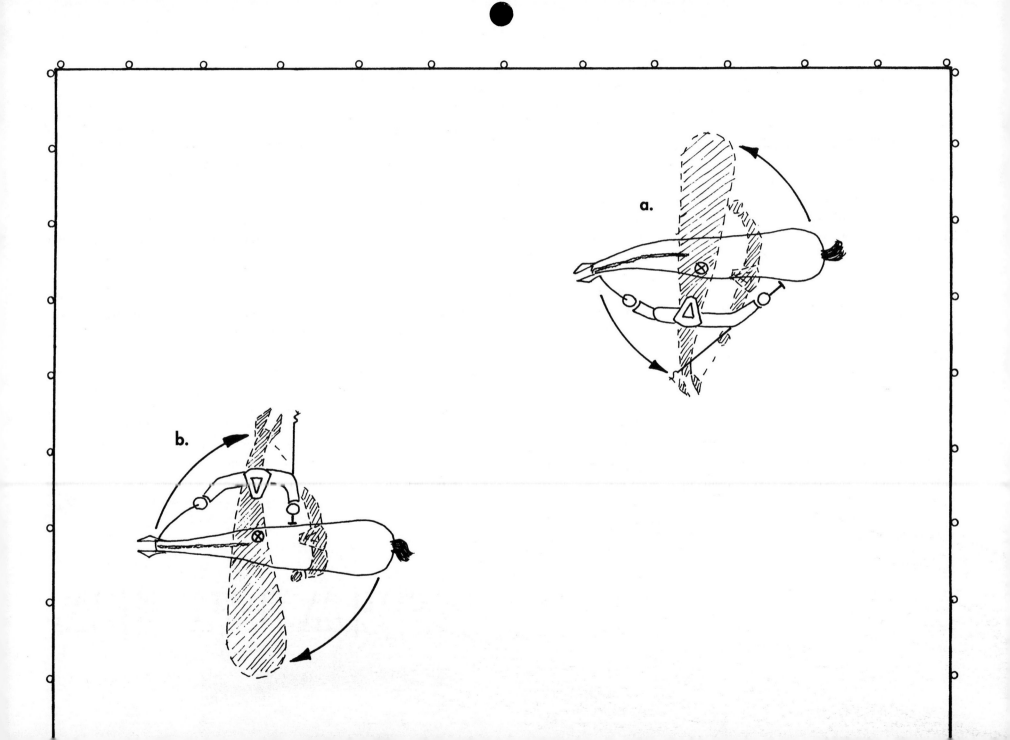

a.

b.

Exercise 11

Turn on the Forehand

You need to be able to position your horse in a variety of ways so that you can set him up prior to longeing and long lining. The turn on the forehand will help you keep the horse from being pushy. It will help you move him away from you when you send him out on the longe line. You have already taught a rudimentary form of the turn on the forehand by moving your horse over when he is tied at the hitch rail for grooming and tacking. He moves his hindquarters in a semicircle while his forehand remains relatively stationary.

a. Working from the near side, stop your horse square. Face the horse's shoulder and hold the lead rope about 8 inches from the halter. Tip your horse's nose slightly toward you. This will weight his left front foot, which is the pivot point for the turn. Using your fingertips or the butt end of your in-hand whip, press his ribs or hip in a light, intermittent fashion.

This will cause the horse to pick up his left hind leg and cross it over and in front of his right hind leg. His next step will be to uncross his right hind leg and step out to the right with it. The hind legs will continue crossing and uncrossing as long as you continue the cues. Meanwhile, the left front leg stays relatively stationary, picking up and setting down in the same spot. The right front leg walks a small semicircle around the left front leg. Teach him to respond to your aid, not fear it or run sideways. One measured step for each pressure on the ribs.

b. The turn on the forehand should also be practiced from the off side.

Note: Some horses (with sensitive reflexes) will curl around a rib cue, which makes them step toward you with their hind legs. This is the oppo-

site of what you want. Alternate spots to cue are the point of the hip and the thigh. To initially show a horse what you want, use one of the alternate spots. Eventually you will want to go back to the rib cue since that will tie in with leg aids when you are riding.

Keep pressure on the halter to prevent the horse from pushing forward, but not so much that it causes the horse to back up. If a horse backs up during a turn on the forehand (a more serious error than walking forward) his legs will cross behind each other rather than in front of each other.

Holding the Lead When performing the turn from the near side, hold the lead rope 6 to 8 inches from the snap with your left hand so you can let rope slide out through your fingers and take up slack by letting your fingers walk the rope. Hold the excess lead rope in a figure-8 in your right hand, as in Exercise 3-**c**.

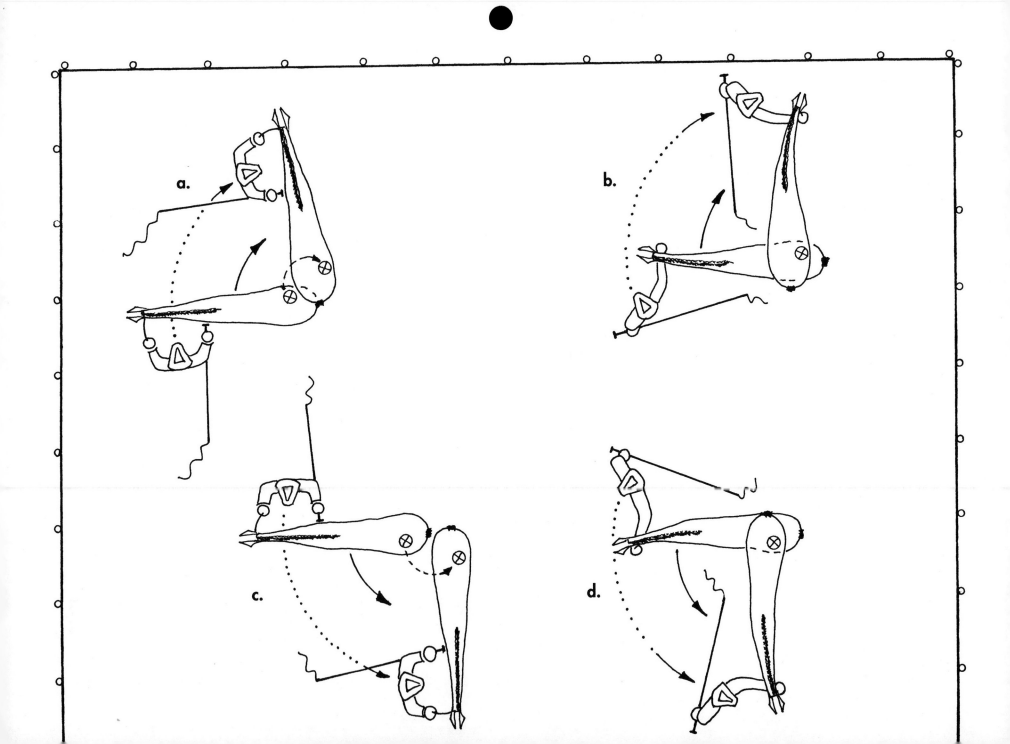

a.

b.

c.

d.

Turn on the Hindquarters

In a turn on the hindquarters, the forehand rotates around the hindquarters. The front feet step a half circle around the hindquarters, specifically around a hind pivot foot or pivot point. In a turn to the right for example, the pivot foot is the right hind. It should bear most of the horse's weight in the turn and be relatively stationary and directly underneath the horse. The left hind walks a tiny half circle around the right hind. The left front leg crosses over and in front of the right front leg, then the right front uncrosses from behind, steps out to the side again, and the sequence is repeated as the front legs move in a semicircle to the right.

a. At first, in a turn on the hindquarters to the right, you can cue the horse on the shoulder to indicate specifically what you want him to do.

Facing the horse's neck, exert a little bit of backward pressure on the halter to settle his weight rearward. Keep his head and neck relatively straight as you apply pressure and release with your fingertips or the whip butt on the point of the horse's shoulder. Walk at the horse and keep his body straight as you rotate his forehand around his hindquarters. His hind feet might walk a small circle rather than rotating on a pivot point or foot. That's okay for the early attempts. Eventually, you want a stationary pivot point (**b**).

b. Now, omit the shoulder cue. Face forward in a more normal in-hand position. Exert pressure back and to the right on the lead rope. Hold the whip parallel to the horse's body to keep him straight.

c. The turn to the left must be performed from the off side. The footfall patterns and aids are reversed. First start facing the horse and use a shoulder cue.

d. Assume the more advanced position and require a pivot foot or point. Take care not to bend the horse in the neck too much; doing so will cause the shoulder to bulge to the right and the hindquarters to swing off the track to the right, and you will lose the pivot point.

Crowd Control If your horse starts to crowd you when you are leading him (this is often a sign of insecurity), tell him to keep his distance by bumping the side of his neck with your elbow.

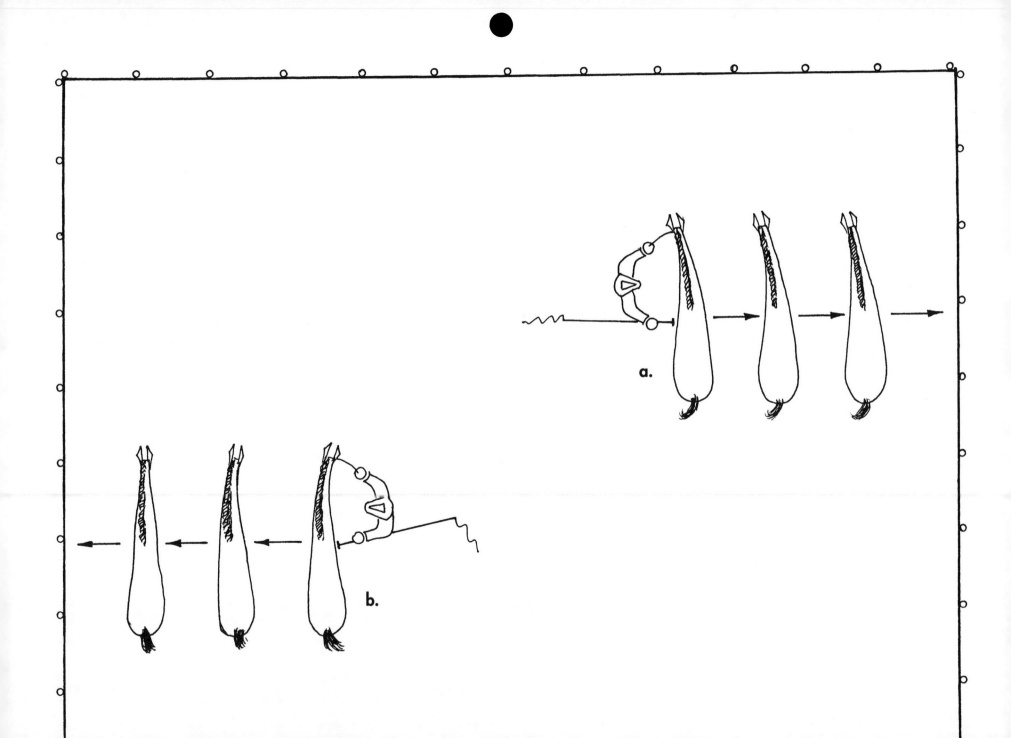

a.

b.

Sidepass

The sidepass in-hand is based on the aids for the turn on the forehand. The difference is that now you want the forehand to move sideways along with the hindquarters.

a. In a sidepass to the right, the horse's head and neck should be straighter than in a turn on the forehand. Especially at first, however, it will be easier if the horse's head is tipped slightly toward you. Your goal is to keep the horse's head in front of his neck and keep his neck anchored securely to his body. You will have to do the "joy stick" adjustment (left-right-back-forward) to keep the body in position. Instead of cueing the horse on the ribs for the sideways movement, as you did for the turn on the forehand, the aid will be applied more at the girth area.

The footfall pattern is two-beat, with the left hind and right front reaching to the right at the same time. Next, the right hind and the left front will step widely to the right. A leg should always cross in front of its partner leg and uncross from behind. This is a valuable exercise for teaching the horse to move his entire body out of a space—handy when you are sending the horse out on the longe line the first time and don't want him to be on top of you!

b. In the sidepass to the left, you must work the horse from the off side. Eventually, the goal is to have the horse's head and neck straight, as in the last stage of **b**.

Stay in position between the horse's head and his shoulder, about an arm's length away. If you use a longer lead, the horse could turn his forehand away from you and his hindquarters toward you. A shorter hold, and you are asking to be stepped on or crowded. Keep your focus forward, alert, yet aware at all times of what the horse is doing.

Variation: Try the exercise over a pole or railroad tie.

What's What and Where Does Sidepass Fit In?

Leg Yield Horse's throatlatch is flexed very slightly away from the direction of travel but his body is straight; horse moves away from the rider's leg or the trainer's ground aid; the line of travel is on a diagonal.

Western Two Step Horse's entire body is bent away from direction of travel; horse moves forward and sideways; the line of travel is on a diagonal.

Sidepass Horse's body is straight or bent slightly away from the direction of travel; full sideways movement.

Half Pass Horse's body is bent into the direction of travel; horse is moving sideways and forward at the same time on a diagonal line.

Full Pass Horse's body is bent into the direction of travel; full sideways movement.

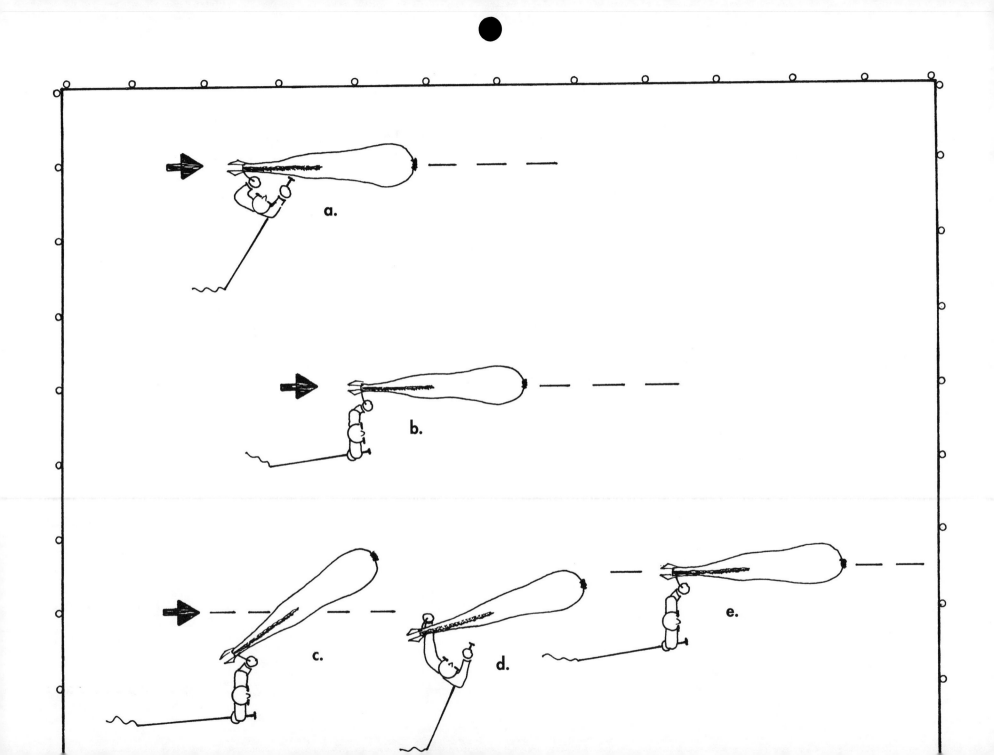

Exercise 14

Back

To teach a horse to back, stop him, turn around, and face the front of his shoulder.

a. When working from the near side, change the lead rope to your left hand. Hold the whip in your right hand, pointing backward. Place the butt end of the whip on the point of the horse's left shoulder. Apply alternate pressure and release to the shoulder point and say, "Baaaack."

The pressure on the shoulder point elicits a reflex action—a natural reaction the horse has when he feels pressure on his shoulder. It is not something you have to teach him.

b. If you try to use halter pressure to teach a horse to back, it usually causes him to raise his head and hollow his back. That is the reflex action to backward pressure on the front of the horse's head. After a horse has learned to back when you use shoulder-point pressure,

however, you can make an association with halter pressure and use it as a "cue" that signals him to back up.

c. When backing from the halter, if the horse's hindquarters start to swing off the path, straighten his body with a slight adjustment of his head position with the lead rope.

d. If his hindquarters start moving off to the right, move his head slightly to the right to align his forehand and hindquarters. You can also point to or touch his shoulder. (If his hindquarters swing left, move his head to the left.)

e. Back a horse only a few strides at a time, and build. Be sure his head stays low and his back level or rounded. If he raises his head or hollows his back, he will likely "lock up." If this happens, review exercises 6 and 10.

The back is a two-beat diagonal gait with the left front and the right hind moving together: picking up, moving back, and landing. The right front and left hind work in unison.

To "show" a horse what you want, you can lead him into an alleyway that he must back out of. The alley can be made of railroad ties; it can be a trailer parked next to a barn; it can be a veterinary stocks, or a row of straw or hay bales placed 3 to 4 feet from the edge of a building or a safe fence. It is best if you lead the horse in and the only way out is to back. Backing a horse along the rail of an arena will also help keep him straight.

Be sure to perform backing from the off side as well.

PART TWO

Free Longeing

Free longeing must take place in a round pen. A loose horse is worked in a circle without a longe line. The pen itself creates the boundary of the circle. Since you have no longe line to signal the horse, you must use body language and whip talk to communicate with him. Free longeing is an excellent way to establish your relationship with a horse in very simple terms.

FREE LONGEING GOALS

- Move forward.
- Stop.
- Turn (the natural tendency at first will be away from the trainer).
- Transitions and all gaits appropriate for the level of the horse's training.
- Turn toward trainer.

(See *Longeing and Long Lining* for training theory and philosophy and more information on tack and procedures.)

Free longeing requires a minimal tack investment but a maximum expenditure for facilities. The only tack you need is a longeing whip. But you

diameter. A 66-foot pen is ideal; it is the equivalent of a 20-meter circle. Because there is no tacking up, prep time for free longeing is relatively short.

Free longeing is the least complicated form of longeing and presents less chance for conflicts from tack. It can be easier on the trainer as there is no longe line to hold, keep organized, or pull on. Free longeing helps teach a horse to face the trainer and be caught. These associations carry over when the horse is free in a pasture as well.

One drawback of free longeing, besides the round pen requirement, is that you don't really have control of the *form* of a horse's movement. Although a well-conformed horse who is an active mover might have pretty good form naturally, most horses have imbalances and stiff areas that cause them to travel counterflexed, hollow, fast, or crooked. Most horses will benefit from the proper use of training aids to help them develop good form.

Another drawback of free longeing is that if a horse does get out of the pen, he is loose. That is why a round pen must be strong and tall enough that a horse cannot escape by jumping or crashing over or through it.

When free longeing, some owners teach the horse to come to them at the center of the pen. I strongly discourage you from doing this. Instead, I encourage you to keep the horse on the longe circle pointed in the direction he is headed unless you ask him to turn. It only takes a few instances of coming to the center to quit work or get a treat for a horse to learn that the center is a pretty good place to be. Such a horse will always be looking for a reason to quit. This is something like a gate-sour horse who wants to stop by the arena gate every time he passes it—he knows that's the way out.

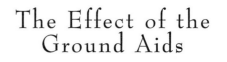

The Effect of the Ground Aids

Body movements Both driving and restraining aids.

Voice Both driving and restraining aid.

Whip Driving aid.

Longe line and driving lines Restraining and shaping aids.

BODY LANGUAGE

Since horses communicate with each other primarily by nonvocal means, you need to be aware always of what your body language is telling a horse. Your stance, attitude, and demeanor often have a greater effect on a horse than the actual aids you use.

Your body language can indicate confidence, strength, and specific expectations from a horse or it can show uncertainty, fear, or inattentiveness.

Your body movements alone can suddenly stop a horse, block him from further movement, "open a door" for a horse to go through, make him gradually slow down and stop, or tell him to hurry up.

Since horses are basically followers, they are willing to accept guidance from you as long as you make your intentions clear and move with sure steps, smooth movements, and confidence.

Your body language includes your attitude, posture, the size and intensity of your footsteps, the direction and intensity of your eyes, and the position and movement of your arms.

When you approach a horse, before you "do" anything, the horse has already read your mood, expectations, state of health, and time schedule. All of this shows up in your overall stance and demeanor. If you march up to a horse briskly with a time constraint first and foremost in your mind, the horse might very likely turn and move away from you. If, on the other hand, you mosey up to him as though you have all day and just want to say "hi," he might likely stay put and greet you.

Your mental attitude has a great effect on your performance and how your horse reads you. The more calm, confident, and positive you are, the better the training sessions will go.

I rarely look a horse in the eye unless I am specifically examining the eye for health purposes. Horses, like many animals, don't like strong direct eye contact. They interpret it as a challenge, a threat, a stare-down. The more indirectly you look at a horse as you work with him, the more comfortable he will be with whatever you are doing.

I have observed that trainers often give accidental, and often conflicting, cues without realizing it. For example, when free longeing, if the horse is tracking left and you are holding a whip in your right hand, you'd better always be aware of what your left hand is doing. If your left arm swings out to the side as you balance or chase a fly, you might without realizing it be asking the horse to slow down, stop, or even turn. As you are developing your longeing skills, you might want to hold your nonactive arm behind your back to ensure that it is quiet until needed.

Your Natural Ground Aids

Driving foot   The foot nearest the hindquarters; when the horse is tracking left, it is the right foot.

Restraining foot   The foot nearest the head; when the horse is tracking left, it is the left foot.

Assertive steps   Large, bold strides and lunges.

Withdrawal steps   Quiet, smooth steps straight back or away from the horse.

Driving arm   The arm nearest the hindquarters; when the horse is tracking left, it is the right arm.

Restraining arm   The arm nearest the head; when the horse is tracking left, it is the left arm.

Free Longeing Suitability

Age	Gaits	Length of Session
Yearling	Walk, trot	5–10 minutes
2-year-old	Walk, trot, canter (to learn departs)	10–15minutes
3-years and up	All gaits	15–30 minutes

Start every session with head down, fiddling, standing, touching.

Free schooling is a variation of free longeing. It can be conducted in an indoor or safely enclosed outdoor arena. If the arena is about 70 × 150 feet, it will be big enough to do a bit of cavalletti work or low jumping but small enough so that the trainer can still control the horse. To free school, the horse must be a trained, experienced horse. Often the horse is worked with a surcingle and side reins but no longe line, which is why it is termed free schooling or loose schooling. The big advantages are that the horse can be worked without the rider's weight, and changes of direction can be made without the constraints of lines.

Longeing Sessions: Plan to spend approximately one month very thoroughly teaching a horse the basics of longeing. For a young horse, the sessions can be held three times a week. Sessions should consist of only five to fifteen minutes of actual longeing per session. With older horses, you can hold longer, more frequent lessons.

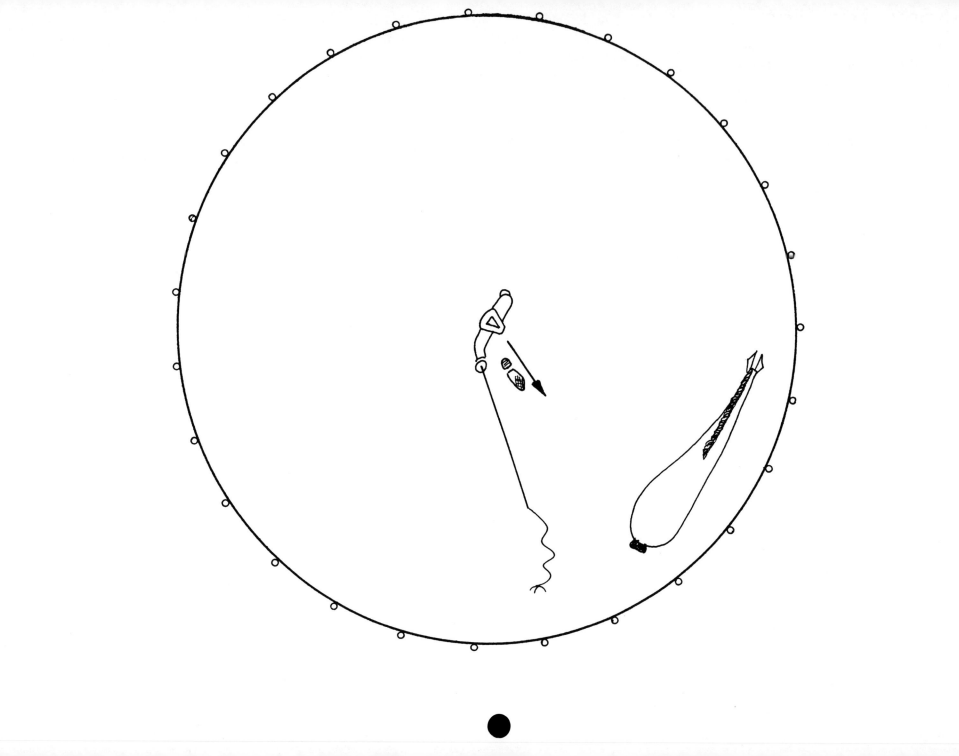

Exercise 15

Go

You basically have three choices in the way to start a free longeing session:

1. You can turn the horse out free in the training pen and stay outside the pen. The horse might race, paw, roll, buck, or call to his buddies. He is making the association that the training pen is also a playpen. This is not a good idea. If you need to turn the horse out, it is best if you do so elsewhere.

2. You can turn the horse loose at the center of the pen and push him out to the rail. With this method the horse tends to rush off, maybe even turn a few times before you can get him to slow down. This is random control but safe because there is distance between you and the horse.

3. You can take the horse to the rail of the pen, stop him alongside it, tell him "Whoa," lower his head, fiddle, handle his halter, leave the halter on but unsnap the lead rope and back away slowly saying "Whoa." Then when you are about 10 feet away, ask the horse to "Walk on." This is the most controlled approach, but

if the horse has not received thorough in-hand work, he could lurch when you remove the lead rope and, because the rail confines him, he could step on you or bump into you.

Ideally, you want to begin a free longe session with the horse walking off calmly. Lead the horse to the center or the rail, unsnap the lead rope, tell the horse "Whoa," and leave him. Don't let him leave you. If your previous ground training was thorough, he will wait until you tell him to move off. If you are working with a horse that trots off when you leave him, you might want to go to Exercise 16 first until you both know it, and then come back here.

With the horse standing and heading to the left, step toward his hindquarters with your driving (right) foot. Use your voice command, "Walk on," and raise the whip slightly from its position on the ground.

You want the horse to respond to your aids, not react wildly. That's why if you have conducted thorough in-hand work, there will be no surprises for the horse.

To *prevent anticipation* at starting, avoid sudden or strange movement that would startle the horse. Review "Whoa" in-hand and "Whoa" on the long line. Ask the horse to ease into a walk—as if you were squeezing a small amount of toothpaste out of a tube rather than banging the last bit of ketchup out of a bottle.

The Walk The walk is a four-beat gait that should have a clear, even rhythm as the feet land and take off in the following sequence: left hind, left front, right hind, right front. The walk has alternating lateral and triangular bases of support. At one moment, the horse's weight is borne by two left legs, and then the right hind is added, forming a triangle of support. Later in the cycle, all weight is borne by two right legs. That's why the walk creates a side-to-side and front-to-back motion.

The speed of the average walk is about 4 miles per hour. The footprints of the hinds should at least touch or land partially on top of the front prints; even better if they land in front of the imprints of the forefeet.

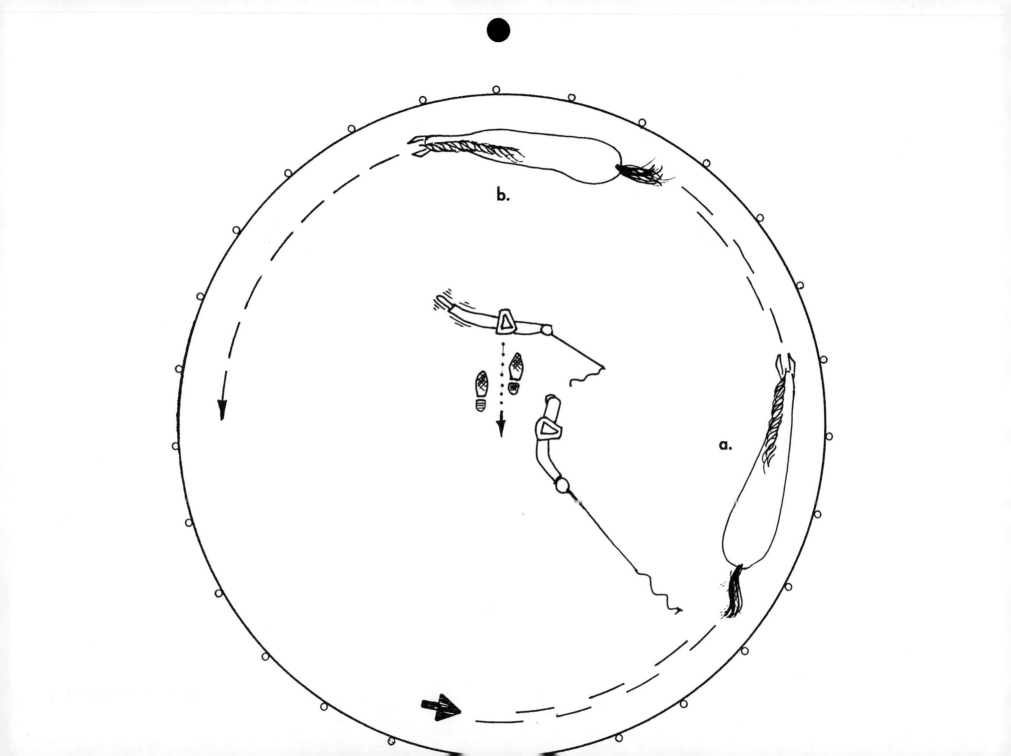

Exercise 16

Slow Down

For best success, start to the left at the trot. Most horses take off at a trot the first few times they are free in a round pen anyway. This is okay at first, but one of the first things you need to teach a horse is a downward transition to a walk. Especially if the trot has deteriorated into a counterproductive trot, the horse needs to be brought down to a walk.

a. The aids for a trot are whip raised to the horizontal position with the driving arm, possibly a step with the driving foot toward the horse to begin the trot, and a neutral restraining arm.

b. If you want to slow a horse down without stopping or turning him, the best way to do it is to put your whip in a neutral position. Either lower it at your side so the tip rests on the ground or rotate it so it points behind your back. In a soothing voice say, "Waaaalk," lower your gaze, and step back a few steps. Often this is all it takes to cause the horse to

walk. With some horses you will need to bring your restraining arm to the horizontal and quiver your hand and fingers to break the horse's intent focus on trotting. As soon as you see that the horse is about to take the first walk step, lower your restraining arm and say "Goooood"; immediately add "Walk on" if the horse questions whether you wanted stop or walk. He will question by starting to stop or turning in to look at you more carefully.

The trot is the gait you will request in 90 percent of early longeing exercises and in 75 percent of advanced work.

The trot is a two-beat diagonal gait in which the right front and left hind legs (called the right diagonal) rise and fall together and the left front and right hind legs (called the left diagonal) rise and fall together. Between the landings of the diagonal pairs, there is a moment of suspension that results in a springy gait. The working trot is an active, ground-covering trot. The average speed of a

working trot is 6 to 8 miles per hour. The hind feet should step into the tracks of the front feet.

"Trot" refers to the gait as performed under English tack with a greater length of stride and impulsion than the Western jog, which is shorter strided and has minimal suspension. The jog is usually performed on a loose rein with a great deal of relaxation.

Since the jog and trot are usually the steadiest and most stable of a horse's gaits, they are useful for developing the horse's rhythm and are the cornerstones of many training exercises.

Sometimes during longeing, a horse will hurry and travel with fast, erratic steps. This is a fast trot, not an extended trot, and it should be discouraged immediately. The horse should be slowed down to a working trot, a walk, or a halt. Then the trot work can resume.

Often an inexperienced horse moves with short, springy strides, with head up and back hollow. This is a quick, hollow trot, not a collected trot. It is not a productive trot and should be discouraged.

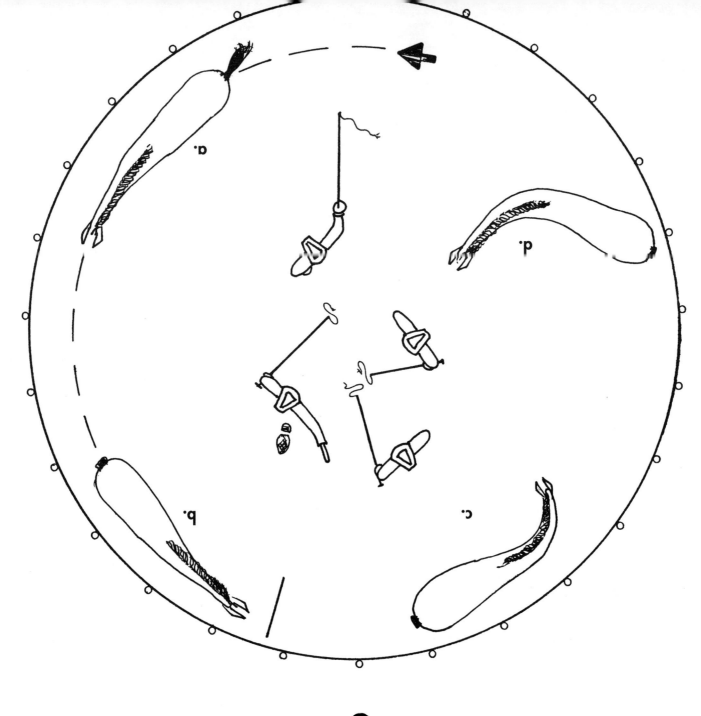

Exercise 17

Stop, Look, and Listen

Be sure your horse has had a chance to warm up sufficiently before you teach him to stop. He is usually warmed up when his topline lowers and he is showing signs of relaxation. You will eventually want to stop a horse from any gait. First teach him from a walk. Once he has stopped you want him to wait patiently and either watch and listen to you for the next set of aids or stand at ease (Exercise 18). First you want to teach him to stop, look, and listen. At first, just require the horse to wait a few seconds, gradually building up his ability to stand for longer periods. If you ask for a full minute the first time you will likely get an explosive burst because with a young horse, the suspense will get to him and he will act as if he will jump out of his skin if he has to stand still for one moment longer (sound familiar, mothers?).

a. The horse is moving to the left at the walk. Your left arm is passive, either hanging at your side or behind your back. Your right arm holds the whip in a following motion on the horizontal to keep the horse moving forward.

b. To stop the horse, rotate the whip behind you and lower it. Reach out with your left arm. Either step to the left with your restraining foot (left) or toward the horse and say, "Whoa."

c. Once the horse has stopped, lower your left arm and stand in a neutral position: whip behind you with the tip resting on the ground, even weight on both feet, arms at your sides. At this point you don't want to stare at the horse's inside eye because it could intimidate him and cause movement. But you do want to make contact with him. If you connect mentally, the horse will notice every nuance of movement. To connect mentally, you need to concentrate and focus on the horse without thoughts of overpowering him. You just want to communicate and get responses. To get the horse to look at you, that is, physically turn his ears or head slightly toward you, choose something that comes naturally to you. I run my fingernail on the rough denim fabric of my

jeans and find that the horse's ears usually point my way. That is all I want. The conversation was: "Hello, are you with me?" "Yes." This will not work if there is a 35 mph wind or the horse is preoccupied with a group of galloping horses in the adjacent pasture. But it is your goal. It is natural to want to use a horse's name to "get his attention"; however, I think it is best to save the horse's name for calling him in from pasture or speaking to him when I enter his pen or stall to catch him. I want him to associate his name with coming to me. This is definitely not what I want in the longeing situation. I want the horse to stay on the rail, body facing straight ahead, and only the head turning in at most. Other attention-getters I have seen used: raised hand or finger, "hey," clicker in pocket, clearing throat, and other noises.

d. A horse should not turn in off the circle track. If his forehand leaves the circle (like this horse), you have lost control of the horse's body. Now you have two things to do: you have to get the horse back into position and you have to teach him to stop, look, and listen. Try to read the horse and prevent this. Often just a step in his direction will thwart him. If you allow or encourage a horse to face you too much, he will be more likely to just turn in and come to you. This bad habit is very hard to change, especially if the horse has been rewarded with a treat for coming to the center. Picture what could happen during long lining! As they say in Hollywood, "That's a wrap!" Never teach your horse to come to you in the center of the training pen. Never feed treats in association with longeing or long lining.

Spooking or Shying Veering or jumping sideways at real or imagined things. Sometimes a horse will veer in because he is spooking at something unfamiliar outside the pen. Take the time to review in-hand work and build up your horse's confidence by working him near and over obstacles. If he is playing or making up boogeymen, use the techniques outlined in Exercise 34.

Problems? All horses can have problems during longeing and the problems all have similar causes. Minimize problems by paying attention to the following:

- Be sure the horse has plenty of regular, free exercise.
- Feed only the grain he requires for his workload.
- Introduce all tack to the horse in a systematic fashion.
- Make sure all tack is clean and well fitted.
- Encourage the horse to move actively forward during all phases of training.
- As you work the horse, be disciplined, consistent, and command respect.

Longe a Yearling? Generally, during the fall of the yearling year, when a horse is about 18 months old, light longeing can be used mainly to develop obedience, responsiveness to your body language, and a familiarity between you and the horse. It should not be thought of as a means of conditioning a horse, building muscle bulk, or tiring him out so you can handle him. That would be too much stress for a young horse.

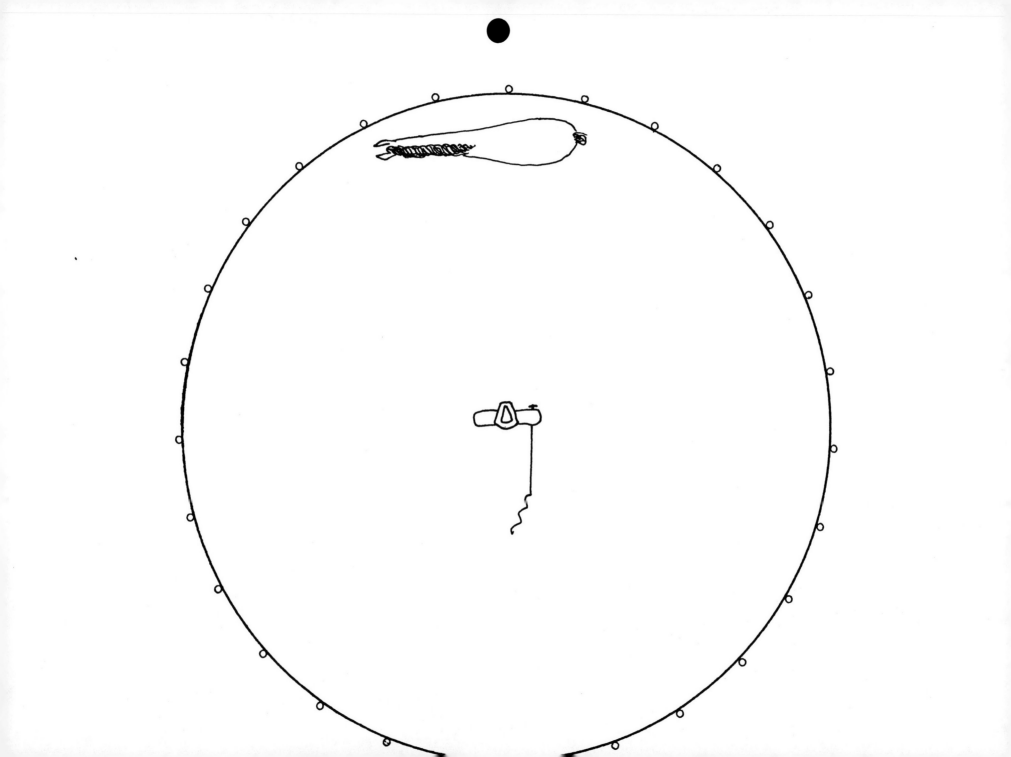

Exercise 18

Stand at Ease

It is good to give a horse periodic breaks. Stop, look, and listen is appropriate for breaks of a few seconds or more when a new action will soon follow. And, if you want to give your horse a more substantial rest break, you can do it by walking him quietly. But the stand at ease is another option.

When a horse stands, he can fill up on air after a particularly taxing work session. This is a primary reward—the horse does not have to learn that this is good. His tired body automatically interprets rest as a reward. But at the same time that he is being rewarded and rejuvenated, he is learning patience and discipline. In fact, the best time to make a pleasant association with stand at ease is when a horse is particularly tired and wants to rest. Then, when you let him stand, he interprets the rest as a reward and the carryover benefit is obedience.

When you ask a horse to stand, assume your neutral position with whip back and low, arms at your side, and weight evenly balanced over both feet. In addition, kick into neutral mentally. Don't think about the horse, how well he has just done or what you have planned next. Empty your mind, lower your gaze, and give yourself a few minutes "off" too.

There is a kind of peripheral monitor that should always be on when you are around horses and that will alert you if the horse starts to move. Your automatic warning tone, "Uh, uh," will probably be sufficient to keep the horse in place. The first few times you allow a horse to have a prolonged stand, the horse might question it because something seems fishy. After all, most horse training is based on stimulus and response and involves motion. That's why "Whoa" lessons are so important.

"Whoa" is usually overlooked and underestimated, but it should be featured and emphasized.

Note: With a confident horse, while he is "at ease," you can give yourself a good lower back stretch. With your feet placed shoulder-width apart and your weight evenly distributed, inhale. As you exhale, squat down, let your chest touch the tops of your thighs. Wrap your arms around your lower legs and arch your back. This takes the kinks out of your back and is a good mental refresher also.

Problem: Rolling The horse rolls when you take him to the training area or during the *Stand at Ease*. It is desirable to keep the round pen and other training areas for training only. If your training pen doubles as a turn-out pen, it is no wonder that a horse would confuse being led to the pen to be turned out with being taken there to work. Many horses roll as soon as they are turned out; that is just natural horse behavior.

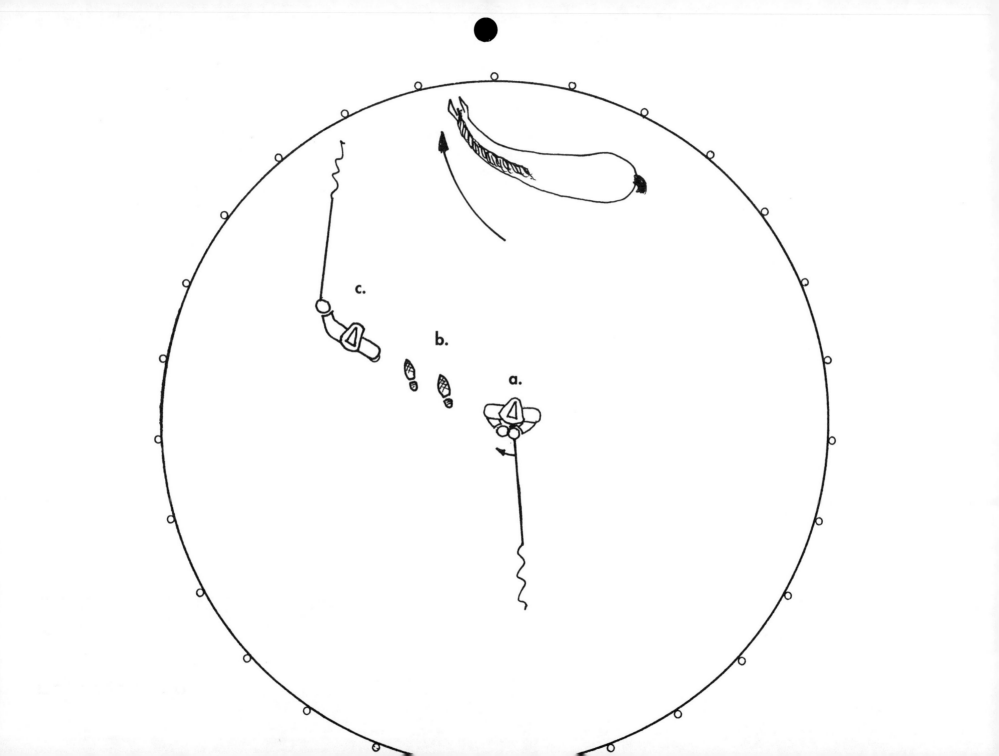

Exercise 19

Outside Turn

Most untrained horses perform an outside turn automatically when you stop their forward motion. In an outside turn the horse turns into the rail. The horse has reacted to being "cornered" or having his movement stopped or slowed. He ducks away from the restraint and heads in the opposite direction. The horse's inborn protective flight instinct makes him naturally turn away from real or perceived danger—this is predator avoidance. Although you are not a predator, the horse reacts to the restriction you place on him in the same way he would to a predator.

You can use the outside turn to help slow down, stop, or control a horse who is racing. Usually, the first few times you turn a horse hard into the rail, he will lope out in the opposite direction. But after the third or fourth turn, he will start to think about what is happening and will look to you for some other clues. That's when you can begin teaching "Walk," "Whoa," and other exercises.

Note: For a hard outside turn, the training pen must have very tall, strong, safe rails.

When an untrained horse turns to the outside, he moves his vulnerable head and throat away from the trainer/predator and presents his best defenses to the potential threat. His first defense is flight. And his second defense is delivering a powerful kick with his well-muscled hindquarters. Although your horse is probably not planning to "kick and run," you do need to be aware of the potentially dangerous habit, attitude, and configuration. That's why you should teach a horse the inside turn as soon as possible. Before you do, however, you should be the "initiator" of the outside turns that the horse does automatically.

a. From a standstill with the horse facing ahead on a left circle, stay at the center of the round pen. While the horse is standing quietly, change the whip behind your back from your right hand to your left hand.

b. Keep the whip pointed behind you as you take a few steps to your left and toward the horse. That puts you ahead of the horse and closer to him.

c. Smoothly bring the whip out from behind your back, take your final step to block the horse's forward movement, and say "Tuuuuurrrrn" with a very drawling, circular sound. If the horse has not stopped too close to the rail, he will more than likely turn to the right and head the other way. Get the whip in proper position for work to the right so you just need to step back toward the center to work the horse.

It is a rare horse who will turn and then stop unless he's trained to do so. That's why at first, you can ask for "Walk on" or "Trot," depending on what you think he is most likely to do. Calm horses might walk on. Those that get cranked up by turning will want to let it out with a trot or canter. Anyway, you know your horse, so ask for what you think you will get and act as if that was your intention all along. Later, you can slow the horse down. This is the psychology of making solid connections with voice commands and aids right from the beginning. In subsequent lessons, you will ask for gait transitions at specific locations in the pen but for now, let psychology be on your side.

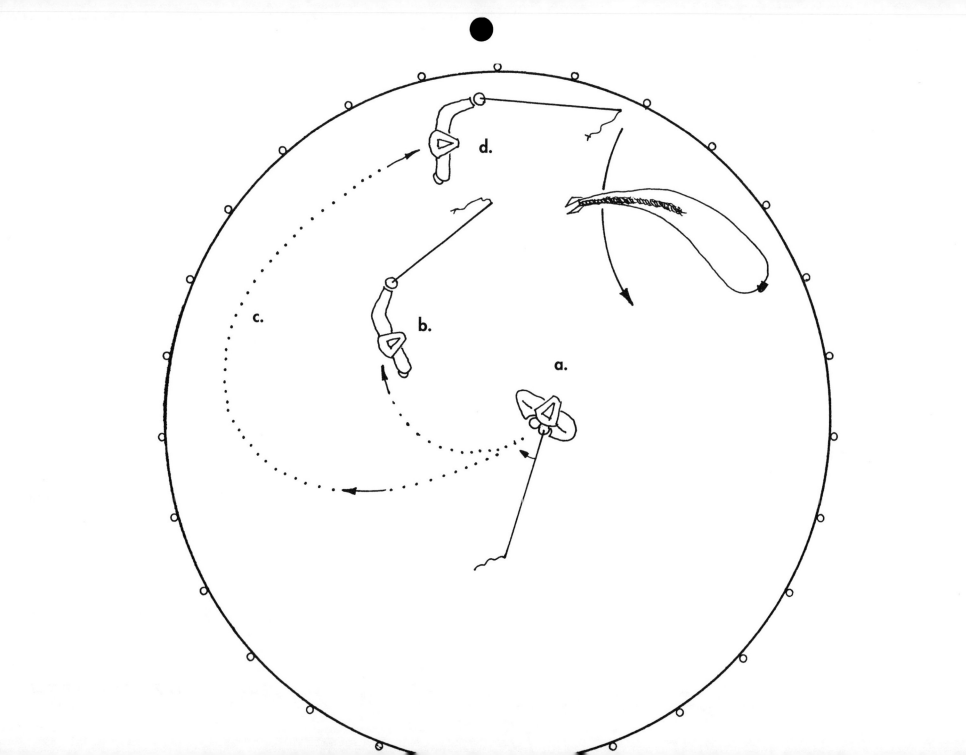

Exercise 20

Inside Turn

Since the inside turn does not come naturally to the horse, you will need to be more astute and read each horse you work so you can design the approach best suited to that horse.

a. As with the outside turn, perform the turn from the halt. In this example, the horse is facing forward on a left circle. While the horse is quietly standing, change the whip behind your back from your right hand to your left hand. If necessary, use the attention-getter you developed in Exercise 17. You want your horse to pay attention to you as you move.

b. With a trained horse, all you will need to do is take one step across the line of vision, use your voice command, and "insert" the whip between the horse and the rail. This is a delicate zone. A misstep here could cause the horse to turn to the outside and bolt and run. So move confidently and make sure you don't inadvertently discourage the horse from turning left by making a strange movement with your right arm.

c. With most horses, the idea of turning to the inside is so odd that they freeze on the rail. Although a horse might already have the stop, look, and listen lesson down, he might need some extra help to figure out just how and where to move. To help him, I really "open the door." I send the horse an engraved invitation in the form of a very wide berth.

d. Then I approach him straight on between his body and the rail. I insert the whip between the rail and the horse's body and "peel" him off the rail.

With both the inside turn and the outside turn, prevent anticipation. Don't ask for many turns at first. Intersperse with lots of stop, look, and listen and stand at ease. Predict which way the horse might turn, and have appropriate aids and body language ready to counteract.

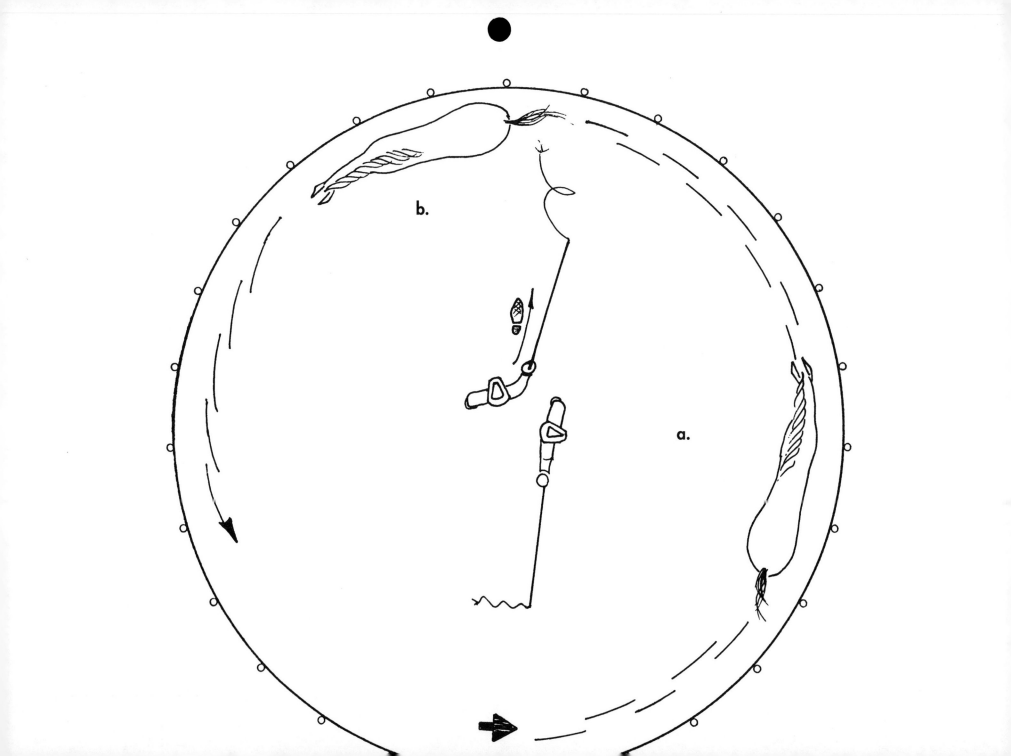

b.

a.

Exercise 21

Trot-Lope

If a horse is at least two years old and has learned basic obedience—"Walk," "Whoa," "Stand"—and he trots with fairly good form and rhythm, it is probably time to begin work at the lope or canter.

a. Make sure the horse is traveling forward at the trot with good energy but is not rushing.

b. For the lope, use the appropriate combination of the following aids:
- Pre command, such as "OK."
- A raising of the whip; a cracking of the whip; or a rolling of the whip.
- A step toward the horse's hindquarters.
- Lope command such as "Let's go!"

The canter (lope) is a three-beat gait with the following footfall pattern:

1. Initiating hind leg or outside hind.
2. The diagonal pair or inside hind and outside foreleg.
3. Leading foreleg or inside foreleg.
4. Regrouping of legs or a moment of suspension.

If the initiating hind leg is the right, the diagonal pair will consist of the left hind and the right front, the leading foreleg will be the left front and the horse will be on the left lead. When observing a horse on the left lead from the side, his left legs will reach farther forward than his right legs. The left hind will reach under his belly farther than the right hind; the left front will reach out in front of his body farther than the right front. When turning to the left, normally the horse should be on the left lead.

The canter has alternating rolling and floating aspects to it. The energy rolls from rear to front; then, during a moment of suspension, the horse gathers his legs up underneath himself to get organized for the next set of leg movements. The horse seems to glide for a moment until the initiating hind lands and begins the cycle again.

A lope is a relaxed version of the canter with a lower overall body carriage.

An extended canter retains the three-beat cadence but is a long, ground-covering stride in which the head and neck reach forward—the horse's form becomes more horizontal. A rushed canter, such as occurs when a young horse gets excited, has a quicker tempo, and is unbalanced and undesirable. A gallop is a fast, ground-covering four-beat gait, not suitable for round pen work.

A collected canter also retains the three-beat cadence but the strides are shorter, the legs move higher, and there is more joint folding (flexion) than in the regular canter. The head and neck are up and flexed and the hindquarters are well under the horse's body. The horse's position creates the impression that he is cantering uphill.

Expression is as important as mechanics.

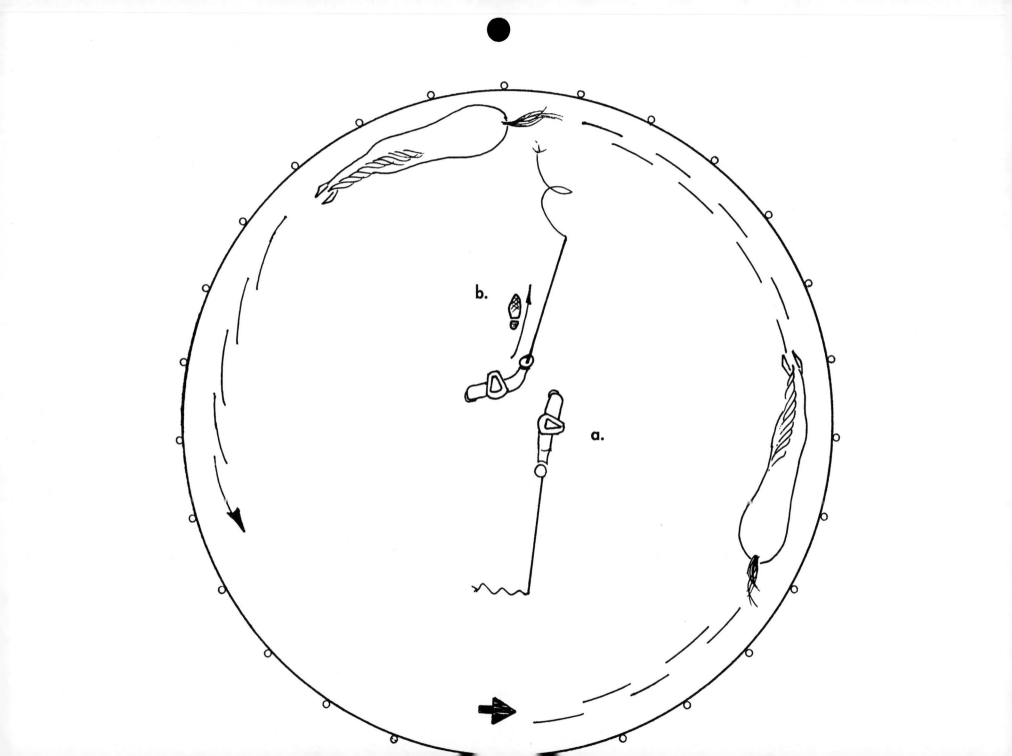

Exercise 22

Lope-Trot

The lope-to-trot transition should be forward and fluid. That will make it more comfortable to ride when the time comes. There is nothing worse than riding a horse who completely shuts down from an active lope to a dead trot; it throws the rider forward and often pitches him off balance. Actually there is something worse: the horse who shifts to a short, quick trot. That kind bounces the rider's kidneys unkindly. If you develop fluid, forward transitions during longeing and long lining, you will be glad you did when it comes time to ride the horse.

a. Just before the downward transition, the horse should be loping or cantering with good energy, balance and rhythm. A horse needs to have active hind legs in order to reach under for a good balanced, smooth downward transition. If a horse is performing a four-beat canter, his hind legs are probably way behind the movement of his body and the transition will be rough and disorganized. So, just prior to the downward transition, don't soothe the horse down and let him die, be sure he is actively cantering.

b. For a downward transition to a trot, in a time sequence and intensity that you will tailor for each horse, do the following:

1. Step back one step.
2. Lower the whip.
3. Raise your non-whip arm and quiver your arm, hand, or fingers.
4. Say "Ta-raaaht" with falling inflection.

As soon as the horse trots, do one of the following:

If the horse is rushing, say "Eeeeeeasy" and continue with the quivering arm and perhaps another step backward.

If the horse "dies" and is performing a lackluster trot, keep your nonwhip arm up but still, raise your whip to a horizontal following without any action from the lash, and say "Trot on!"

Once the horse has trotted for a circle or two, you should be able to assess whether the work to this point has been correct and productive.

THE SIGNS OF RELAXATION

- Head and neck held low and reaching.
- Rhythmic breathing.
- Back slightly arched and swinging.
- Tail held off anus and swaying rhythmically.
- An even tempo movement.
- Contented snorting or blowing through nose.
- A calm, inwardly focused eye.

Relaxation will help preserve a horse's self-esteem and a good attitude about his work.

59

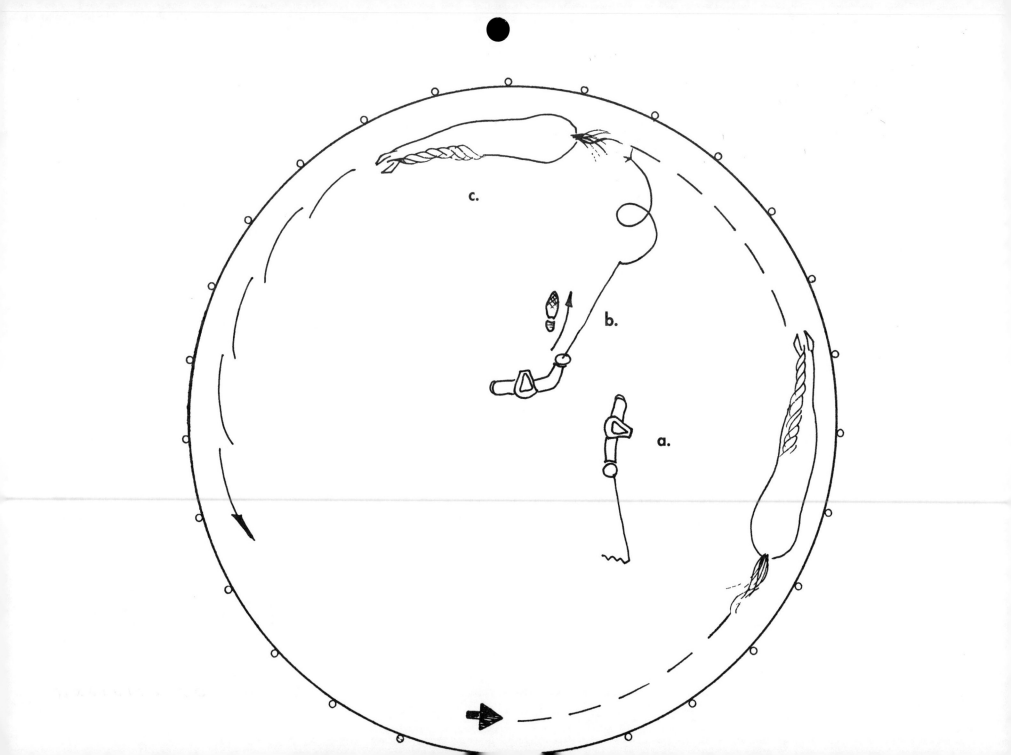

Exercise 23

Walk-Lope

The walk to lope transition is quite an advanced movement. The horse must already have a good basis in the collected lope or canter in order to strike off without any trot steps in between. This lesson might be better left until after side reins have been used. If this transition is asked of a horse too early in his training, you might luck out and "surprise" the horse into a canter from a walk once or twice, but the horse will likely lose his state of relaxation and his form and rhythm will suffer. For horses with naturally collected conformation and for trainers who like to do more at the free longeing stage, I include it here.

a. The horse's walk must be pure, unhurried, and with good reach with the hind legs in order to be in the right place at the right time for a strike off. If the horse is walking calmly but stepping well under himself, apply the following aids:

b. Just prior to asking for the lope, "gather" your horse. With your body language (slight clockwise shoulder tilt and possibly a half step toward the horse's forehand with your left foot) ask for a slight compacting of the horse's frame. This is similar to a half halt or a check in riding. This is a very momentary shortening that should occur just a fraction of a second before the lope depart. At the same time, you might want to give your precommand, such as "OK." All of this should just take a fraction of a second as you don't want the horse to break or turn and look at you.

c. Then, simultaneously, step to the horse's hindquarter, raise, pop, or roll the whip as necessary, and say "Let's go," or whatever your lope command or sound is.

If the horse trots instead of loping and you feel he is advanced enough to know the distinction, bring him back down to a walk and start again.

If he lopes but the rhythm is quick, use "Eeeeeasy" aids.

If he strikes off at a collected canter and lope, tell him "Goooood" but keep the driving aids present. (Also give yourself a pat on the back because you prepared the horse properly for this difficult free longe lesson.)

Problem: Anticipation The horse lopes before you ask. Once a horse has learned what usually comes next, he might automatically perform what he expects will be asked. This is a symptom of a nervous horse or a rushed training program. It also can be a symptom of a very keen horse that is so "tuned in" that he gets himself in trouble! The horse's excellent memory and keen senses have allowed him to pick up signals from a particular place in the arena, the feel of a specific piece of tack, your body language, breathing, heartbeat, even your pheromones. All these are clues that he instantly pieces together and then reacts to before you even know you have cued him. Although anticipation of a few steps or so might seem harmless or even novel at first, if left unchecked, it can develop into a habit that makes a horse virtually uncontrollable via the traditional aids. To prevent anticipation, vary the sequence of the lesson maneuvers, the location of the lessons, and keep things moving forward in a progression.

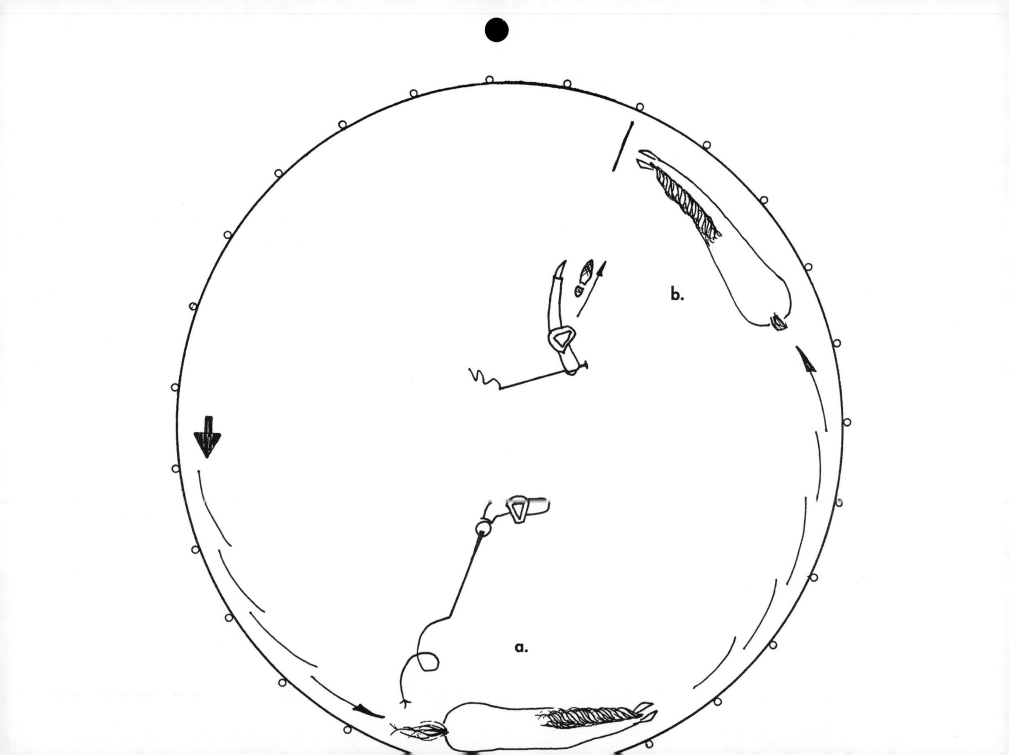

b.

a.

Lope-Halt

The halt from a lope or canter is an entirely different animal than the technique you use to stop or slow down a racing animal. Often that type of exercise results in a quick outside turn and the horse just lopes in the opposite direction.

This exercise is a controlled, balanced, advanced exercise. In it, you want the horse to go from a collected lope to a balanced, square halt with all four legs under his body. There should be no trot steps in between. Just like the lope-trot transition, you want the lope-halt transition to be smooth and forward. A forward halt? Yes, that means the hind legs are reaching forward under the horse's body at the moment of the halt. If the hind legs are behind the movement, the horse's back hollows, the front-end action is stiff and stilted, and ultimately the horse must move his hind legs under himself after the stop—all undesirable elements.

Here's what you do to get a forward halt:

a. Keep the horse loping forward energetically but in a collected frame, using whatever body language and whip aids you normally use. Mentally pick a spot you want your horse to "plant."

b. When the horse is a few strides from that spot, swivel on your driving foot and take a big step toward the "plant" spot with your restraining foot. At the same time, say "Whoa" in a low tone with a punctuated end, and put out your restraining arm.

Footing Notes: Footing is important for all movements but critical for a good stop without injury. Footing should have cushion and should not be too deep, slippery, or sticky. Footing is composed of the base, surface material, and additives. The base must be a thick enough layer so that stones don't work up from the earth underneath. A four- to six-inch base is usually adequate for a round pen or arena. The layer over the base is the cushion or the surface material. Often it is a mixture of sand, silt, clay, topsoil, and wood or rubber products. Additives are soil conditioner and aerators that keep the surface material from getting packed or dusty.

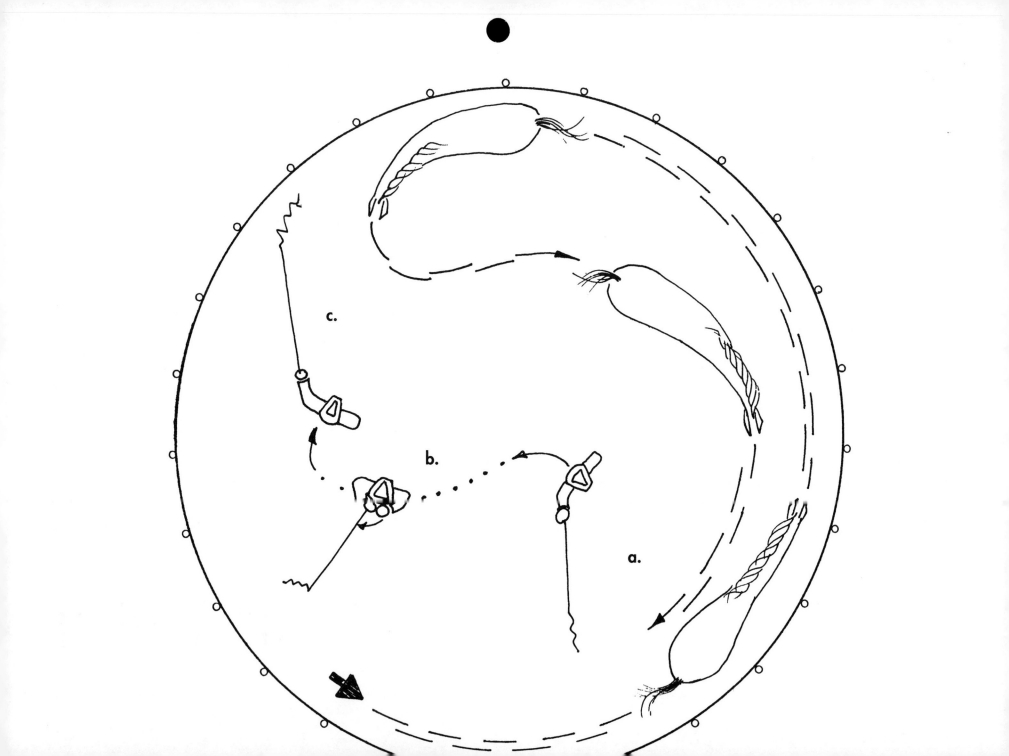

Reverse to the Inside at the Trot

You've taught your horse a turn to the inside from a halt, which is much like a turn on the hindquarters. Arcing turns, on the other hand, can be performed at any gait and are valuable for the horse's upcoming driving lessons. You'll probably have the best luck at maintaining impulsion if you start the exercise first at the trot. Later you can try it at the walk and lope. Many horses lose their momentum at the walk and just at the critical point of the turn, hesitate and ask, "What?" A reverse at the lope requires a lead change, so should be reserved until the horse is ready for such a lesson.

a. With the horse trotting actively forward, mentally pick a spot where you want the turn to begin. That spot might be directly behind you. Keep the trot aids on your horse.

b. When the horse is about two strides from the spot, begin backing up to give the horse some room. You are "opening the door." At the same time you are backing up, change the whip behind your back as shown in Exercise 2.

c. Many horses will begin to turn in response to your backing up, but with some you might need to step a little bit in front of the horse's line of travel. At the same time, present the whip calmly. Be sure you have given the horse enough room so he can turn without breaking to a walk.

As soon as the horse has turned, begin to follow him as you work your way back to the center of the round pen.

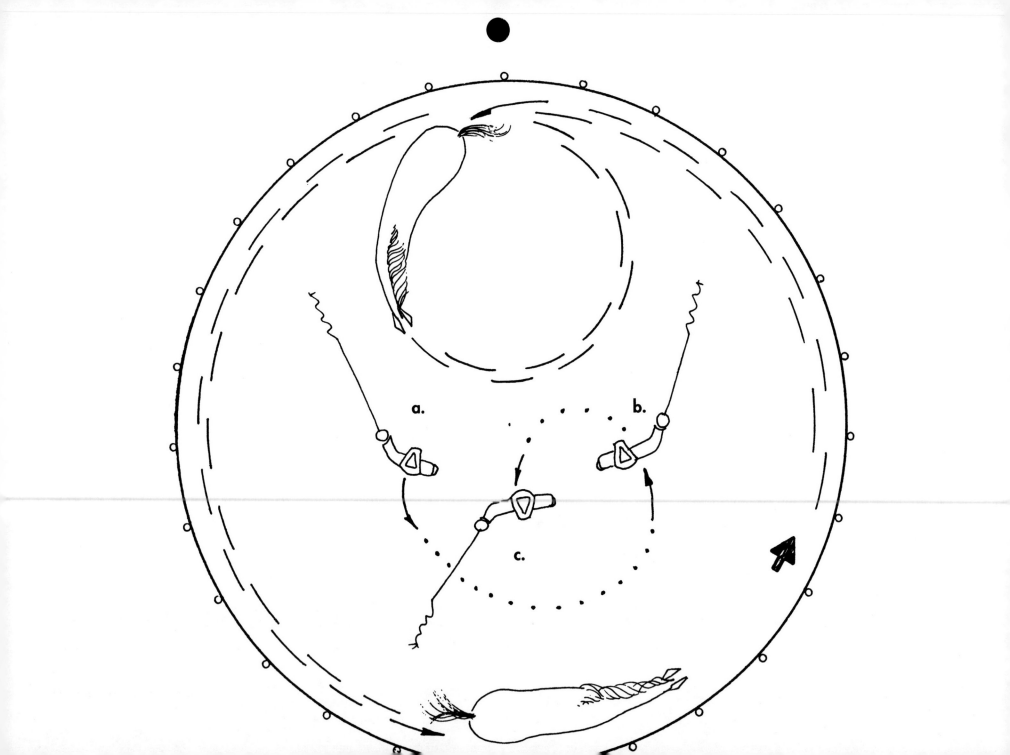

Exercise 26

Trot-Circle-Trot

In this exercise, the horse performs a complete circle that sends him back to the original large circle at the point he left it. He maintains the original direction of travel throughout the exercise. If the horse is tracking to the left, keep the whip in the active trot position—on the horizontal. Stay in the normal longeing position, facing the horse's mid-rib area. As the horse approaches the place where you want him to come off the rail, begin backing up and moving to the left. As you do this, switch the whip behind your back from your right hand to your left hand. Raise the whip in your left hand. The horse will see the open door combined with a forward block from the whip and he will turn in off the rail.

a. At the point where the horse has come off the rail, the amount of room you give him will determine the size of the full circle he will make. The smaller the circle, the more collected the trot will have to be. Begin working your way over to the other side of the small circle by walking a bit backward (to mirror the horse's circle) and in the same direction as the horse is moving.

b. When the circle is the size you want, switch the whip behind your back to your right hand. You should be in a position to send the horse back to the rail of the round pen.

c. Return to your position at the center of the round pen and aid the horse around the pen in a normal manner.

Collected Trot: A collected trot is performed at the same tempo as the working trot but with shorter steps, more marked cadence, more joint flexion, a rounded back, well-engaged hindquarters, and subsequently, a naturally (not forced) elevated neck and more vertical flexion in the poll. This is an energetic trot with the balance shifted rearward, which allows free shoulder movement. This trot has the shortest moment of suspension. Therefore it covers the least ground and the hind feet usually do not reach the imprints of the front feet. Some breeds of horses will naturally perform a collected trot during free longeing, but it is rare.

The smaller the circle, the more collected the trot will have to be.

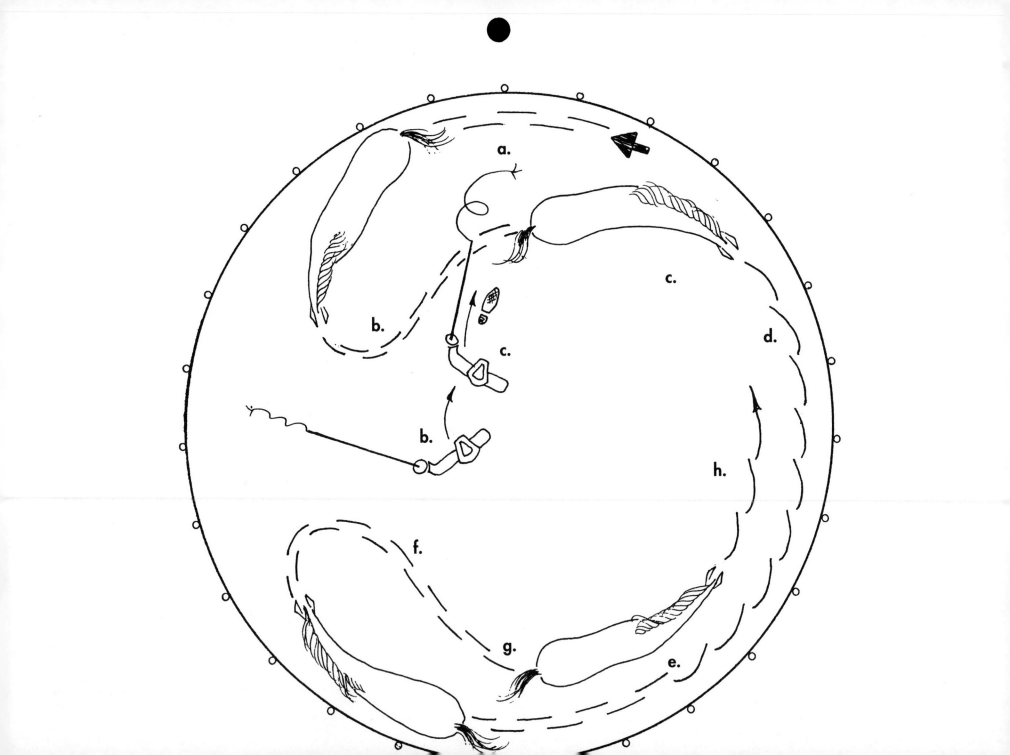

Exercise 27

Trot-Reverse-Lope

In this exercise you will be combining the elements of exercises 21, 25, and 22. The horse will trot, reverse, lope as he is returning to the rail, lope until you ask for a trot, and then repeat the exercise.

This is an excellent way to "dance" with your horse while you are free longeing. But be sure you are the one who is "leading"!

a. Horse is trotting in a circle to the left.

b. You ask the horse to turn in off the rail, using the techniques in Exercise 25.

c. Just as the horse is about to join the rail again, tracking right, you ask for a lope depart as outlined in Exercise 21.

d. Have the horse lope between one and three times around the round pen. Work on maintaining form and an even three-beat rhythm.

e. Ask for a downward transition to trot, as outlined in Exercise 22.

f. After the horse has trotted a few strides, ask for an inside turn, as in Exercise 25.

g. As the horse is about to join the rail, tracking left, ask for a lope, as in Exercise 21.

Have the horse lope until you want to repeat the exercise or ask for a different one.

Protective Boots Because of frequent missteps caused by the horse's inexperience, lack of coordination, and lack of conditioning, it is usually wise to protect his front legs with boots. Splint boots with hard strike plates may prevent a fractured splint bone if the horse raps his inside cannon area with the opposite hoof.

Depending on their design, the boots might also protect the rear of the horse's leg—the flexor tendon area—from the blow of a hind toe if fractious behavior or uncontrollable galloping causes him to overreach.

Bell boots will protect the bulbs of the front heels from overreaching of the hind hooves. Bell boots will also minimize trauma to the coronary band if the horse inadvertently steps on himself.

Sport boots are designed to support the flexor tendons during hyperextension, especially in deep footing at the canter or lope.

Before applying sport boots, both the boots and the horse's legs must be very clean. Sport boots should be put on very snug to provide support and to keep debris from entering the boot. Because most sport boots are made of neoprene, which is heat concentrating, they should be used only for a period of about an hour.

Problem: Rushing A horse takes short, quick steps. A horse in a hurry is either afraid or out of balance. Be sure the horse is familiar with all equipment and does not fear you. Work him at the walk and trot only, with lots of transitions. Have the whip ready to use in front of his chest to slow him down. Or step in front of him and face him to slow him down. Stop. Stand. Regroup.

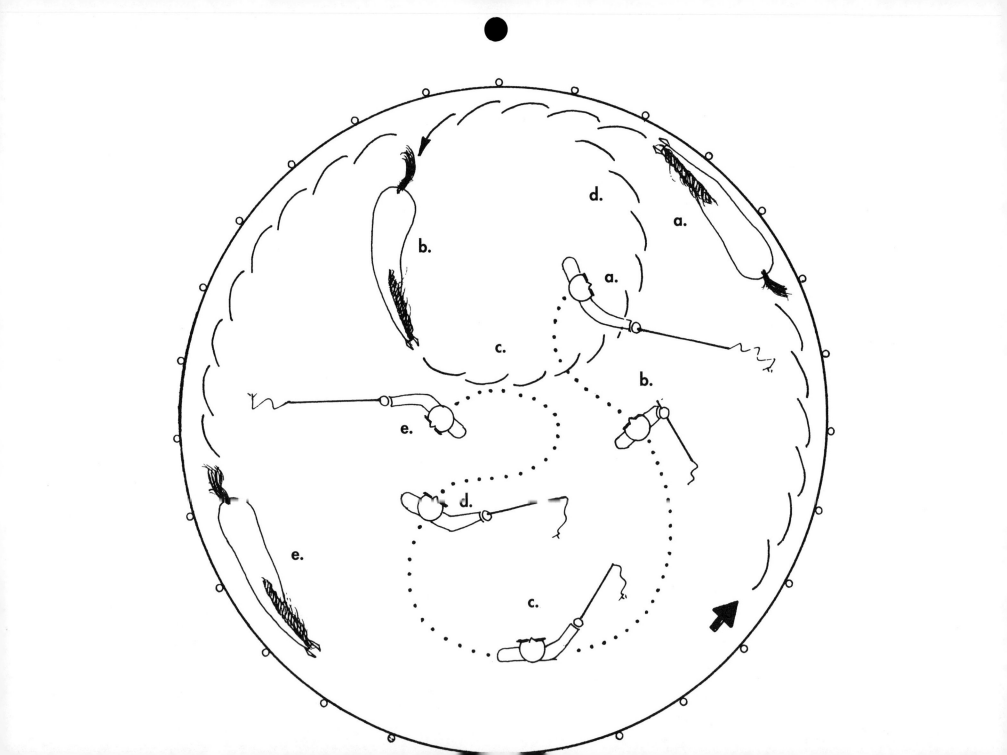

Exercise 28

Lope-Circle-Lope

This is an advanced free longeing exercise. It requires that the horse be very familiar with and confident in your body language, voice commands, and aids. The horse must be paying attention to you. To perform this exercise, it is essential that the pen be at least 66 feet in diameter because you will be asking the horse to make, at a lope, a full circle of about half that size. For a horse to be able to lope a 33-foot diameter circle, he must be balanced, conditioned, and be loping in a relatively collected form.

a. The horse is loping a circle to the left.

b. You start backing up to open a space for the horse to come in off the rail. By now, the horse should not need you to come way over to the left to ask for the inside turn. He should be watching you and know that when you back up, he is to come through the door.

c. You might need to back up almost all the way to the opposite rail of the round pen to give the horse maximum room for the lope circle. Otherwise, he might feel cramped or get out of balance and break into a trot.

d. As the horse is finishing up the circle, reassure him that you do not want a change of direction and help him close up the circle by moving over to the right.

e. When he has finished the small circle, resume your normal longeing position at the center of the pen and have the horse continue the lope for at least one full round before you change gaits or perform a different exercise. If you ask for a trot immediately after completing the small circle, the horse will tend to associate that with the finish of the small circle and will be more apt to trot each time he completes the smaller circle. This "follow through" technique is another anticipation prevention method.

Note: During this entire exercise, the whip is in your right hand. Instead of switching it to your left hand in **b.**, you've just lowered the whip and pointed it behind you. This should be enough of an indication to the advanced horse, along with your body language and possibly the voice command, "Tuuurrrn," that you want him to turn inside.

PART THREE

Line Longeing

Even if you don't have a round pen, be sure to read all the exercises in the free longeing section. They contain goals and techniques that you will need in line longeing.

If you have a round pen, hold the first longe line lessons in the round pen. This will help your horse easily make the transition from free longeing to line longeing.

If you don't have a round pen, start the longe line lessons at the end of an arena, using three sides (or at least two) to help you control your horse as he learns.

Eventually all horses should have longe lessons in the arena and in the open.

Line longeing lessons are suitable for horses two years of age and older.

A longe line gives you added control over your horse, but it is one more thing you have to keep track of. The line gives you a definite means to teach your horse not to turn his hindquarters toward you when you ask him to stop and turn. You will be able to prevent the horse from ducking to the outside and turning into the rail. You can also begin to correct counterbend and add inside bend by using tugs on the longe line. The concept of inside bend can be a simple series of takes and gives to get the horse turning slightly into the circle.

Once your horse is trained, a longe line will allow you to longe him in an open area, such as an arena or pasture, or at a show ground.

A longe line presents several potential safety hazards. Your horse could become wrapped up in the line, which can frighten and even injure him. He could also just step over the line and get his leg caught, which could result in a rope burn. That is why sacking the horse out to ropes is essential because it shows the horse that ropes are not panic materials and that rope restriction should mean stop, not fight.

A longe line could also tangle your feet or arms and if it were attached to a frantic horse, you could be injured. So be careful. Prepare your horse and develop good habits.

Longeing with a halter and longe line is a rather unsophisticated way to casually longe a well-trained horse but it is not a suitable way to *train* a horse to longe. You would have very little control using a halter and you would not be able to influence a horse's form while he is working. Also, if you absolutely have to stop a horse, you will probably find that the amount of jerking or pulling required is hard on you and is very ineffective.

Longeing with a bosal is a viable option. If the headstall, fiador, and bosal were well fitted, they would be a great improvement over a halter and might be more suitable for certain horses than a cavesson.

Longeing with a cavesson is the most traditional English method of longeing and provides you with good control via the weighted nosepiece of the cavesson.

Methods of Attaching the Longe Line

To a Halter: Although a halter is not the best choice of headgear for longeing, it is probably the most common. For a halter to be used at all, it must fit perfectly. In the case of longeing, this means fairly snug so that it will not shift. The hardware must not contact the cheekbones or cause rubbing.

The longe line should be attached to the inside cheek ring of the halter, which means you have to change attachment each time you change direction. If you attach the longe line to the throat ring, you will have more "whoa" power than with a cheek attachment and you won't have to change attachment when you change direction, but the halter will tend to swivel on the horse's face. If you really need to "communicate" with a horse, your "Whoa" from 30 feet away won't have much impact with a halter. That is why so many people use chains with halters: a halter, by itself, is simply not "enough." Yet, a chain is not appropriate for longeing because it does not release (reward) the horse when he is performing correctly. The chain pressure tends to always be there because of the weight of the longe line, which makes effective training more difficult.

To a Bosal: A properly fitted bosal rig is especially good for slowing down and stopping a horse. That's because the longe line is attached at the heel knot of the bosal, located at the rear. When the longe line is tugged, the pressure is transferred to the nose of the horse. This signal is very similar to the in-hand halter pressure the horse has known since early halter training, only stronger, so the bosal has good "whoa power." There is no reason a horse cannot be longed in a bosal all the time, once

he has had basic lessons. If, however, the horse is at a stage where he fights or tries to pull away, you might find the bosal delivers some nasty skin rubs on the nose and jawbones when he jerks or pulls against the pressure on the longe line. It would be better to use a cavesson until the horse accepts the longeing process, and then switch to a bosal if you want.

To a Cavesson: Before you attempt to longe your horse in a cavesson, let him get used to its action with some in-hand work. Attach the line to the middle ring on the noseband. At first the sensation of the weighted nosepiecc will be unfamiliar and the horse might raise his head, push into the pressure, or freeze. Let him slowly become accustomed to the feel and find a way to balance and respond to the cavesson.

Generally, the center ring of a cavesson is used for longeing. This point of attachment does not have to be changed when you change direction.

You can also attach the longe line to the inside ring of the noseband but then you will have to change the point of attachment each time you change direction. You might want to use the inside ring for a horse who counterflexes on the circle. The pull from the inside ring will help you flex the horse to the inside of the circle.

LINE LONGEING GOALS

Whoa on the longe line.
Walk.
Walk to halt transition.
Look at me, not necessarily face me, but pay attention.
Turn to the inside with longe line.
Walk to trot (or jog) transition.
Working trot.
Trot to walk transition.
Trot to canter transition.
Working canter.
Canter to trot transition.
Lengthened trot.
Spiral in and out at the trot and canter.
Canter to walk and walk to canter.
Canter to whoa.

(See *Longeing and Long Lining* for training theory and philosophy and more information on tack and procedures.)

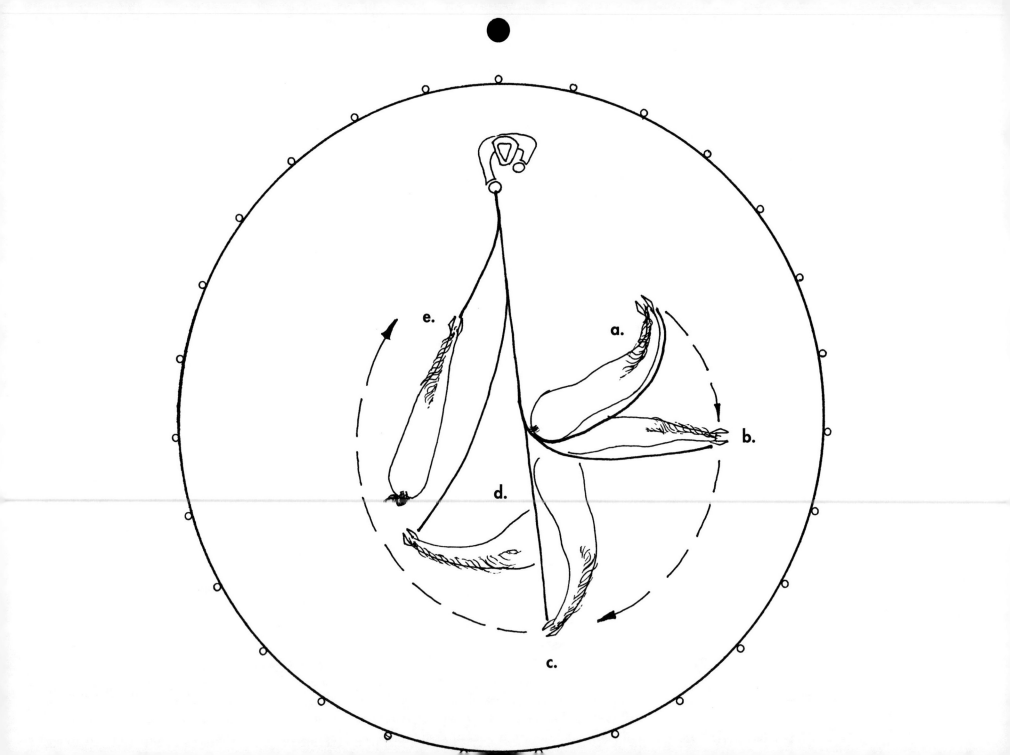

Exercise 29

Turn on the Long Line

Before you attempt to longe your horse with a longe line and a halter, cavesson, or bosal, teach him how to bend to the left and right on a long rope. This will get him used to a long rope controlling him from a distance and will give you an indication of how he might react on the end of a longe line.

Standing on near side, snap a 15- to 20-foot rope to the bottom ring of the horse's halter, to the center ring on the cavesson noseband, or to the fiador loop that hangs below the heel knot of the bosal.

You can attach the line to one of the halter's cheek rings or to the side rings of the cavesson if you feel the horse will require more of a lateral cue, but then you will have to change the point of attachment each time you change direction.

Tell your horse "Whoa," and then step to his hindquarters on the near side as in Exercise 9, *Whoa on a Long Line,* and give a soft tug on the rope, which should cause him to turn and face you.

Do this on the off side as well.

Repeat until the horse is comfortable with the procedure.

Then stand on the horse's near side and place the rope over his head and neck so the rope runs along the off side of his body. Remind him to "Whoa," if necessary, and step to his hindquarters as you draw the rope along his off side.

a. Then, if necessary, again repeat "Whoa" and step at least 10 feet from your horse's near side. The rope will be running along his offside ribs, hips, around his hindquarters and to your hand. He will probably face you, wondering what is going on. Be sure you have enough tension on the rope so that if your horse tries to turn to the left, he can't.

b. Lightly tug on the rope, which should cause the horse to move his neck to the right and straighten it. The rope pressing on the right side of his hindquarters aids you in straightening the horse's body for the turn to the right.

c. Stay where you are standing and gather up the rope, which will cause the horse to turn to the

right. Let the horse find the answer slowly the first time you do this. At the point where the horse is facing directly away from you, you are in his blind spot and you are also in a potentially dangerous kicking zone. That's why you want to be sure there is ample distance between you and the horse as you perform this exercise.

d. Continue giving soft tugs on the rope until the horse turns around to face you.

e. When the horse is facing you, you can stop reeling in the line. Walk up to him and say, "Goooood."

Now step to the off side and perform the same exercise. Continue to alternate sides until the horse bends equally well in both directions without resistance. Every horse will initially be smoother in one direction and stiffer in the other. Many horses will hold their heads up and their bodies stiff in one direction. This will alert you to potential tendencies and problems in the upcoming work.

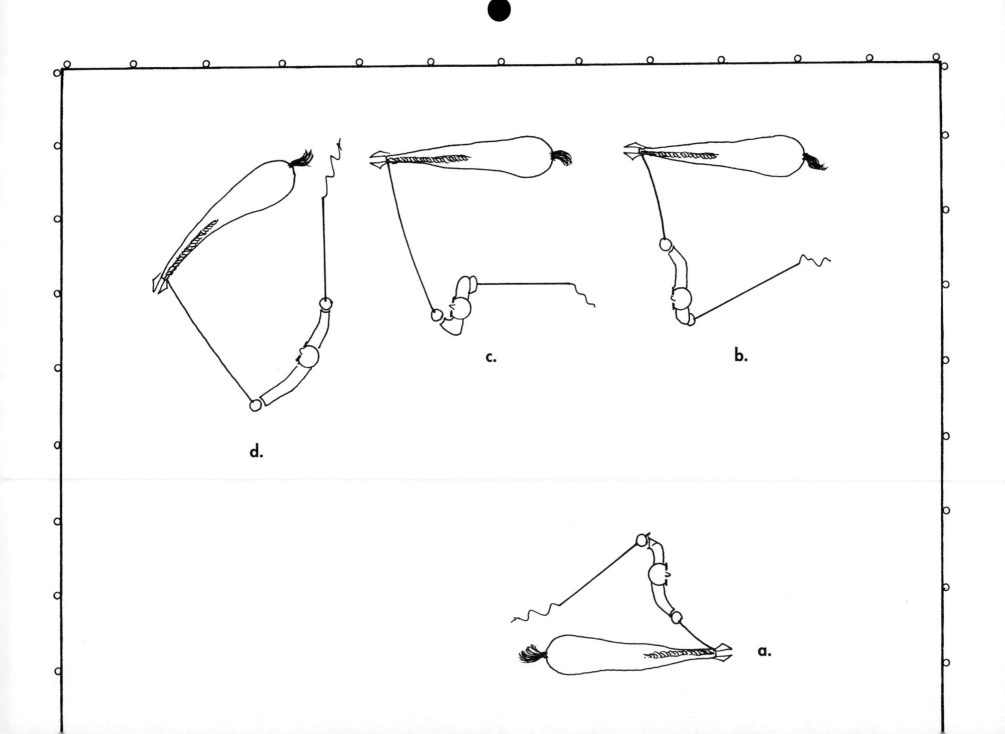

Exercise 30

Changing Position

After completing the previous exercise, your horse will be better pre-pared for the sensations that he's likely to encounter in longeing and he will tend to respond with cooperation rather than resistance.

Before you begin line longeing, you should sack the horse out to ropes (Exercise 69), work him frequently from the off side, and make a strong connection between in-hand voice commands such as "Walk on," "Whoa," and "Easy." All of these things will help the line longeing lessons go more smoothly.

It's time to go from the in-hand position to the longeing position. If you have free longed your horse, the transition should go smoothly because he is already used to you being off at his side while he is working. If you are starting from scratch, you'll need to pay very close attention to your posi-tion in relation to the horse, your whip use, and the tension on the line.

a. Begin by leading the horse in the normal in-hand manner. If you are working in an arena, work down the long sides.

b. Start letting out a little bit more line until you are holding the horse on 4 to 6 feet of lead line.

c. Switch the whip to your other hand behind your back and face the horse slightly. Refer to Exercise 2 for help.

d. When you get to the corner of the arena, use the side to help you turn your horse as you step back toward his hindquarters. Use the whip as a driving aid to keep the horse moving forward. Be sure you don't get ahead of the horse's shoulder. Keep contact on the longe line so that you can turn him as you step backward toward his rear. You can walk along with the horse in the longeing position and negotiate the short end of the arena. Then perhaps you will assume the normal in-hand position. Switch to the longeing position several times until you are coordinated and the horse is relaxed with the procedure. Now you are ready to move to the round pen for some actual longeing.

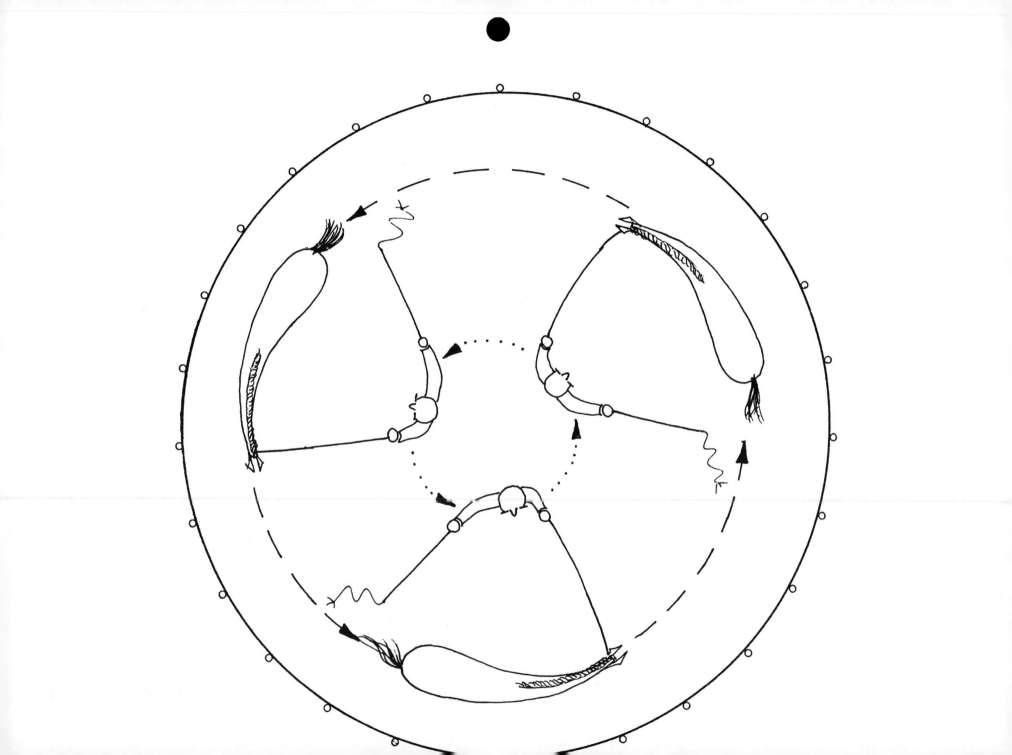

Concentric Circles

The closer you work to a horse, the greater the effect your aids will have on him. The farther away you work, the more diluted their effect.

Although the end goal is to have the horse work around you in a circle, at first you might have to work concentric circles with your horse. With some horses, you might have to resort to this technique each time you introduce a new variable.

Concentric circles are two circles that have the same center. The circle you make and the circle your horse makes should have the same center—it's the point where you will later stand when the horse is better trained and will longe around you. The advantage of concentric-circle longeing is that the horse works on a large circle, which minimizes stress to his limbs and allows him to keep in balance. The trainer must keep walking, which means more exercise—a highly regarded benefit!

First review in-hand work on a long line, Exercise 10.

For concentric circles, you will walk alongside your horse with the longe line out about 10 feet. This takes some talent on your part. You have to keep the piece of pie configuration, be effective in driving and guiding, face the horse, and walk sideways all at the same time!

This gives you good control of the horse while you develop in him the idea of forward motion.

Gradually, you will be able to let out more line and work your way toward the center of the circle while the horse maintains his path on his own.

Save the concentric circle technique for when you need to increase the horse's impulsion or for when you want to use it to teach him to extend or move out in a particular gait. If you constantly stay after a horse by always using the concentric circle, he will become dependent on it and your signals from the center will lose their effectiveness.

LONGE LINE LENGTH

The goal is to work a horse in a circle 20 meters (66 feet) in diameter. That means the horse is 33 feet away from you, which is why you need to use a 30- to 35-foot longe line (10 to 12 meters). The common 24-foot longe line, even when extended full out, puts the horse on a 48-foot circle *(maximum)*. A 24-foot longe line is too short for working young horses or for cantering any horse but may be appropriate for ponies.

AVOID RHYTHM AND IMPULSION PROBLEMS

As you work a green horse on the longe line, aim to develop pure, unhurried gaits that have plenty of energy from the hindquarters. If you allow a horse to rush or work with an uneven or impure rhythm, it will carry over to his saddle work. Influencing the tempo of a horse's gaits on the longe line is one of the most difficult yet one of the most beneficial aspects of longeing. You must encourage energy and action from the horse, using your body language and the whip, and at the same time contain the horse with the action of your body and the longe line. By using a 35-foot longe line and working the horse on a 66-foot circle, you give the horse the best chance for finding his balance and rhythm. When a horse loses his balance, he takes a quick step.

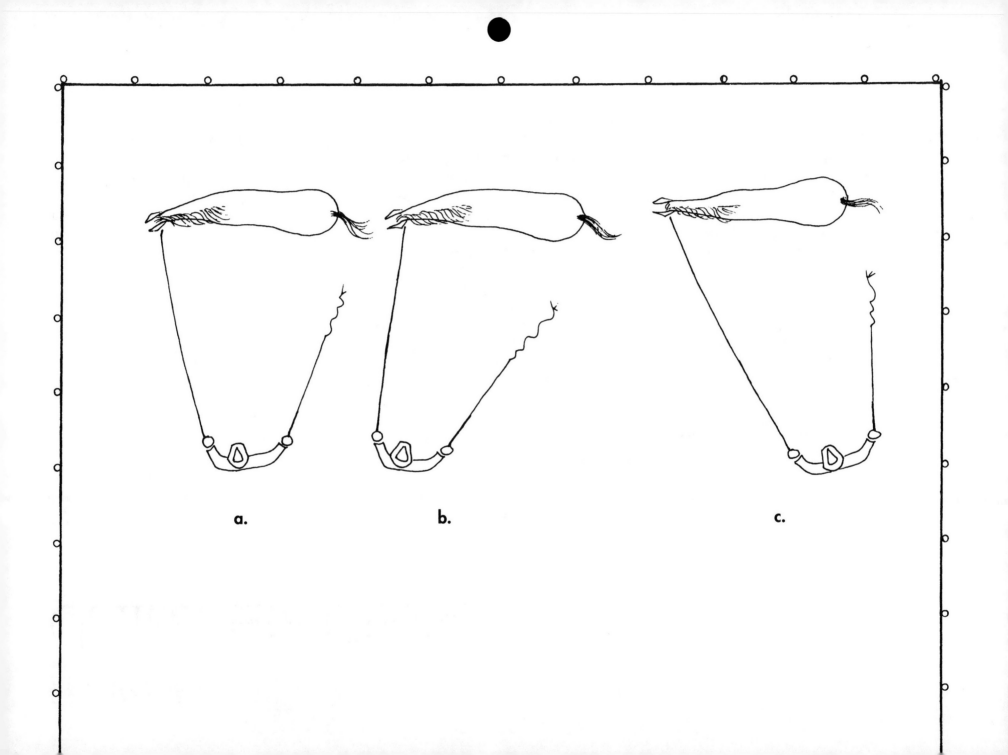

a.

b.

c.

Exercise 32

Position Control

Where you stand in relation to the side of the horse's body has a tremendous effect on *whether* he moves and *how* he moves or whether he stops, faces you, or turns. Refer to the free longeing section for more information on body language.

a. For most longeing maneuvers, you want to face a point on the horse's body approximately at the center of his ribs. The arm holding the longe line should invite forward motion yet maintain contact with the horse via the headgear. The whip should encourage impulsion. This central position is called the "control triangle" and the "piece of pie configuration." In the central position, you have the best chance of regulating and balancing the driving and restraining aids. You are in the best position to move the horse on or bring him back, when necessary.

b. If you get ahead of the central position, you run the risk of thwarting the horse's forward movement. Of course, if that is your goal, then step to the horse's head by all means! But under normal circumstances, you'd only want to be in this forward position momentarily to effect a change. The forward position is used to slow down, stop, or turn a horse. In the forward position it is much more difficult to effectively move the horse forward.

c. If you get behind the horse's movement, aiming at his hindquarters, you could lose control of the horse's head. Since this is more of a "chase" position, if a horse bolted while you were behind the movement, you could experience the sport of sand skiing. You would have no mechanical ability to stop the horse if you got this far behind him. Even with a lazy horse, this is not a recommended position because the horse could more easily swing in and kick you.

A Piece of Pie When longeing with a line, the configuration that the trainer and horse make is like a piece of pie rotating around a pie pan. The longeing circle is the pie pan. The horse is the crust, the trainer the point of the slice of pie; the longe line is one side of the piece, and the extended whip is the other side. The hand holding the longe line guides the horse, regulates impulsion, and helps to balance and shape the horse. The hand holding the whip provides impulsion. The trainer's position in relationship to the horse should be at or behind the midpoint of the horse's body. This lets the trainer "catch" the horse between the driving aid (whip) and restraining aid (the longe line).

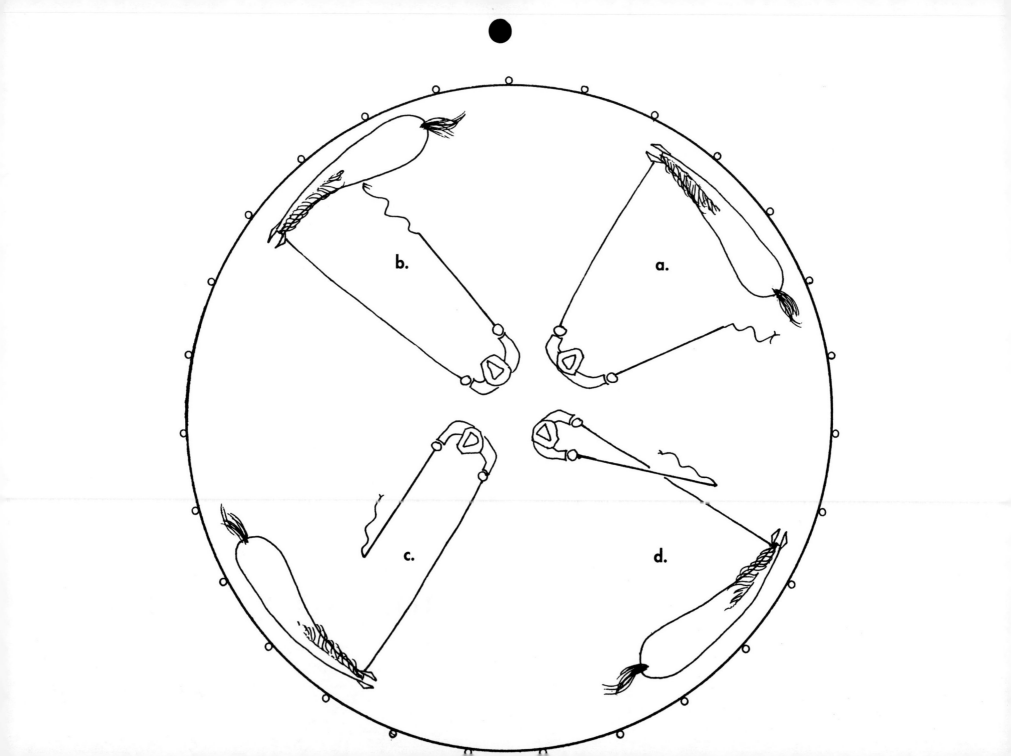

What Whip Where?

Where you point the whip is going to have a great effect on the type of response you will get from the horse.

a. In the normal position, the whip is aimed just behind the horse's hindquarters. This is the position that allows you to actively move the horse forward and balance him between the driving and restraining aids. It's most suitable for young horses and routine longeing and should be used unless you need to "fix" something.

b. In the rib-tickler position, the whip aims at approximately the place where a rider's leg might give a cue for bend later, during riding. This position is fine for horses who are pretty bombproof about longeing and will accept the whip aimed here. Some horses find this position a little curious and attempt to look at the whip. The rib-tickler position gives you the best bending effect, as the horse's body responds by curling in one continuous arc—around the point of the whip.

c. Aiming the whip at the horse's shoulder or neck is suitable for pushing the horse out onto a larger circle and asking for bend in the shoulder and neck. This technique should be used with caution and with experienced horses. A whip this close to the head would cause some horses to stop or turn. This forward position helps when you are teaching the spiral (Exercise 40) and also helps push a horse that cuts in back out to the rail.

d. Crossing the whip over or under the longe line is a definite restraining command that means slow down or stop. When the whip comes in front of a horse's field of vision, he most likely will not want to run through it. Whether you go over the longe line or under it will depend on your height and the height of the horse you are longeing.

WHIP TALK REVIEW

- Point or make a small movement (jiggle or wave) to get a horse to move over or forward.
- Send out the lash to lick the horse on the barrel to cause him to move out or forward.
- Send out the lash to lick the horse on the hindquarters to cause him to move forward. It may cause him to kick.
- Never send the lash out to hit the horse ahead of the girth. It could hit him in the eye.
- Roll the whip in circles after a lazy horse to keep him loping.
- Crack the whip by moving it forward and then quickly back, to wake up a horse!

See Exercise 2 for more on whip works.

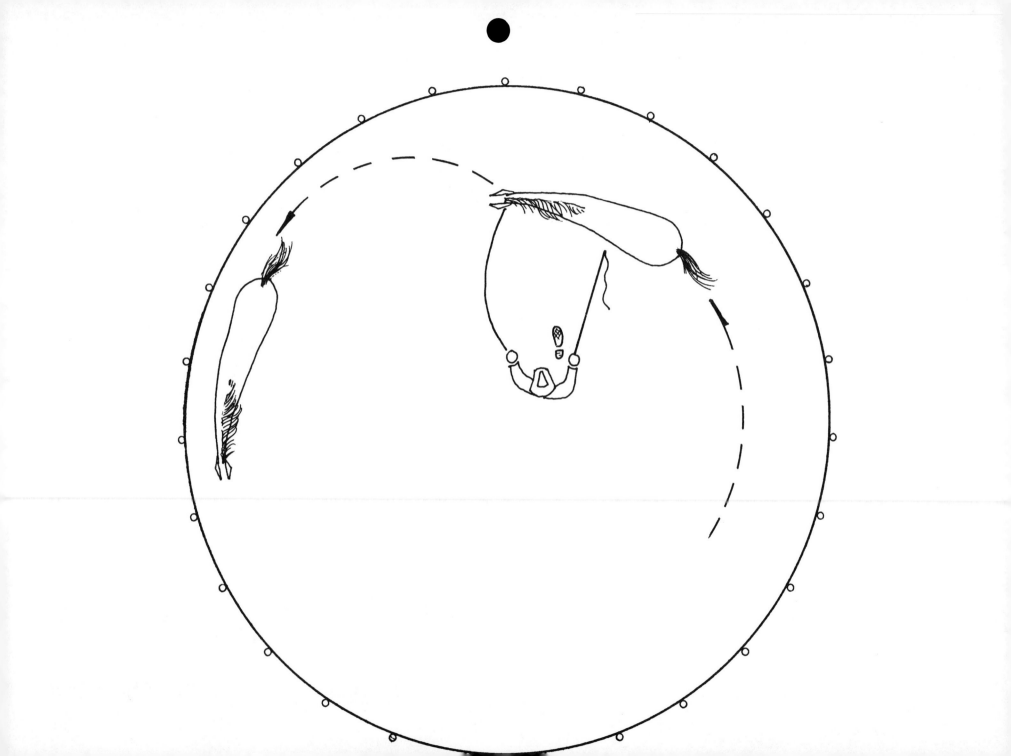

Exercise 34

Pushing the Horse Out

You will need a technique to push a horse out on the circle for spiral exercises and also to gain control of the horse that cuts in on a particular portion of a circle. A horse might cut in for any of the following reasons:

- Something along the rail is frightening him.
- He is insecure and wants to get to a safe place more quickly.
- He started cutting in when he first was longed, it was not corrected, and now it is habit.
- The footing in a particular portion of the training pen is too deep, slippery, or difficult to negotiate.
- He wants to get to the gate and quit work.
- He likes to be near his buddies, so works on the rail when he is near them and cuts into the circle when he is farthest from them.
- He hasn't yet learned the enjoyable, relaxing feeling of working in a continuous circle.

To move a horse back onto the rail, use any or all of the following techniques:

- Step assertively toward the horse's forehand with your driving foot. You might have to take several steps toward the horse: right, left, right.
- Point the whip at his midsection and lunge at him, pushing him out.
- Give him enough slack on the longe line so that he can move away, yet retain some contact so that you can control him.
- Direct the whip toward his neck or shoulder if he tends to cut in abruptly at a certain point.
- Anticipate where he usually cuts in and take his mind off the option by driving him actively forward and assertively stepping toward him to keep him on the rail.

Problem: A Horse that Cuts Corners   The horse consistently shaves off one side of the circle, making a flat spot. Nip this one in the bud. The horse is not receiving benefits from the longeing and he is learning that he can take control. Take an assertive giant step toward him while sending a wave through your longe line to pop him on the shoulder at the same time you lunge with the whip at his hindquarters. An appropriate voice command would be "Go on." *Never compensate for your horse's irregular circle by backing up when he travels closer to the center.* Instead, make him move out and take contact with the longe line. Side reins, with the outside rein adjusted slightly tighter, will keep a horse on the track of the longeing circle. (See the section on longeing with a bridle and side reins, starting page 125.)

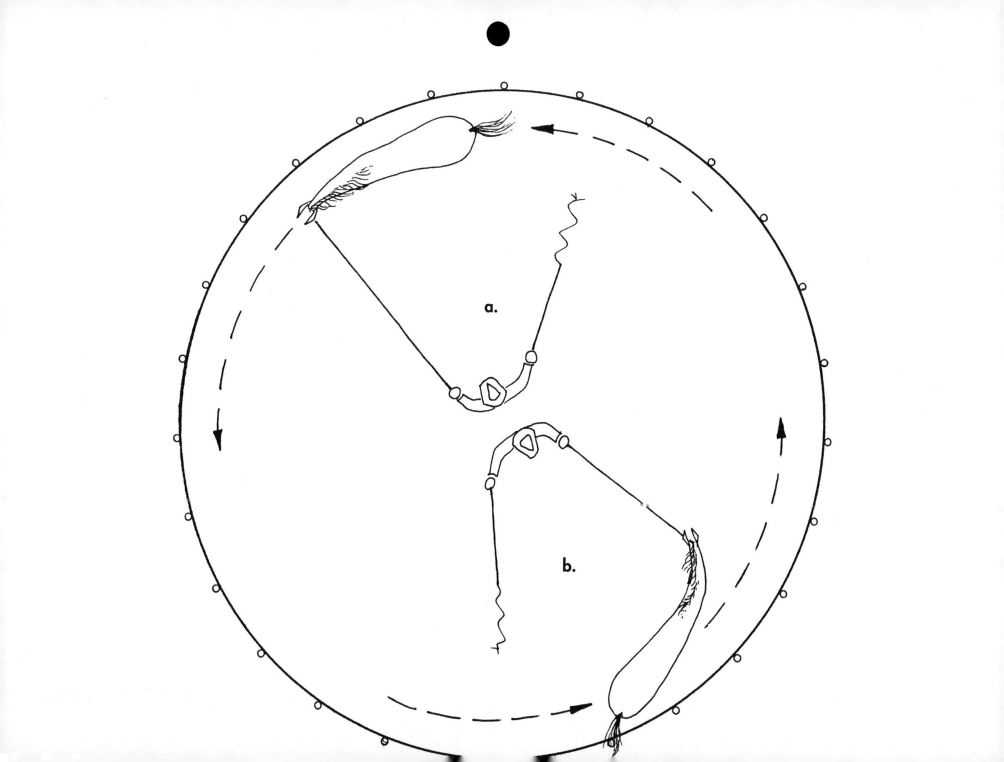

a.

b.

Exercise 35

Correct and Incorrect Bend

Longeing is circle work. Circles and circular figures require turning. The turn can involve an almost imperceptible arcing of the horse's spine on a very large circle or an extreme inward curving for a very small collected circle. Turning requires proper flexion and bending.

Lateral flexion is a turn of the horse's head to one side or the other. The movement takes place at the joint of the axis vertebrae: the junction of the neck and the head, more commonly referred to as the poll or throatlatch area. When a horse is described as flexed (in contrast to bent), the rest of his spine (from the poll to the tail) is straight. Flexion is created with side rein aids in longeing and with long lines in ground driving. There can be lateral flexion without lateral bend, as in the case of leg yielding. Generally, however, a horse who is flexed is also bent.

a. Lateral bend is the arcing of the horse's entire body. When circling left, the horse will be bent to the left. Correct lateral bend requires lateral flexion. The bend must be uniform from poll to tail. When a horse tracks correctly on a circle, the hind legs follow in the tracks of the front legs. This is the most stable, vertical configuration and results in the fewest interference problems.

b. The horse's neck is more flexible than the back, so the tendency is for the front of the horse to overbend and shift the hindquarters off the track. If a horse carries his shoulder to the inside of the circle and his hindquarters off the track of the circle, the hind legs are not following in the track of the front legs. The horse is leaning inward, which is an unstable posture. When a horse is unstable, he is off balance and has erratic rhythm. This leads to poorer muscular development and a higher incidence of interference. Overbending is one of the main cautions when you use side reins. If they are used too early in the horse's development or are used incorrectly (too short an inside rein, for example), they can create improper bend and lead to a host of other problems. This must be avoided.

Problems: Incorrect Bend, No Bend, Stiffness
The horse does not bend correctly when traveling in a circle. It is okay if a young horse is a bit stiff on a 20-meter circle. Once the horse gains some experience, however, he should start lowering his entire frame and bending inward. *Be certain you are working the horse on a 20-meter- (66-foot-) diameter circle. Smaller circles exaggerate and reinforce an untrained horse's natural stiffness.* If you see that a horse carries himself stiff to the outside, with his head up or his back hollow, you'd be better off postponing his longeing lessons until he's at an age when you can introduce side reins and a surcingle or use ground driving. If you let a horse repeat stiff circles over and over again with poor carriage and movement, these habits will not only carry over in his memory patterns but his body will develop undesirable muscular patterns as well.

When a horse overbends to the inside, he puts more weight on the inside shoulder, loses contact with the longe line, and possibly swings his hindquarters off the circle. It might be a normal symptom of his level of training. If it is time to address the problem, there are several ways to do it,

87

using side reins (see Exercise 59). In the meantime, you should use the techniques in Exercise 34 to push the horse out on the circle.

When a horse falls out, he is usually stiff, bends little, if at all, and pulls out of the circle, putting more weight on his outside shoulder. He needs to be brought in on a small concentric circle or spiral to learn bending.

Imbalances and improper bending often occur because a horse does not want to engage his hind legs (and back). Engagement means stepping under the body with the hind legs and rounding the back. The stiff horse and the horse who has not yet developed hind leg strength will swing the hindquarters off the circle and not use his hocks.

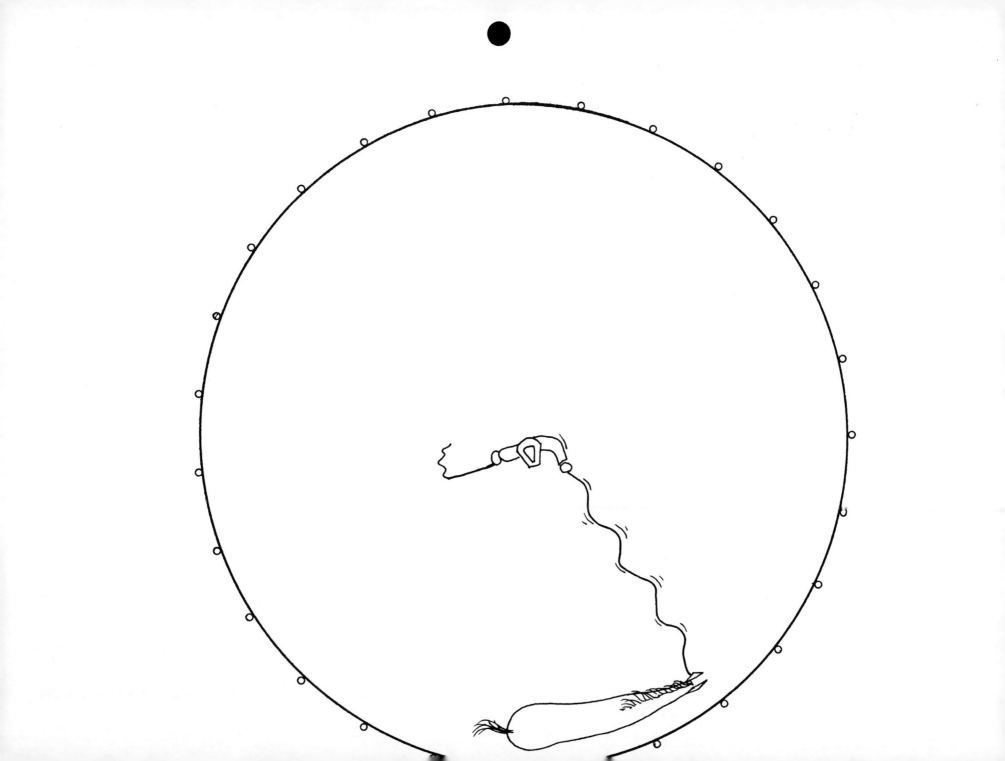

Exercise 36

Easy

"Easy" is an important all-purpose lesson that can help you calm a horse in a variety of situations. You can use it to help you:

- Calm a horse who is rushing.
- Make a transition within a gait, such as from an extended trot to a jog.
- Make a transition between gaits, such as from a trot to a walk.
- Stop a horse who has become tangled in a line or has a broken piece of tack.
- Relax a horse who has just been startled.

"Easy" starts with a soothing, drawling voice command: "Eeeeezzeeeeeee." It's as if you are trying to put the horse to sleep with your hypnotic voice. As with many commands, it helps if you have made the association during in-hand work when you are near a horse and can stroke his neck to soothe him as well.

Along with the voice command, you will want to assume a fairly neutral body position. Depending on the horse and the situation, you might want to hold the whip to the side or behind you.

The calming wave in the line should arrive at the horse as a gentle vibration that helps to break up any tension or resistance. The wave should not be abrupt, as if it were a punishment. The combination of the "Easy" aids should make a horse more relaxed, not more nervous.

Suppleness and flexibility depend on the horse being relaxed. Excess muscular tension leads to fear, quickness, and injury.

Cavesson Weight: "Breaking" cavessons are generally made of stout leather, have heavy metal nose pieces, and straps to fasten them securely and keep them in position on the horse's head. During "breaking" it is often necessary to tug or pull quite hard on the line to control the horse. When a light aid is given, it has more "weight" with a cavesson than it would with a halter. Lighter, simpler cavessons are also available for the very young horse, the already-trained horse, for use with a bit or bridle, and for use as a dropped noseband.

Problem: Disobedience The horse cannot be stopped, wraps himself in the longe line, whirls, is willful, kicks, or otherwise misbehaves. First give the horse the benefit of the doubt and rule out fear and a hasty training progression. Is he afraid of the longe line, the whip, his headgear, or you? If so, assess and review. This is where the use of "Easy" might be appropriate to calm the horse who has a legitimate fear. Check the fit of all gear.

If you have determined that the problem is, in fact, disobedience, then actively drive the horse forward. You may have to temporarily sacrifice rhythm and tempo, but at least the horse is going forward and not sideways or upside down. If a correction is necessary, be prompt and effective. If a horse kicks while free longeing, immediately turn him hard into the fence (rollback) at least twice so that he is then traveling in the same direction he was initially. Act as if nothing has happened. If he kicks again, repeat. If a horse kicks on the longe line, use the cavesson to immediately discipline him with a sharp jerk and turn him into the circle. If the problem persists, seek the help of a professional who might choose to use a different technique for that particular horse.

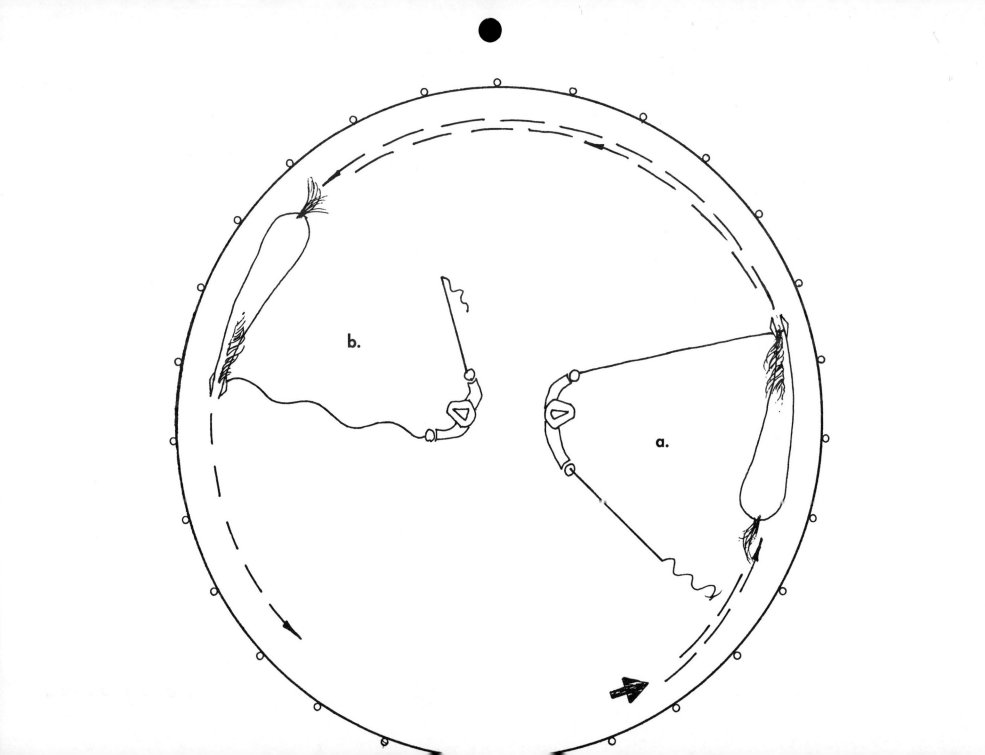

Trot-Walk

Although it might seem as though walking would be the first gait you would teach your horse, often it is not. If your horse is very calm and well mannered, asking him to walk in each direction with a couple of halts here and there would be an appropriate first longeing lesson of about five minutes.

Because of the lack of impulsion at the walk, however, many horses inexperienced at longeing on a line tend to turn or stop. This you want to avoid. If you think your horse will stay calm, begin the trot after a few steps of walk. Your horse may begin the trot without your asking. This is okay at the beginning. The trot results in fewer stall-outs and unwanted turns, and less confusion. Your horse will learn to keep going forward with continuous motion.

a. Once your horse is trotting, when you want him to walk or stop, use the aids you used in free longeing.

b. Lower your whip or put it in a neutral position at your side or behind your back.

Speak soothingly, "Waaalk," and step back a few steps.

Use a gentle wave action on the longe line to ask for the downward transition. Too harsh a line action could cause him to stop.

Even at the walk, keep a good longe line contact. If you have no contact, you have no control. A longe line that sags and drags on the ground wears out prematurely but more important, you do not have that instant connection that allows you to communicate with your horse.

Caution: When you start a horse out during a longeing session, you must stay back far enough to drive the horse forward. This, however, puts you near the hindquarters—a dangerous place to be if the horse kicks. To minimize the chance of the horse making contact, turn his head in toward you as you begin. This moves the hindquarters out on the circle away from you.

Cavesson Fit: For routine longeing, the cavesson noseband is generally positioned about midway between the prominent cheekbones and the corners of the horse's mouth—approximately two fingers below the prominent cheekbone and about three to four fingers above the nostrils. In this position, the noseband will be effective but won't interfere with the horse's breathing or risk damaging the fragile tip of the nasal bone.

Free Walk: A free walk is characterized by long strides, a relaxed back, and a lowered head and neck. The horse should be allowed to carry his head and neck as low as he'd like. The free walk is a good way to check whether the previous work has been correct and the horse is relaxed.

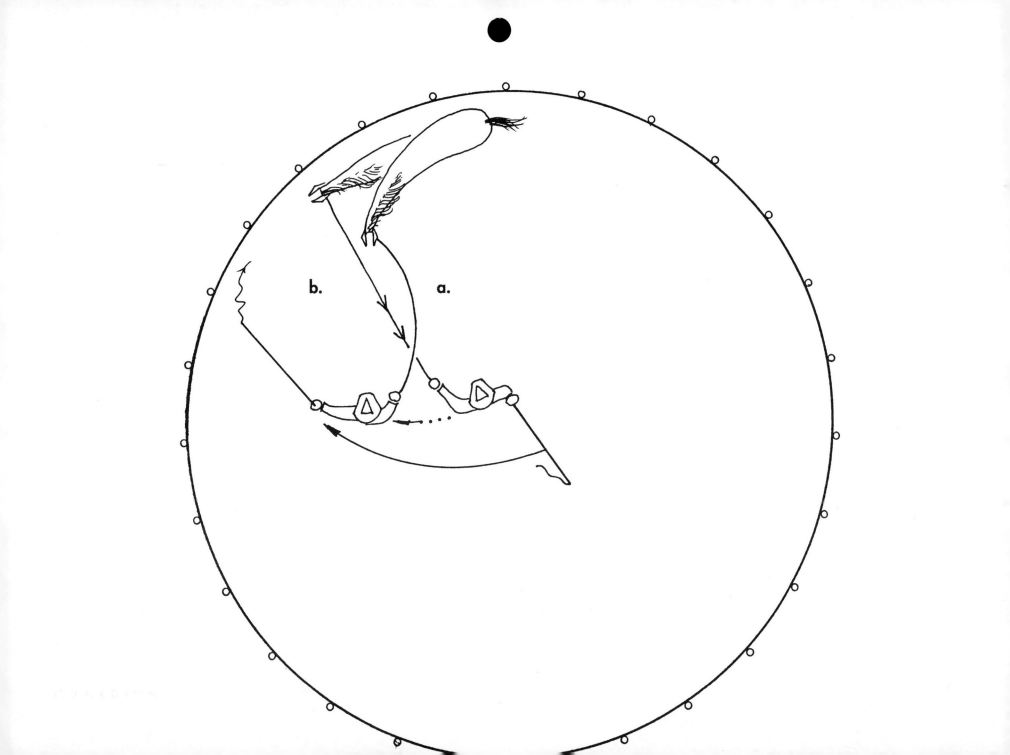

Turn

When you add a longe line, you immediately gain a positive way to control which way a horse turns when you call for a reverse. The turn on the longe line must be to the inside. An outside turn is not possible because the horse would become tangled in the line. But be prepared that a horse might try to perform an outside turn.

Now that you have a line to help control and guide the horse, you can easily teach him an inside turn. If you free longed your horse, you might have had difficulty establishing an inside turn in both directions. Often a horse will easily learn to turn inside when tracking left but may also want to turn left when tracking right and so has trouble learning an inside turn to the right. If you didn't complete this lesson in free longeing or if you don't have a round pen and didn't free longe, the longe line gives you the means to teach that lesson here.

a. Always make the first inside turns from a halt. Stop the horse on the circle track. Point the whip behind you.

b. Switch the whip behind your back while maintaining some tension on the line. Give the voice command "Tuuuuuurn," using circular sounds as you step to the horse's forehand and present the whip as a cue to turn.

With some horses, the first turn comes easier on a 30-foot line than on a 10-foot line. Many horses feel crowded and stiffen when facing you and a whip in close quarters. Other horses are too far away to control at 30 feet and so learn better at 10 feet. You will have to experiment.

WHIP SWITCH

When changing hands on the whip, here is another method that works okay with shorter longe whips:

- If the horse is tracking left, tuck the whip under your right arm with the butt end facing forward and up. The tip of whip will be on ground behind you.
- Change the line from your left hand to your right.
- Reach behind your back with your left hand and retrieve the whip.
- Now you are set to change the horse's direction.

Problem: Horse Turns Away The horse turns away from you and turns his hindquarters toward you. It is normal for a horse to turn away from you when you first teach him to free longe. If the habit persists during line longeing, however, you will need to go back to the bending and flexing exercises in-hand. With a cavesson, you can snap the line on the inside ring.

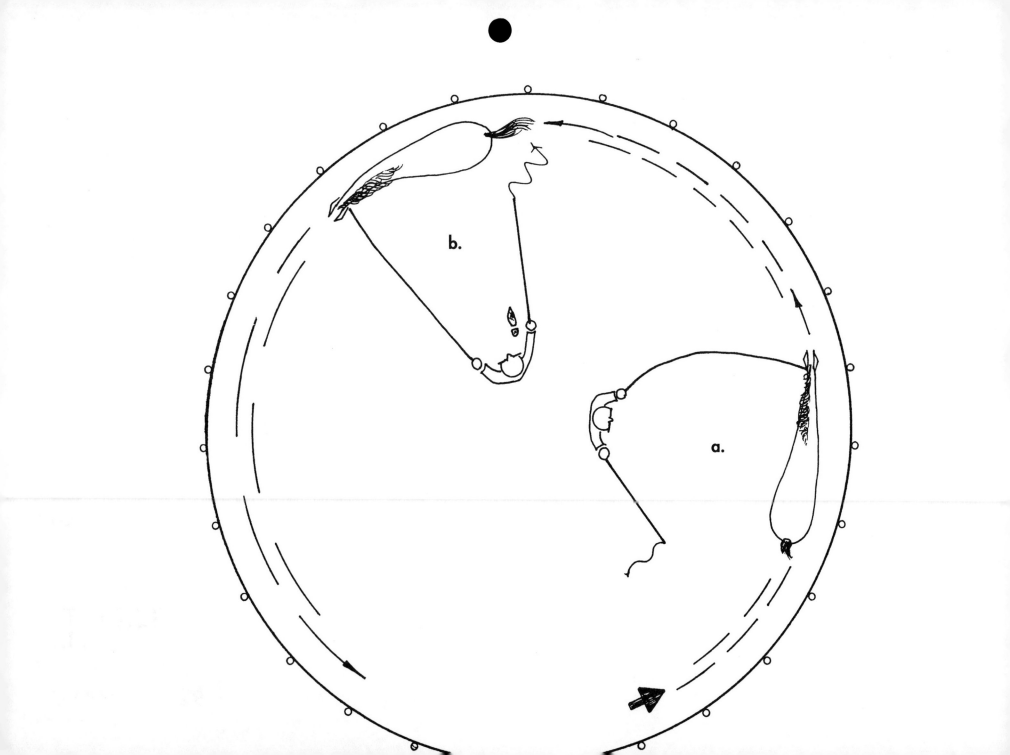

Exercise 39

Trot On

Since the trot is often the main gait you use in longeing for both training and exercise, you need to attend to it constantly. A horse's trot can deteriorate if ignored. If you let a horse go round and round on automatic pilot, he will choose the physical parameters that are mechanically easiest for him. If left unchecked, a poor trot can become a habit.

The most common problems with the trot are:

1. Rushed but not extended: the stride has shortened and become quick, and is usually accompanied by an inverted topline (high head, hollow back, hindquarters behind the motion).
2. Too slow: the stride has lost all its impulsion and has deteriorated into a *wog*—half walk, half jog.

Interestingly, the cure for both problems is the same. And it is a cure for many problems in ground training and riding. Increase forward impulsion.

Forward impulsion is the desire to actively move forward. It is the thrust or manner in which the horse's weight is settled and released from the supporting structures of the limbs in the act of carrying the horse forward.

Driving aids encourage forward impulsion. In longeing you can increase a horse's impulsion with your body language, voice commands, and whip position.

Forward impulsion is diminished in an exhausted or frustrated horse or one who is confused or intimidated by the improper use of headgear or training devices.

a. When a horse is performing an unglued or pokey trot, often it is because the trainer has tuned out and is haphazardly holding the whip and line. The whip is limp or erratic in its motion. The line is dragging or slack. All that is needed is a tune up.

b. Invite the horse forward by leading with the longe line. In order for a horse to feel a lead, there must be contact on the line. Step toward the horse's hindquarters. Activate the whip but keep it horizontal and following or "chasing." You want to drive the horse on but not up into the next gait. I use the voice command, "Trot on," spoken as though I am really saying, "Wake up!" With a good feel on the line, you can hold the horse in the trot gait but liven it up with your driving aids. Tell the horse "Gooooood" when you see a positive effort. Don't expect a horse to trot on forever at first. This is something that has to be developed gradually, especially in a horse who has been allowed to dawdle or trot in poor form.

Problem: Horse Breaks into a Canter This is not as big a problem as you might think. At least the horse is making an error on the side of more impulsion! You should pay attention to the tendency, however, to keep it from becoming a habit. You might have to go back to concentric circles and an even stronger contact on the line, coupled with an actively following whip. "Skate" along with your horse with your knees bent.

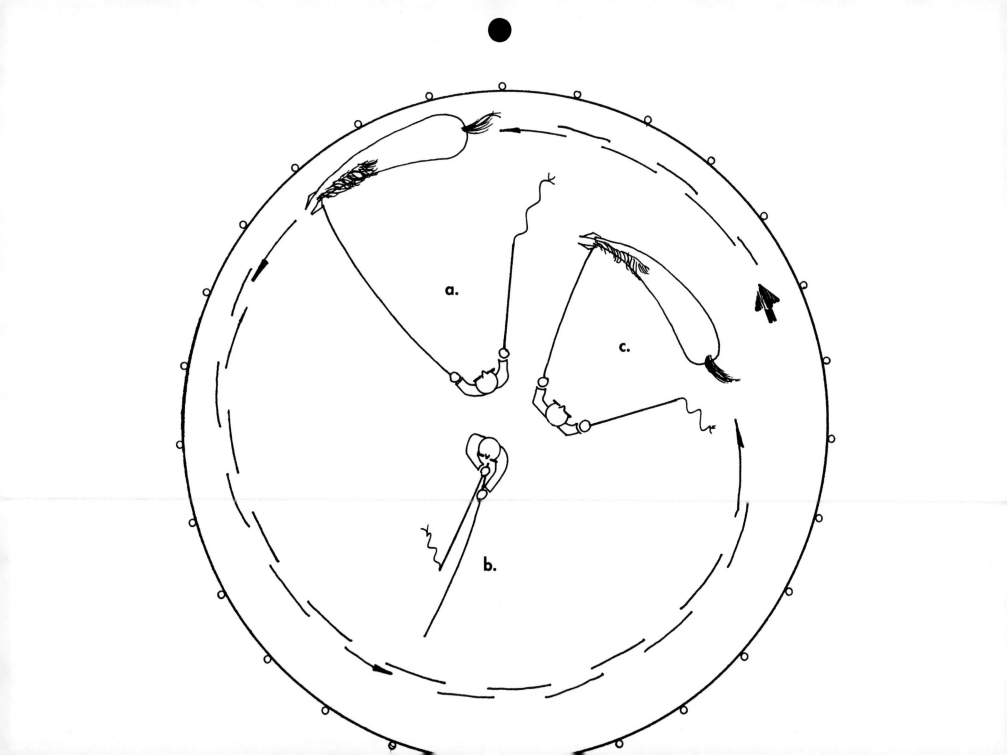

a.

c.

b.

Exercise 40

Spiral-In Trot

One of the main purposes of a spiral is to get a horse to track straight. You work him in a smaller circle so you can bring his head in and push his hindquarters out.

a. Until now, the horse has mainly been worked on a full 20-meter (66-foot) circle.

b. As the horse is trotting, bring your hands together in front of you, (Exercise 5), so you can shorten the line in increments. If you have a hard time gauging 5 meters, make a mark on your longe line. Some longe lines have distance tags.

c. As a horse gains his balance, he can be brought in gradually for short periods of time to work on a smaller circle. First, spiral-in at the trot; the horse is brought into a 15-meter circle. As you reel in the horse, do so in small increments, with a give-and-take feel, not a sudden pull. You want the horse to retain his balance. Work the horse on the smaller circle for only about one or two circles the first time. The smaller circle will increase the horse's

chance of interference if he is unbalanced. If you note any speeding up or resistance, let the horse spiral out. This may indicate that it is too early in the horse's physical development to work in a smaller circle.

Problem: Should You Spiral a Horse First on His Strong Side or on His Weak Side?   Horses, like humans, usually have a side preference. That is why most horses initially travel stiff in one direction and overbend in the other. This is referred to as a horse's natural stiffness and hollowness, or a horse's strong and weak sides.

Many horses are stiffer (stronger) on the left side of their bodies. The left sides of their bodies tend to curl inward to the left and strongly resist stretching to the right or straightening. When such a horse travels to the left, its strong left side may tend to overcurl the horse to the inside.

When traveling to the right, the same horse will have difficulty counteracting the strong pull from the left side, so will have difficulty bending to the right. This can show up in several ways: head up, carried to the left, body held at an angle with the front feet outside the tracks of the hind feet,

hindquarters shifted in to the right, weight falling out on the left shoulder. If *made* to bend to the right, the horse would overbend to the right and bulge (or pop) his left shoulder out or carry his entire body to the left to relieve the stress from the stretch on the left side.

Until a horse is systematically developed, he often has a difficult time bending his entire body uniformly in both directions. So, at the beginning, it's best to start longeing on the horse's stronger side, usually the left. And it's better to introduce new concepts to the left as well. That way, fewer problems will pop up. With most horses, it's best to first spiral in left.

After warm-up, you can switch to the weaker side but you may find, at first, that you cannot work the horse as long in this direction. As the lessons progress, you will gradually increase the amount of time the horse can work to the weaker side. And eventually you will begin to start some of the sessions on the weaker side. But remember, developmental exercises are not by nature confrontational. They are gradual progressions to a desired state, not a showdown.

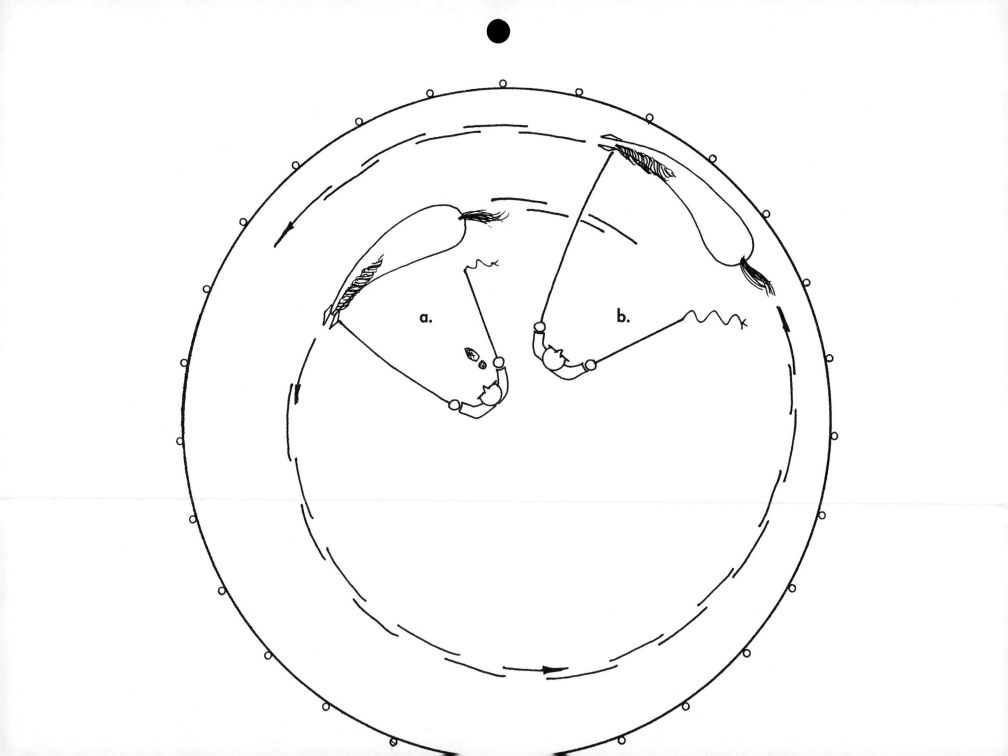

a.

b.

Exercise 41

Spiral-Out Trot

As you spiral the horse back to the original 20-meter circle, be aware that you want to maintain an even bend throughout the exercise. The horse should travel "straight" ahead in all aspects of the spiral exercise.

a. Move toward your horse with a small, driving footstep. Point the whip at the horse's hindquarters or ribs to push him back out to the large circle.

b. Maintain contact on the longe line but open your fingers and allow the line to slip through in small increments as the horse gradually works his way back to 20 meters.

If you give the horse too much slack with the line all at once, his forehand will turn "flat" to the outside, off the circular track, and he will make a "beeline" back to the rail of the round pen. This you do not want.

Remember: the goal is a consistent rhythm of the trot throughout the exercise and a consistent bend. The horse must stay straight on the track of the circle. This increases the flexion and engagement of the inside hind leg.

CROOKED OR STRAIGHT?

Most horses move naturally "crooked," as doing so requires less effort than moving straight. Most training strives for *ordinary straightness*, where the spine (midline) is in a straight line. Because a horse's hips are wider than his shoulders, the hind feet do not step directly in the tracks of the front feet when the horse is straight by *ordinary* standards. Dressage strives for *relative straightness*, where the inside hind follows in the exact track of the inside front.

Most horses (80 to 90 percent) travel naturally crooked in this fashion: the right hind travels in a track to the right of the right front and thus sends more weight diagonally to the left shoulder, causing the horse to fall in to the left. The left hind leg carries more weight and the right hind pushes the body to the left. This results in the left side being stiffer and stronger than the right side.

So, when going to the left, the horse tends to overbend to the left with a curling stiffness, weighting the left shoulder, and swinging the hindquarters off the track to the right. The correction for this is to first drive the horse actively forward. Then, if you are experienced with side rein use, you can counterflex the horse slightly to the right, using side reins (see Exercises 51-67).

When going to the right, the horse tends to counterflex to the left with a straight stiffness from a strong pull by the left side. The hindquarters swing in to the right. The correction for this is, once again, to drive the horse actively forward. If you are experienced in side rein use, you can work the horse "in position" to the right with a somewhat shorter inside rein. Another correction is shoulder-in, which is easier to achieve with long lines than with side reins.

About 10 to 20 percent of horses travel crooked in the opposite way.

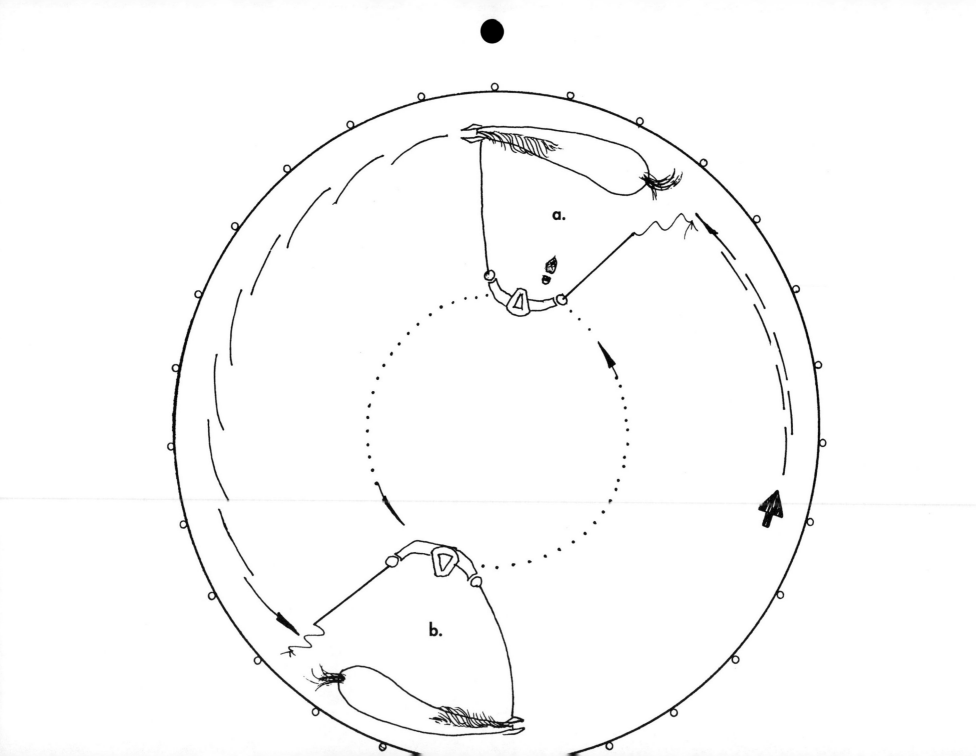

a.

b.

Exercise 42

Trot-Lope Concentric

When you first teach a transition to a lope or canter, you have the best chance for success from the trot. A balanced, active trot has a good deal of impulsion, so it should be easy to shift the horse up into the higher gear. Going from an unbalanced, fast trot into a lope, however, usually results in a fast, unbalanced lope. And moving from an extended trot into a canter results in strung-out canter with risk of interference during the transition. The best transition will occur from a relatively balanced working trot into a canter.

Prior to asking for the lope transition, be sure the horse is trotting in an energized, compacted frame, not rambling or dawdling. Do this by stepping up your active driving aids: step to the horse, active whip, but do not ask for a "Trot on." You want to contain the horse's movement by a strong contact on the longe line, just as you would with a half halt when riding. You want to hold the horse in the enhanced energized state for only a few brief moments. Just before you ask for the transition, use your preparatory voice command, such as "OK."

a. Ask for the upward transition by a combination of the following aids:

- A step to the horse's hindquarters.
- A raising, popping, or rolling of the whip.
- A voice command such as "Let's go."

b. Some horses benefit from your working a concentric circle while they learn transitions in balance and gain their form. Working in a concentric circle has the following characteristics and benefits:

- The horse works the full 20-meter circle.
- You are close enough to "aid" him with the whip directly if required
- You are close enough to maintain a good contact on the longe line
- You get some additional exercise!

LOPE A TWO-YEAR-OLD?

Before you longe any horse younger than 24 months of age, examine his knees and fetlock joints. Some young horses have "open" knees; the growth plates of the bones are still actively adding on bone. With such a horse, postpone longeing until the summer of the two-year-old year when the horse is at least 24 months old. Pasture turn-out would be a better exercise option until then.

Problem: Horse Changes Leads Sometimes a horse will strike off on the correct lead and then switch to the wrong lead. Frustrating! This is usually because the horse is so tired, lame, or stiff that he changes leads to get relief. If he has been worked to the left quite a bit during a particular session, for example, it would not be surprising that he is seeking relief from the left lead by switching to the right lead. If the horse is lame, of course, even though his training reflexes have him take the correct lead for a few steps, his self-preservation will kick in and he will switch because it hurts. Quit the session and take the appropriate health-care or conditioning steps. You might need to go back to lots of walk-trot transitions with side reins until the horse has learned to bend equally in both directions.

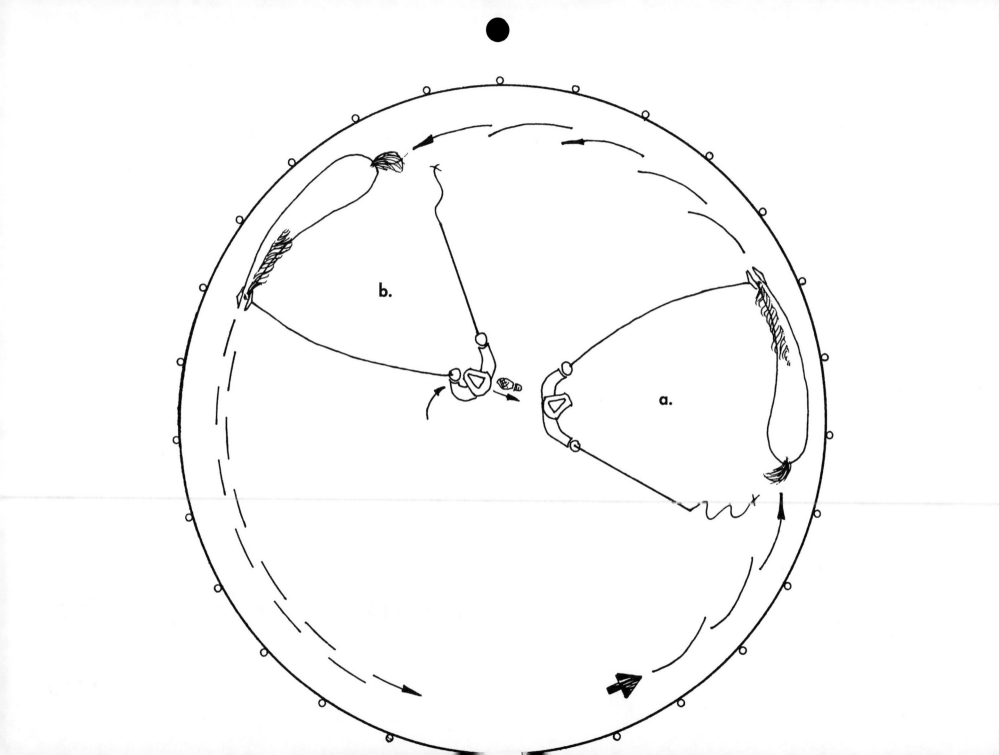

b.

a.

Exercise 43

Lope-Trot

As you know from riding, the canter/lope to trot transition can be unsettling. That's because most horses are not collected enough to perform a balanced downward transition—one in which the hind legs drive deep under the horse and support him.

A transition is a shifting of gears. A *downward* transition is a change from a gait that is more ground-covering or faster to one that is less so. Examples are canter to trot, canter to walk, trot to walk, and walk to halt. Downward transitions can also indicate decreases within a gait, such as extended canter to collected canter.

Good transitions are prompt yet not sudden. A horse *must* be prepared for every transition. No transition is correct without the proper use of preparatory commands.

Transitions are a smooth balance between driving aids and restraining aids. Although the net result of these forces should be near zero, indicating that they approach being equal, there should always be a tendency for more driving energy so that the transitions are forward.

The lope to trot transition should be forward and fluid. If you emphasize fluid, forward transitions during longeing and ground driving, you will be glad when it comes time to ride the horse.

a. Just before the downward transition, the horse should be loping or cantering with good energy, balance, and rhythm. A horse needs to have active hind legs in order to reach under for a good balanced, smooth downward transition. If a horse is performing a four-beat canter, his hind legs are probably way behind the movement of his body and the transition will be rough and disorganized.

b. So just prior to the downward transition, don't let the horse die. Be sure he is actively cantering. Then, in a time sequence that you will need to tailor for each horse, do the following:

1. Step back one step.
2. Lower the whip but keep it active.

3. Raise the hand holding the longe line and hold, quiver, or snap the line back, depending on the horse.

   Say "Ta-raaaaaat," with falling inflection and ending on a low tone.

As soon as the horse trots, do one of the following:

If the horse is rushing, say "Eeeeeeasy," and cast a gentle wave on the line (see Exercise 36).

If the horse "dies" and is performing a lackluster trot, keep a contact on the line, raise your whip to a horizontal following position without any action from the lash, and say, "Trot on!" (see Exercise 39).

Problem: Horse Is on the Wrong Lead The horse is being worked in a circle to the left and is on the right lead. Or the horse is *disunited*, that is, he is cantering on one lead with the front legs and the opposite lead with the hind. It is the rare horse who takes the wrong lead when being free longed in a 66-foot round pen. As soon as you add a longe line, halter, cavesson or bridle, however, you are changing that horse's balance. When side reins are not being used, you will see a horse's natural tendency to left-right balance and suppleness.

Most horses take the wrong lead occasionally but usually take the correct lead when brought back to a trot and asked again for canter.

If a horse consistently takes the wrong lead in a particular direction, he is exhibiting stiffness. With a horse like that, it would be best to wait until you introduce side reins before working on the lead. But although side reins can help to develop suppleness and left-right balance and teach a horse to take the correct lead, if side reins are used too early or improperly they can actually teach the horse to take the wrong lead at the canter. For example, if your horse is tracking left and you have a tighter inside side rein to try to "make" the horse bend to the left, the horse may very likely take the right lead when asked to canter. The same horse, with head left free, quite likely would hold his head off to the right and take the left lead!

Problem: Horse Is Disunited   At first, the disunited horse can be treated in the same manner as the horse who takes the wrong lead. Usually, however, I move a disunited horse forward with strong aids for a moment, and that causes the horse to "unite." It's as if the horse is "popped" into synchronization. If you feel the horse would be frightened and

rush uncontrollably from strong driving aids, it might be better to bring the horse back to a trot or walk and then reestablish the canter, hopefully on the right lead and united.

JAQUIMA ALTERNATIVE

A properly fitted and balanced jaquima delivers its pull from the heel knot area of the bosal and can be suitable for longeing the Western horse. The bosal is the heavy rawhide nosepiece of the entire "jaquima," or hackamore rig. The bosal is suspended from a browband headstall that has had the throatlatch removed. A knotted rope fiador is substituted for the usual throatlatch. The fiador is a rope throatlatch with three knots: the hackamore knot, the fiador knot, and the sheet bend. The hackamore knot is tied and affixed to the heel knot of the bosal. The fiador knot is tied and positioned 4 to 6 inches above the hackamore knot and is positioned at the horse's throatlatch. The ends of the fiador pass through the headstall at the poll and are secured with a sheet bend knot at the horse's near cheek. A bosal can deliver an effective "Whoa" signal. Care must be taken to ensure that the bosal is of the right size and diameter for the particular horse. The nose portion of the bosal should fit the contour of the horse's nose very closely. There should be two to three fingers' room between the sidepieces of the bosal and the horse's jaw. This will allow the bosal to swivel back when the longe line is pulled, and relax and drop down when the longe line tension is slack.

Problem: Horse Faces You   The horse stops and turns in and faces you or starts walking toward you.

This is a serious fault to avoid. Unfortunately, many people think it is "sweet" when a horse wants to come to the trainer and, in fact, train the horse to come to the center of the training pen, rewarding him with treats and petting. Do not do this. Training a horse to come when he is in a stall, pen, or pasture is an entirely different matter, however, and is to be encouraged.

When a horse comes to the center of a training pen, he has negated the effect of this exercise. Your goal is to keep the horse facing forward on the track of the circle and moving forward at all times, except when you want him to turn. When he halts he should stop on the line of the circle. Make sure you are not causing the horse to turn in by inadvertently getting ahead of him or stepping backward as you longe and pulling the line toward you.

With problem horses, you should always walk forward as you longe. If a horse further challenges you by charging you, you must lunge toward the horse and back him down, or this could turn into a very serious problem. See Exercise 34 and the "Side Rein Longeing" section for help with this problem.

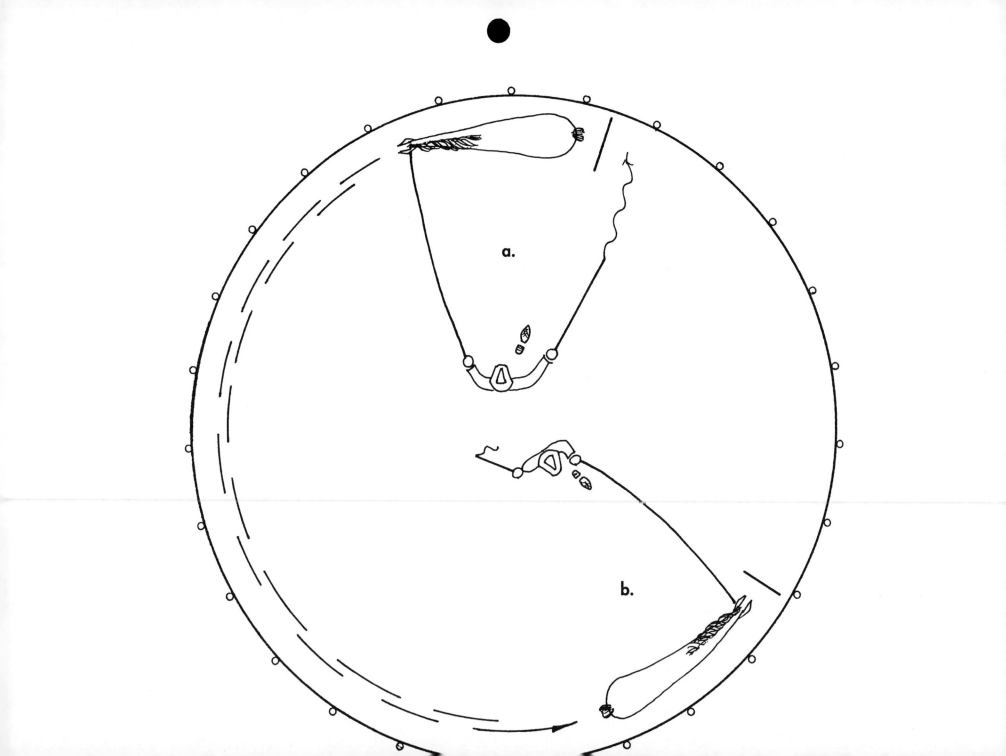

Halt-Trot-Halt

In preparation for some collected work, teach the horse this, one of my favorite riding exercises, on the longe line. An impeccably performed halt-trot-halt exercise goes a long way toward rounding a horse's topline and getting his hind legs under his body.

Throughout the entire exercise you are aiming for front-to-rear balance as well as left-to-right balance. Overall balance is the harmonious, precise, coordinated form of a horse's movement. It is composed of equal distribution of weight from the left side of the horse's body to the right and an appropriate relationship between the weight-bearing functions of the forehand and the hindquarters. It is balance that gives the horse the ability to spring from a standstill into a trot and to smoothly power-down from a trot to a square halt.

a. From a halt, you are going to have to create a brisk scenario so that the horse differentiates your upward aids from those for a walk. With some horses, however, if you make it too brisk, you will get a canter. Generally, you start from a square halt with contact on the longe line.

Simultaneously, you step with your driving foot toward the horse's hindquarters, cue with the whip, and briskly say, "Ta-rot!" The trot you are asking for and hope the horse performs is a more collected version of his working trot and a more animated version of his jog.

b. Since the benefits of this exercise are greatest when the transitions come with little trotting in between, let the horse trot only a half circle or so before asking for the halt. Although you can use a preparatory voice command for this exercise, you will want to use it close to the actual command. Therefore, the basic instructions are to simultaneously step forward with your restraining foot, put the whip in a neutral position (behind is best), and say "OK, Wo!" In this case, the "Whoa" sounds somewhat like a dog's woof.

See Exercise 33 for extra help with whip positions.

Problem: Horse Is Lazy The horse has to be prodded continually to make him move and keep him going. Causes are varied: the horse is underfed, overworked, has parasites, has a disease, is tender-footed, is being worked on poor footing, or simply has learned that he doesn't *have* to work.

First, all health, nutrition, and hoof problems must be ruled out or attended to.

If a horse is mentally lazy, the kindest yet most effective way to encourage him to move out and get in shape is with one well-applied whip aid.

Usually just the sight and sound of a whip cracking will get a horse moving. But the chronically lazy horse has learned to ignore the whip. You will need to remind him that the whip can reach him. (Exercise 2). If you merely come at a horse with a wiggling whip or tap him lightly with it, he will become desensitized to it and you will lose this very important driving aid. It is more humane in the long run, and definitely more effective, to use a whip once, in the correct place and with optimum intensity. For a time, instead of staying in the center of the circle and pivoting around, you will have to walk a medium-sized concentric circle while the horse works on the larger circle.

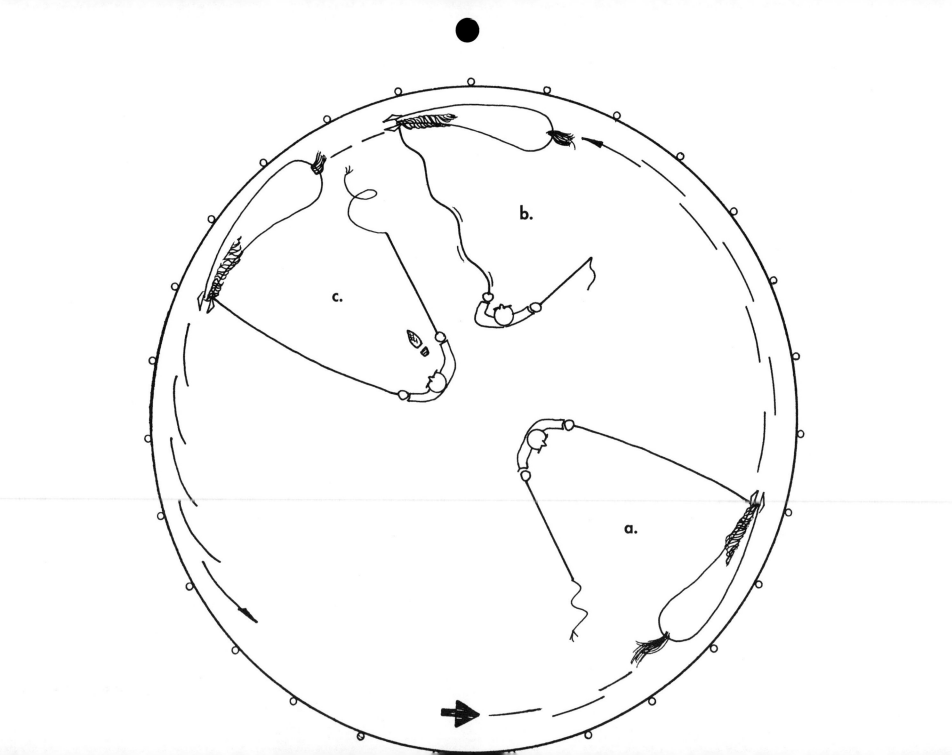

Trot-Walk-Lope

Now you will teach your horse his first quasi-collected transition, a lope from a walk. The secret is to use a few walk steps strategically placed between the trot and the lope. It is important that there be just a few *steps* because if you wait a few *strides* or more, the horse might lose the impulsion benefits from the trot.

In essence what you are doing is waking the horse up to the idea of actively moving forward, using a brisk trot, then having him walk a few steps before asking for a canter transition. This is much like the exercise you will use later when you're teaching the horse a walk-canter transition when mounted.

When performing an upward transition, a horse should be calm and relaxed yet balanced and collected. The transition should be "up in front," which means the horse should drive under with the hind legs and round the topline so that the forehand is elevated. That's a tall order for a young horse but is a requirement as a horse progresses in physical development.

An *upward* transition indicates a change from a standstill or a slower gait to a gait that is more ground covering. Examples are halt to walk, walk to trot, trot to canter, and walk to canter. In addition, an upward transition can indicate a change in the movement within a gait. For example, a trot can be regular (often called working), extended, or collected. The change from a working trot to an extended trot would be considered an upward transition.

a. As you trot the horse, keep contact on the longe line and use an active forward-driving whip aid.

b. Prepare for the downward transition because many things will happen quickly. Simultaneously, say "Waaalk," cast a gentle wave in the line, and put the whip in a neutral position at your side. In this case, don't put the whip behind your back because in a split second you will need it! As soon as the horse walks, establish a solid, steady contact on the longe line.

c. For the lope/canter depart, step to the horse's hindquarters with your driving foot as you slightly bend the horse to the inside with the line, and say "Let's go!" as you give the lope signal with your whip. I don't use the preparatory command here because the horse should be quite alert from the downward transition and should not need a "warning" that something is happening.

If the horse trots instead of loping/cantering, bring him down immediately to a walk and try again. If the horse is flustered, you will need to go back to trot work to reestablish rhythm and relaxation.

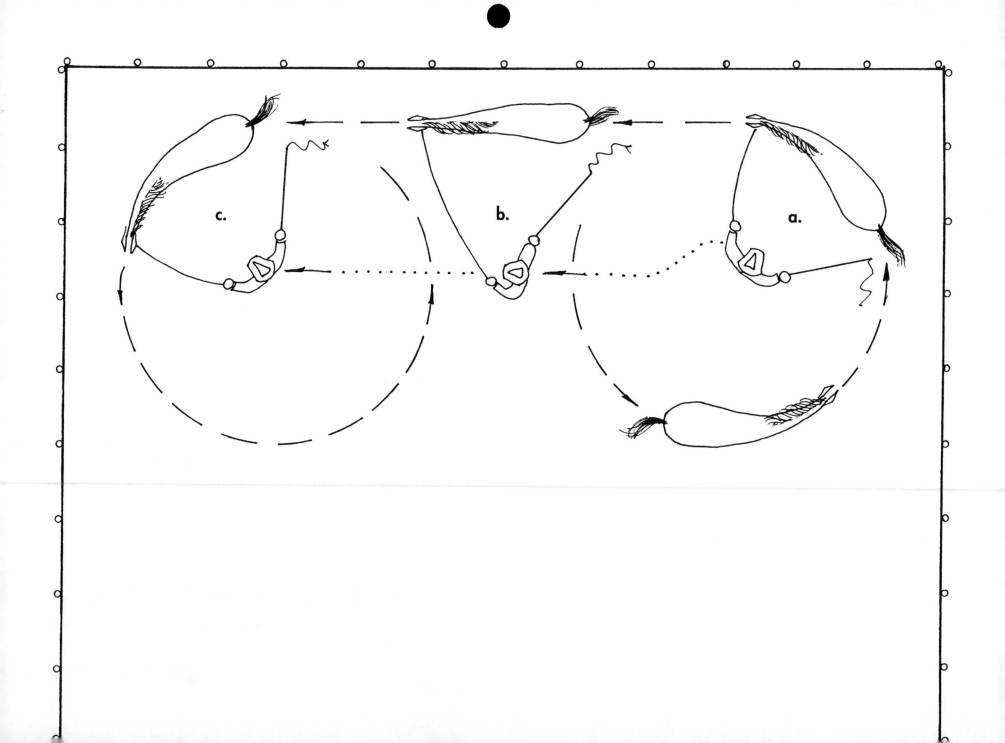

a.

b.

c.

Exercise 46

Spectacles

Provided that a horse is sufficiently under control, conducting longe lessons in a large arena further tests and solidifies his training.

One of the simplest and safest first exercises, other than going round and round at the trot in the corner of the arena, is Spectacles, which is performed at the trot. It is a circle with a straight piece along the long side, followed by another circle.

You will get more exercise here but unless your horse is an unusually long-strided horse and you are very short, you should have no trouble keeping up.

a. When you perform the first 20-meter circle, you will have two sides of the arena to help you contain the horse. But when the horse comes to the "open" sides of the circle, you will see how thorough the training in the round pen was. Circle at the trot as you have in the past. When the horse is warmed up and ready, head him down the long side.

b. You'll be half turned to face your horse and half turned to watch where you are walking. You'll need to stay in position as he trots alongside you. In some cases you may need to trot to keep up, especially if you ask for a lengthening here. If you are lengthening the trot, use the aids described in Exercise 39, Trot On. You will only be asking for three or four steps of lengthened trot here.

c. When you get 40 feet or so from the opposite end of the arena, settle yourself and work the horse around you again in an ordinary longeing circle.

Note that for this and other "active" training exercises it might be helpful to wear running shoes rather than boots. And no spurs!

If the arena is wide enough, you can continue the pattern around the arena, making a pair of spectacles on the short end, then the other on the long side, etc.

If the arena is not wide enough, you can ask for an extension down the centerline of the arena and connect the two circles that way. This is more difficult, however, as you do not have the arena rail to help guide you.

You will want to return to this exercise after you have taught the horse to work in side reins.

Problem: Horse Pulls You feel as though you are water skiing instead of longeing. If you are longeing in an open area or a large arena and the horse pulls on the line, don't just pull back. This is one tug of war you will definitely lose. Dig your heels in and lean back, but use intermittent tugs or jerks on the line so that the horse feels pressure and release. It is something like pumping the brakes to stop your vehicle. Be sure your whip is in a neutral position (or on the ground, if you have taken hold of the line with both hands) as you try to regain control. If the horse tends to pull to the outside of the circle, snap the longe line on the inside ring of the cavesson or the inside ring of the snaffle.

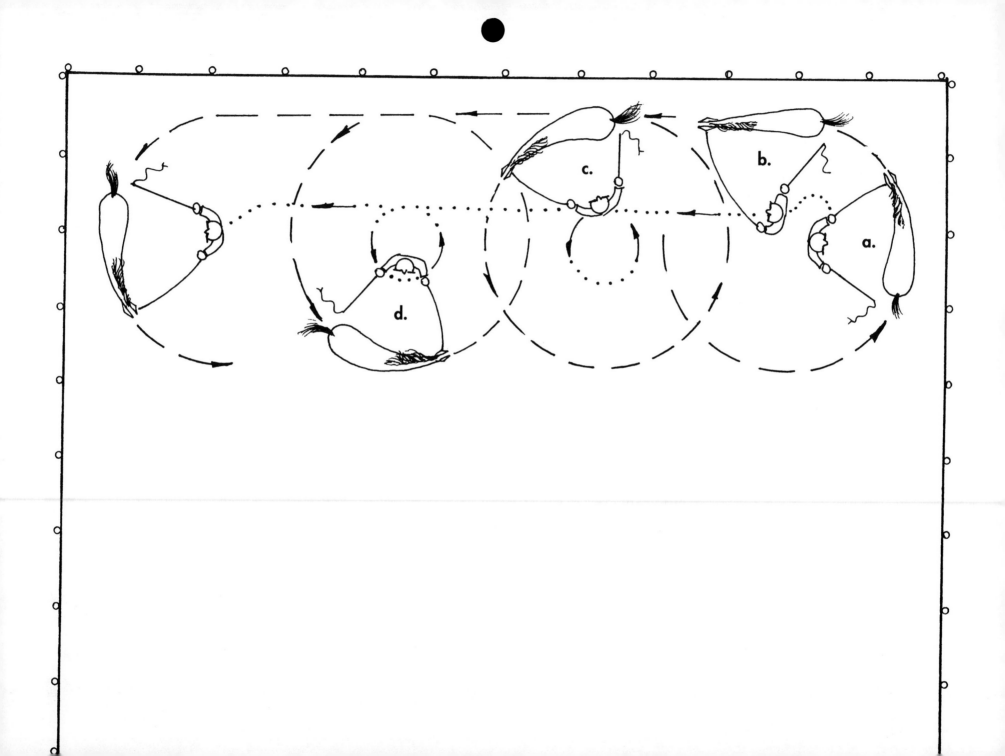

Exercise 47

Wagon Wheels

This series of circles always makes me think of "Rolling, rolling, rolling, keep those wagons rolling, Rawhide! Crrrack!" so I call it Wagon Wheels. It *looks* like a series of wagon wheels rolling along because inside the horse's circle (the wheel), the trainer makes a small concentric circle that looks like the wheel hub. Now that you have the picture clearly in mind, here's the reason for performing this exercise.

It diminishes the boredom of going round and round in one circle on the same spot as in traditional longeing. Yet the great benefits of a circle are still here. You stretch the horse out for a stride or two and then begin another circle. I can fit eight to ten circles along the long side of my arena. You can perform any size circle, from a 30-foot-diameter circle that would be appropriate for a collected trot to a 70-foot circle for a working canter. The ultimate goal? An absolutely steady rhythm throughout the entire exercise.

The steadier a horse's rhythm, the more relaxed and balanced he is. Steady rhythm is composed of several elements. Rhythm, per se, is the cadence of the footfall within a gait, taking into account timing (number of beats) and accent (of the beats). Evenness is the balance, symmetry, and synchronization of the steps within a gait in terms of weight-bearing and timing. Regularity is the cadence, the rhythmical precision with which each stride is taken in turn. Tempo is the rate of movement, the rate of stride repetition; a faster tempo yields more strides per minute.

a. Start the first circle in the arena corner and establish the size of the circles you will be using. Get a solid contact on the longe line and begin working in a concentric circle.

b. At the point the circle is tangent to the arena rail, walk forward and ask the horse to do the same by releasing the bending aid on the line and driving the horse forward with the whip.

c. After about two strides of straight trot, ask for inside bend with a tug on the line and begin a new circle. It should be the same size as the first one. Again work a concentric circle.

d. As you work the backside of the circles, be sure you are getting the same bend and control that you get along the arena rail.

In a Longeing Cavesson, Cheek Is Essential A cheek or jowl strap is like a second, lower throatlatch. Fastened snugly across the horse's cheek, this strap prevents the cavesson from twisting around and causing the side pieces to bump into the horse's eye when the longe line is pulled.

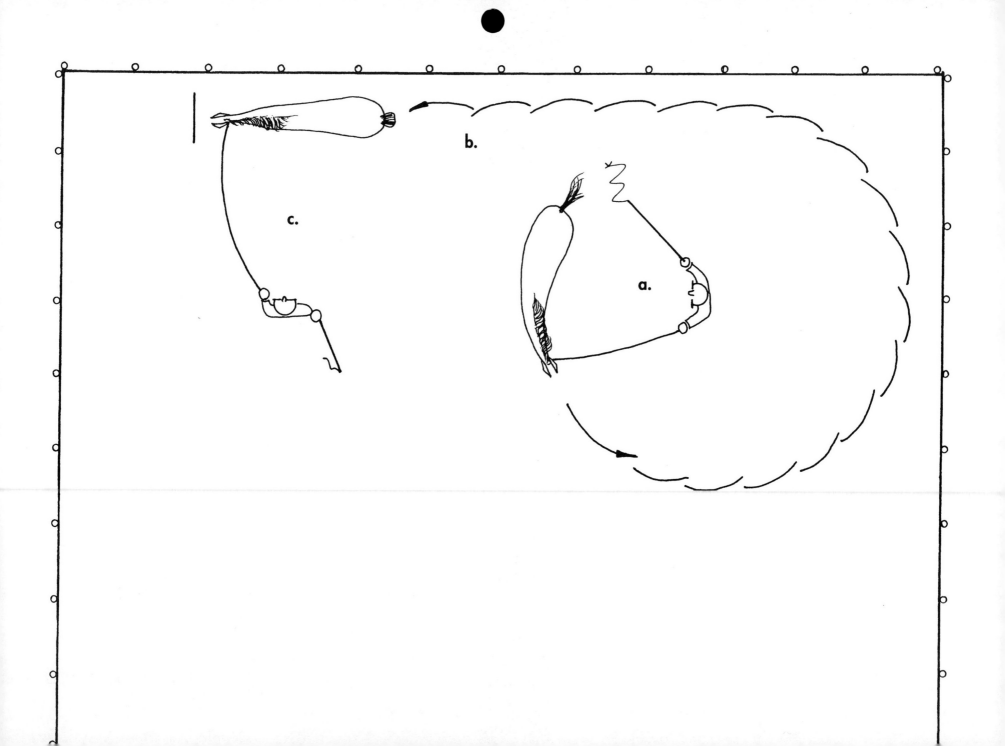

b.

c.

a.

Exercise 48

Lope-Whoa

Conducted in the arena, this is an advanced exercise. The horse must already be fairly collected and light. You will be utilizing a half halt or check to ready the horse for the halt.

a. Lope a large circle at the end of the arena. Continue working the circle until you feel the horse is collected, cadenced, and balanced.

b. Lope the horse down the long side of the arena. You shouldn't have trouble keeping up if the horse is somewhat collected. You won't be loping him very long down the straightaway—about three to four strides. With each stride on the straightaway, you can deliver a half halt at an intensity that gathers and organizes him but not so strong that it causes him to trot.

c. To bring the horse to a prompt, straight, balanced stop, use the aids for a prompt halt as outlined in Exercise 44. The rail on the side of the horse and the end rail in front of his face will help you. Be sure to give (yield) with the longe line as soon as the horse has stopped.

"Half Halt or Check"

Just as in riding, a half halt organizes the horse's mind and body for a brief instant before a transition or a new bend. A combination of driving and restraining aids, a half halt gets the horse's attention and rebalances him. Activate your whip, spring forward and plant your feet, and lift up and back on the longe line.
You can also use your preparatory voice command, such as "OK."

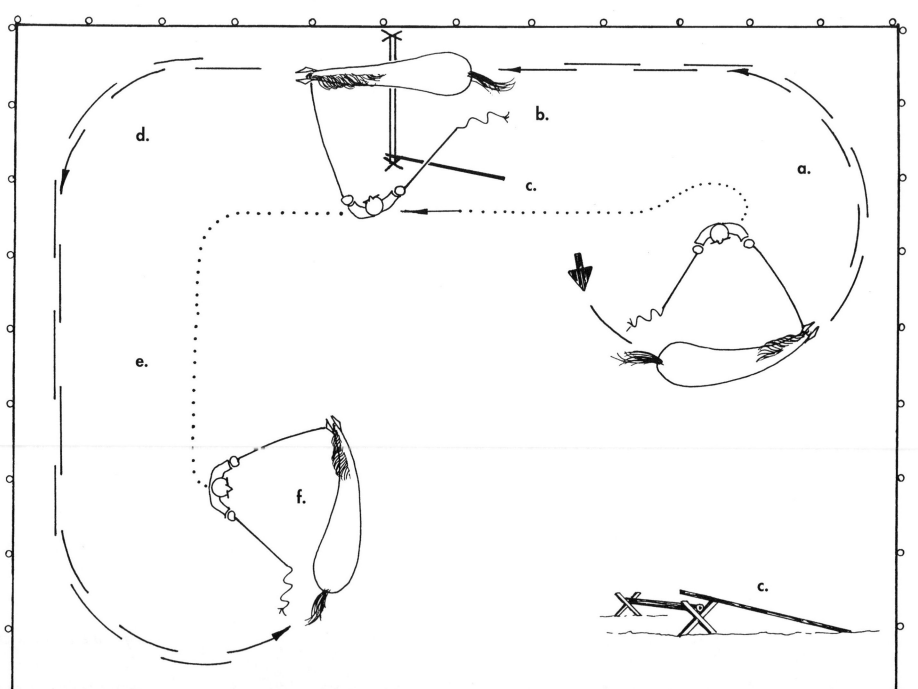

a.

b.

c.

d.

e.

f.

c.

Exercise 49

Trot Jump

In previous exercises you have taught your horse all the necessary components of this exercise except negotiating the pole. It will be convenient to have an assistant help with setting up and adjusting the pole.

Place a jump standard or jump block up against the arena rail. If you are going to use a 10-foot pole, place the other block 10 feet from the rail. A smooth block on the inside is nice because your longe line won't get caught on it. If you are using cavalletti or a jump standard, add a ramp pole on top (see **c**). The longe line will run along the ramp pole and over the top of the cavalletti and not get caught on the **X**.

First, work the horse between the blocks with no pole on the ground. Lead the horse between the two blocks.

Now set the pole on the ground between the two blocks.

Lead your horse over the pole until you feel he no longer has any apprehension. The horse should cross the exact center of the pole with his body perpendicular to the pole.

a. Longe your horse at a trot at the far end of the arena in a 20-meter circle. When you feel he is sufficiently ready, straighten him and head to the pole that is lying on the ground. If you are using cavalletti, set the cavalletti at its lowest setting.

b. You might want to call for a downward transition to a walk, and walk over the pole the first time. If you and your horse do well, you are ready to try it at the trot. Although the goal is for the horse to cross the pole dead center, you might be better off insisting on an absolutely straight body and controlling the horse along the rail. Later you can work on dead center. Be sure you move along with your horse over the pole so that you don't pull him just as he crosses the pole or prematurely pull him into a small circle after the pole.

c. A ramp pole from the ground to the top of the cavalletti not only prevents your longe line from getting snagged just at the crucial moment when the horse is going over the pole, but also helps guide the horse to the jump.

d. Try to keep the horse's body straight for at least three strides before you turn for the corner.

e. After the corner, work the horse straight as long as you can keep up or until you come to the other side of the arena.

f. Bring the horse into a circle and continue trotting, or bring him down to a walk.

You can use this same exercise to familiarize your horse with jumping. If you raise the pole to 18 inches, the horse will likely still trot over it. If you want the horse to hop or pop over the pole, you will need to raise it to 2 to 3 feet. Realize that if the horse pops over the pole, he will likely land in a canter. This excites some horses and you will need to stay in control and keep up.

Tip: To help your horse find his way to the pole, especially if you are asking him to jump, make an invitational alley with one or two poles acting as wings.

Option: Instead of using one pole raised to 2 feet, you can use cross poles. The two poles will be set at 3 feet on one end and on the ground at the other. The center point where they cross and where the horse should negotiate the jump will be only about 1 1/2 feet high.

Option: You can use this same format with three trotting poles. Start with the poles set 4 feet 6 inches apart and make adjustments to suit your horse. If your horse is very large or you want to extend his stride, increase the distance. If your horse is very small or you want to collect his stride, decrease the distance.

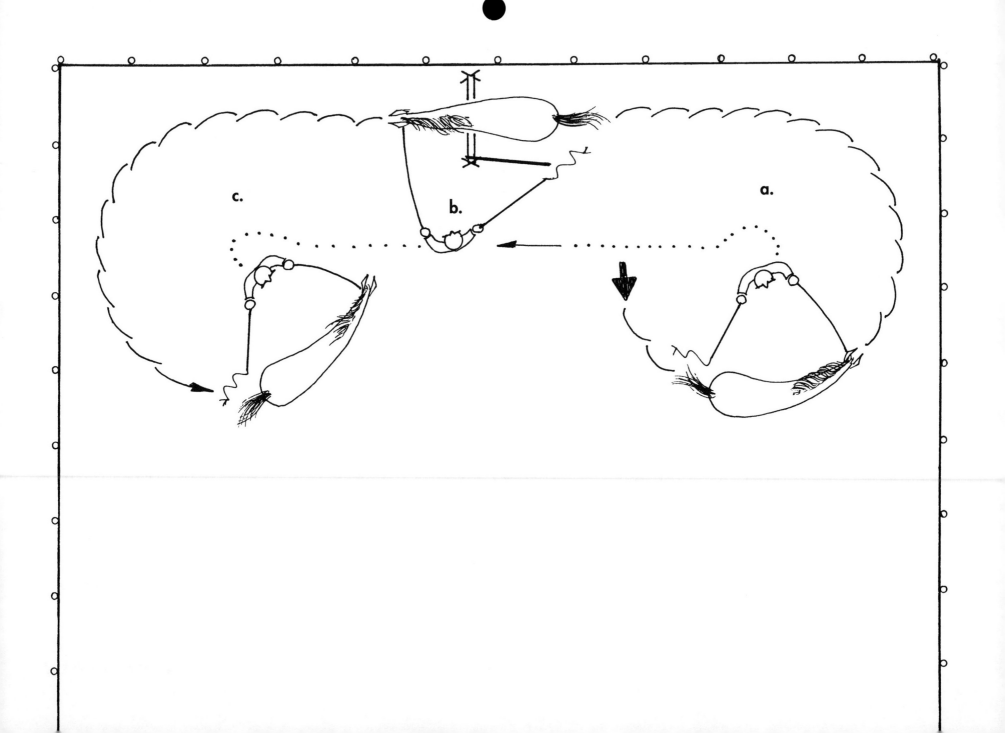

Exercise 50

Canter Circle-Jump-Canter Circle

B e sure you're wearing shoes in which you can easily and safely run.

This exercise can be performed loose in a round pen or with a trained horse in a small arena.

Even with a trained, conditioned horse, limit the jumps to a maximum of five. Just two jumps per session are plenty for the learning horse. Start with an 18-inch jump and work up in 4 to 6-inch increments. A sound horse of any breed should be able to easily jump an 18-inch jump initially and learn to jump up to 3 feet.

a. Longe your horse in a circle at a canter to warm and loosen him up. If you are working in a large arena, you might have to work your way closer to the jump with Wagon Wheels (Exercise 46). The closer you are to the jump before you straighten your horse from circle to straight line, the easier it will be for you to keep up on foot. In fact, you'd better be right alongside the horse as he is approaching the jump. If you get ahead of the horse's eye, you could cause him to break gait or stop.

b. Be sure to loosen the contact somewhat on the longe line as the horse approaches and goes over the jump. It is essential there be only light contact while the horse is jumping so that he can freely use his head and neck. As the horse is jumping, you must again get ready to keep up so that you can keep him tracking straight after the jump for at least 2 to 3 strides.

c. If you circle the horse prematurely after the jump, it will teach him to duck out after a fence, which is a difficult habit to break and eventually can negatively affect his approach, takeoff, and landing.

Benefit: Teaches a horse to jump and use his neck and back without the weight of the rider.

Caution: Be sure the longe line cannot get snagged on the jump. (See Exercise 49, section **c.**) You don't want the line to deliver a discouraging bump on the horse's nose or mouth just as he is going over the jump.

Note: When first teaching a horse to approach the jump straight, you can use wings to encourage him to hold his body straight. Later, you should require him to approach and jump the pole at the center without wings.

Tip: Putting a pole on the ground at the base of the jump helps the horse see where the ground is in relation to the jump. This is called a ground line.

Problem: Horse Refuses Jump   If the horse refuses the jump, try to keep him from whirling around or bolting past. If you can stop him facing the jump, go up to the horse, lower the pole, and lead him over. Repeat until you feel he has calmed. Be sure the refusal was not caused by your action or an action of the tack. If the horse does not jump after this review, he is likely just being naughty and will need to be driven forward. If you do not feel confident, get help.

PART FOUR

Side Rein Longeing

Side reins are adjustable, usually stretchy reins designed for longeing. They help show a horse the proper form in which to work and can assist him in overcoming stiffness and imbalance. You can forgo side reins altogether but if you do, be sure to still practice all of the exercises in this section. You can use side reins as a temporary stepping stone to help you accomplish certain goals with your horse, or you can use side reins as a regular part of your horse's training program. No matter which course you choose, you have instructions here on how to proceed correctly.

In order to use side reins, you will need to tack the horse with a surcingle or a saddle. This, then, is the progression I follow:

1. Longe from the middle ring of the cavesson. Horse wears a surcingle. No side reins.
2. Longe from the middle ring of the cavesson with the side reins attached from the surcingle to the side rings on the cavesson.
3. Add a snaffle bridle without noseband or reins. Longe from the middle ring of the cavesson with the side reins attached from the surcingle to the side rings on the cavesson. Let the horse just carry the bit to get used to it.
4. Longe from the middle ring of the cavesson. Attach side reins from the bit to the surcingle.
5. Only when necessary to correct a problem and with very experienced horse and trainer: Longe from the bridle with side reins from bit to surcingle. If an inexperienced horse were to misbehave while being longed with a bridle he could injure his mouth if he pulled, bolted, fell, or had to be sharply reprimanded for his behavior.

Longe line to bit attachments include the following:

a. Buckle-style strap around noseband and inside bit ring. Distributes pressure. Must be changed each time direction is changed.

b. Curb-style longeing strap. Not as good lateral pull as **a.**, but doesn't have to be changed when direction is changed.

c. Through inside bit ring, over the poll, and snapped to the outside bit ring. Severe: acts like a gag bit. Must be used by experienced trainer. Must be changed each time direction is changed.

d. Through inside bit ring, under chin, to outside ring. Collapses the bit and can create great pressure on bars. Not recommended.

e. To the inside bit ring alone, between the headstall and the side rein. Bit could be pulled right through the horse's mouth. A full-cheek snaffle bit would prevent this. Only for trained horse and experienced trainer.

(See *Longeing and Long Lining* for training theory and philosophy and more information on tack and procedures.)

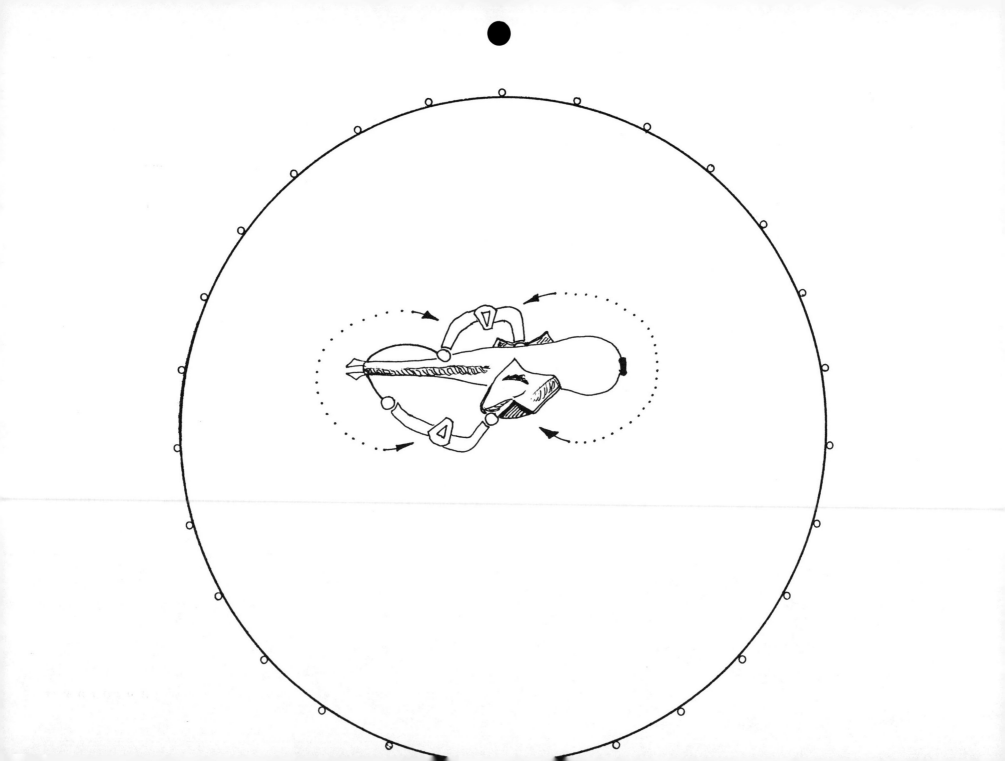

Exercise 51

Sacking and Tacking

Sacking out is a continuation of the lesson "Whoa." Once the horse has learned to stand, you need to begin building his tolerance for stress. Stress is a demand for adaptation and is necessary for growth. You should gradually increase a horse's ability to withstand various stresses so that when later confronted with them, he will be able to cope. You don't want your horse to spook every time he sees a plastic bag. And you wouldn't want him to panic if he got his leg caught in a rope or a fence, because he would most certainly injure himself.

Self-preservation has taught the horse to be wary of unusual motions, sounds, sights, smells, and of unfamiliar objects touching him. Setting up a specific group of lessons to help a horse overcome his natural fears will pay off in the long run. When working specifically on building confidence in the horse, never trigger active *resistance*. In other words, do not stimulate him beyond his ability to cope. If you see the horse ready to blow up or flee, ease up and gradually work back up to his actual tolerance level. Add more stress on another day.

Take the horse into a small training pen and show him a soft cloth jacket or a saddle blanket. Allow him to smell it. Then rub the blanket over the horse's head, neck, back and croup. Softly flap the blanket all over the horse on both sides. Stop and let the horse regroup if he seems ready to explode. Once the horse has accepted the soft, quiet item, substitute a raincoat or slicker and begin the process again.

Showing the horse that he must submit to certain restrictions is not meant to be harmful, but rather to protect him from his own natural instincts. Horses who have gone through well-planned sacking out and restraint lessons are more likely to remain calm when tangled in longe lines; have better manners for veterinary and farrier work; and tend to "test the limits" less often. Once a horse knows the meaning of the word "Whoa" with the aid of restraint, he is much safer for himself and his handler in all routine handling and management situations such as tying, hoof handling, grooming, and tacking.

You may want an assistant to help you with the first lesson in surcingle (or saddle) sacking and tacking. The horse is groomed and tacked with a cavesson. Let the horse smell and inspect the surcingle or saddle. Gently place the blanket and surcingle in position. Peak the saddle blanket in the gullet to prevent pressure on the withers when you tighten the surcingle. Fasten the girths. Be sure the girth or cinch is tight enough to prevent the saddle or surcingle from slipping under the horse's belly if he runs or bucks. Let the horse stand for a few moments, until he has relaxed somewhat. Tighten the girth a bit more. Many accidents occur from a too-loose girth or cinch, which allows the surcingle or saddle to slip back or roll under the horse's belly.

Then untrack (move forward) the horse, taking care to stand well to his side in the event he lunges forward in a reaction to the girth pressure. After walking for several minutes in-hand, send the horse out on the longe line at the walk. Keep things quiet until you sense that the horse has let out the breath he has been holding!

Practice all line longeing lessons with just the surcingle. Then add side reins.

SURCINGLE STABILITY

If a horse has a good set of withers and is not fat, a surcingle should stay in place provided it is fastened snugly. If you are working a round or fat pony, or a horse with low withers, however, you might want to consider stabilizing the surcingle with a breast collar and/or a crupper.

WESTERN SADDLE OPTION

If you are using a Western saddle instead of a surcingle, always fasten the front cinch first, then the breast collar (if used), and finally the rear cinch. It might be best to leave the rear cinch for a separate lesson. When removing the saddle, unbuckle in the reverse order.

Problem: Bucking   The horse crow-hops, rounds his back, tucks his croup, and bogs his head. If the horse is very fresh and bucks when you longe him, you may not have been turning him out often enough and before you longe. If the bucking is a reaction to girth pressure, be sure the girth is not too tight, pinching, and does not have foreign material pressing into the horse's skin. If a horse bucks out of playfulness or freshness, just drive him forward. If a horse bucks out of sheer disobedience, have headgear on him that will allow you to reprimand him sharply when his feet are off the ground. A well-fitted cavesson or jaquima usually does the trick. It's best to stop bucking before it becomes a habit. As soon as the horse quits bogging his head, drive him actively forward.

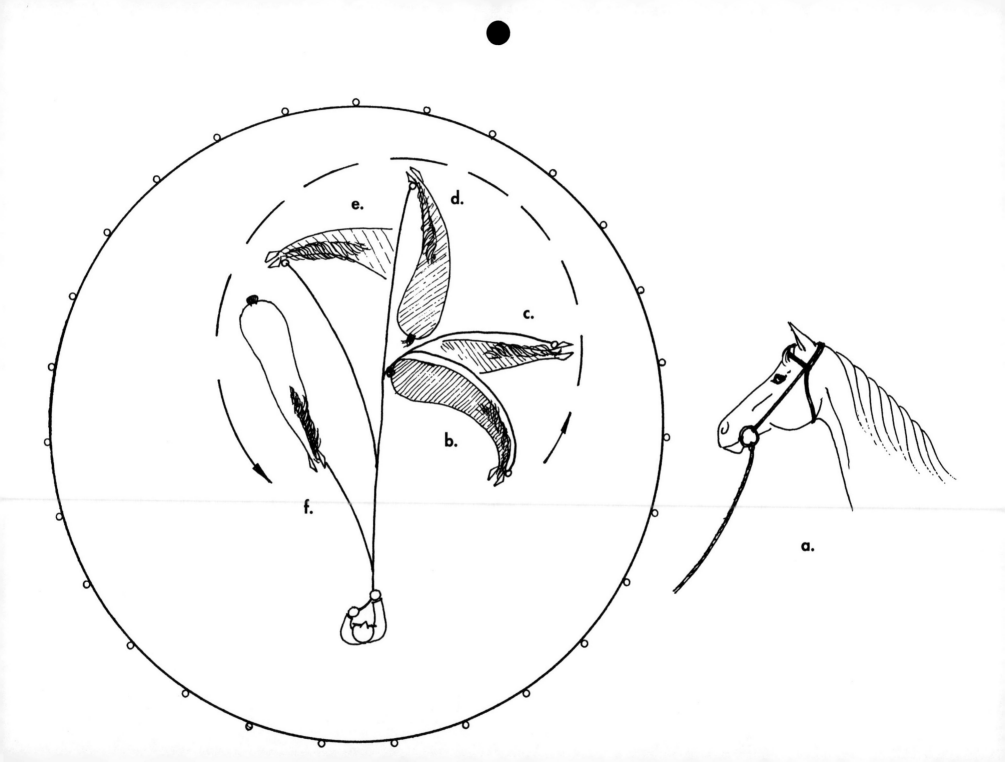

e.

d.

c.

b.

f.

a.

Exercise 52

Introducing the Bridle

A standard browband snaffle bridle is fine for ground training lessons. The adjustment should take into account a horse's tendencies, such as mouthing the bit, putting his tongue over the bit, chewing the bit, or holding the bit in his premolars. The sidepieces of the bridle should be adjusted so that the mouthpiece of the bit makes light contact with the skin at the corners on both sides of the horse's mouth and extends about 1/8 inch to 1/4 inch on each side.

HOW TO MEASURE FOR A BIT

The standard width for most English snaffles is 5 1/2 inches and for most Western bits 5 inches. Bits are available in 1/2-inch increments. To measure a bit, suspend it from a headstall so the rings are vertical. Let the mouthpiece rest flat on a table and, using a tape measure, determine the inside dimension from one ring/mouthpiece junction to the other.

HOW TO MEASURE A HORSE'S MOUTH

Using a piece of doubled baling twine, make a knot about a foot from one end and another knot 5 1/2 inches down the twine, leaving at least a foot on that end as well. Simply slip the twine bit into your horse's mouth and see where the knots lie in relation to the corners of the mouth. If your horse wears a 5 1/2-inch bit, there should be from 1/8 inch to 1/4 inch between the corners of his mouth and the knots on each side. If you try to use a wooden dowel or some other rigid measuring device, it's hard to get a reading since the horse's tongue is in constant motion.

SHOULD YOU USE A NOSEBAND?

Often a cavesson, flash, or dropped noseband is used with a snaffle bit. By keeping the mouth closed and the tongue under the bit, and by stabilizing the bit's location, nosebands prevent the horse from avoiding the action of the bit. Nosebands apply pressure to the nasal bone and chin groove. A tight noseband does not allow mouthing of the bit.

When using a flash noseband, the top portion should be located about two fingers below the prominent cheekbone. The lower strap is fixed below the bit. The buckle should be positioned on the side of the nose, not near the bit or in the chin groove where it can cause rubbing and collect saliva and ingesta.

REVIEW TURNING

Review the turning lesson in Exercise 29, using the snaffle bit. This time the exercise is described from the off side. You will need to practice it from both sides.

Standing on the off side, snap a 15- to 20-foot rope to the off snaffle ring of the bit. Snap it behind the sidepiece of the bridle. With this turning lesson, you will need to change the point of attachment each time you change direction.

Tell your horse "Whoa" and then step to his hindquarters on the off side and give a soft tug on the rope, which should cause him to turn and face you. Do this several times on both sides.

a. Then stand on the off side of the horse, attach the snap to the near bit ring. Place the rope over his head and neck so the rope is on the near side of his body. Tell your horse "Whoa," step to his hindquarters on the off side, and draw the rope along his topline and croup so the rope runs along the entire length of his near side.

b. Then, if necessary, repeat "Whoa" and step at least 10 feet from your horse's off side. The rope runs along his near side ribs, hips, around his hindquarters and to your hand. Be sure there is enough tension on the rope so if your horse tries to turn to the right, he can't.

c. Lightly tug on the rope, which should cause the horse to turn to the left and straighten his body.

d. Stay where you are standing and gather up the rope as the horse quietly turns to the left. Let the horse find the answer slowly the first time you do this. At the point where the horse is facing directly away from you, you are in his blind spot and you are also in a potentially dangerous kicking zone. That's why you want to be sure there is ample distance between you and the horse as you perform this exercise.

e. Continue exerting pressure on the rope until the horse turns around to face you.

f. When the horse is facing you, you can stop reeling in the line; walk up to him and say "Goooood."

Now step to the near side, change the point of

Continue to alternate sides until the horse bends equally well in both directions without resistance. Every horse will initially be smoother in one direction and stiffer in the other. Many horses will hold their heads up and their bodies stiff in one direction. This will alert you to potential tendencies and problems in the upcoming work.

After completing this exercise, your horse will be better prepared for the sensations he will encounter from the bridle.

LEADING WITH A BRIDLE

When leading a horse that is wearing a bridle you have the following attachment options:

- Snap lead to halter or cavesson for a horse that is unfamiliar with a bit.
- Snap lead to bit ring and noseband for a transition between halter and bit, or use a leather buckle-style longeing strap around the bit ring and noseband.
- Snap lead to bit ring behind the headstall for a backward (whoa) pull; note that the pull will tend to twist the bit.
- Fasten to the inside bit ring in front of the headstall for an upward (half halt) pull.
- Use a curb-style longeing strap for a backward pull that pulls more evenly on the bit than snapping to one ring.

Bit Antics Young horses often exhibit odd behavior due to lack of familiarity with the bit. A young horse starts by carrying his head high and/or his nose extended out and the bit touches only the cor-

his mouth and try to spit the bit out. This does not necessarily indicate dental problems. With more experience, he will accept the pressure of the snaffle on the bars and tongue. At that point, his head will lower with a slight convex curve to the topline of his neck and he will flex vertically at the poll.

Caution: Headstall Too Long When the headstall is too long, it positions the bit too low in the horse's mouth. If the horse has not learned to pick up the bit and carry it, using suction of his tongue against the roof of his mouth (see Exercise 65), the bit will just hang low. In a male horse, an extremely low bit could hit the canines. In any horse, a too-low bit invites a horse to put his tongue over the bit. Also, signals to the bit could be disjointed and abrupt because the bit must first be lifted up in the mouth before it contacts the corners of the mouth.

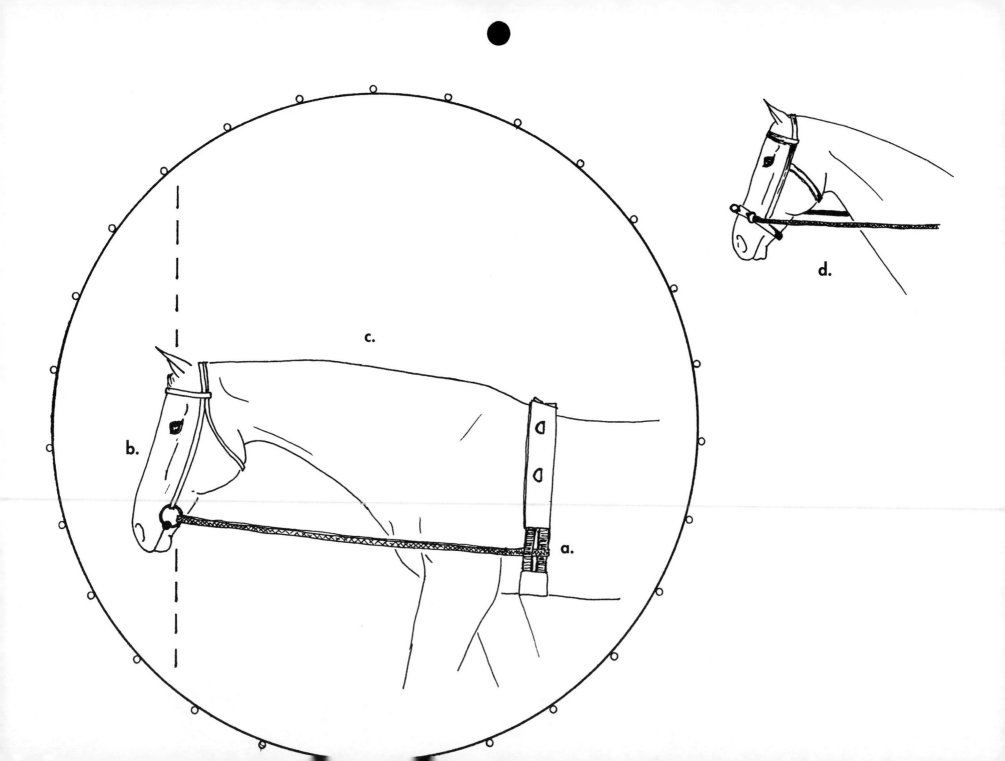

a.

b.

c.

d.

Adding Side Reins

The addition of side reins should be approached carefully. First, side reins should be used on the horse's halter or the side rings of the cavesson (**d**) to accustom the horse to the idea of restriction. This is safer than using them for the first time on a bit. If a horse panics when he feels the pressure of the side rein restriction on the padded nose of a cavesson, he might raise his head or rush, but he won't injure himself. If a horse panics the first time he wears a bridle, he could injure his mouth.

So, practice all exercises in this section first with the side reins attached to the side rings of the cavesson. Meanwhile, the horse can carry the bridle to get used to it.

SIDE REIN SAFETY

- Never lead a horse with the side reins attached.
- Never tie a horse with side reins attached.
- Never leave a horse unattended with side reins attached.

- Carry side reins to training area.
- Warm the horse up at the walk, then fasten the side reins.
- Fasten the outside rein first.

BEGINNING CONTACT

In the early side rein lessons, encourage the horse to stretch his topline and neck forward and down (**c**). This helps to develop the muscles that will gradually be collected upward and rearward. His nose should be 10 to 30 degrees in front of the vertical (**b**).

To encourage the horse to stretch forward and down, attach the side reins with loose or light contact, depending on the horse.

Points of attachment for this stage include:

- Billets of surcingle (**a**). *Tip:* to keep the side reins from sliding down, run the rein under the first billet and over the second one.
- Girth of English saddle.
- Cinch rings of Western saddle.

TOO LOW OR TOO HIGH?

If a horse carries his head very low, don't try to *lift* it up by using higher, tighter side reins. Instead, drive the horse forward! At first he might be too quick, but you can work on that.

Too low a head position (mouth below the point of the elbow) puts too much weight on the forehand, preventing the hindquarters from engaging properly.

If a horse carries his head too high, don't use the side reins between his forelegs. Instead attach the side reins at a regular height and let him work at a trot without strong driving aids. He will eventually find a lower position to carry his head.

Tack Tip: Choosing Side Reins Side reins can have no elastic inset, or they can have elastic elements (elastic strips, rubber donuts, or rubber rods) that range from stiff to "boingy." Very springy side reins invite a horse to play and root into the bit. Side reins with no elastic have no give, so are most suitable for advanced horses. Side reins with moderate elasticity are the most versatile and are suitable for training young horses.

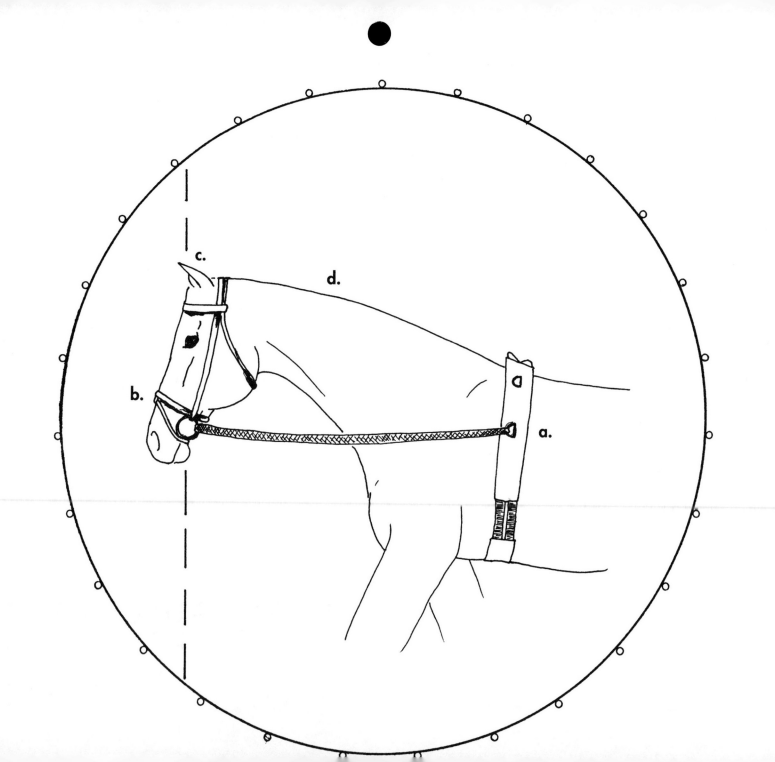

Working Contact

Work your horse in his normal repertoire of exercise as he becomes familiar with side reins. Gradually, over a period of weeks, months, or even years, make changes to the length of the side reins and the point of attachment on the surcingle or saddle. This, if done correctly, will aid the horse in the development of a functional and attractive physique. It will encourage the development of a rounded topline (see **d**) and engagement of the hindquarters, the goal of any style of horse training.

Through the majority of the horse's early and intermediate work, he should carry his nose in front of the vertical (**b**). How far in front of the vertical will depend on his conformation and your goals. The more thorough you are at *gradually compacting* the horse's frame, however, the more solidly the horse will be on the bit when it comes to the advanced, highly collected work.

As you shorten the side reins, you gradually elevate the horse's head. Several things to keep in mind:

1. The line from the bit to the point of attachment on the saddle or surcingle should be horizontal (**a–b**).

2. The horse's poll should always be the highest point of his topline (**c**).
3. The side reins should be adjusted appropriately for each gait. The reins must be longer for a free walk than a collected trot or canter.

At this stage, appropriate points of attachment include:

- The middle rings on the surcingle (**a**).
- Rigging rings of Western saddle.
- Billets of English saddle.

A noseband (**b**) at this stage is appropriate.

Caution: Keep the Poll Up!   The poll is the area *between* the horse's ears (**c**), not 3 to 4 inches behind them. A horse that breaks at the top third of his neck instead of flexing at the poll is avoiding contact with the bit and is either behind the bit or headed that way.

Note to Western Trainers: If you are training a stock horse, this stage might be your end stage. If your goal is an "up in the bridle," highly collected Western horse in the Spanish tradition, the horse might benefit from the judicious use of side reins for collection. This will depend on the bosal and bit training progression you are using, however.

GOALS IN A HORSE'S PHYSICAL DEVELOPMENT

- Gradually change the horse's flat or hollow topline to a rounded topline.
- Develop suppleness and strength evenly on both sides.
- Gradually shift the weight of the horse from the forehand to the hindquarters.
- Improve the style or expression of the horse's movement.
- Improve the quality of the gaits.

Safety Tip: Snug It Up   Always give the surcingle or saddle a check and tightening once you reach the training area and are ready to work the horse.

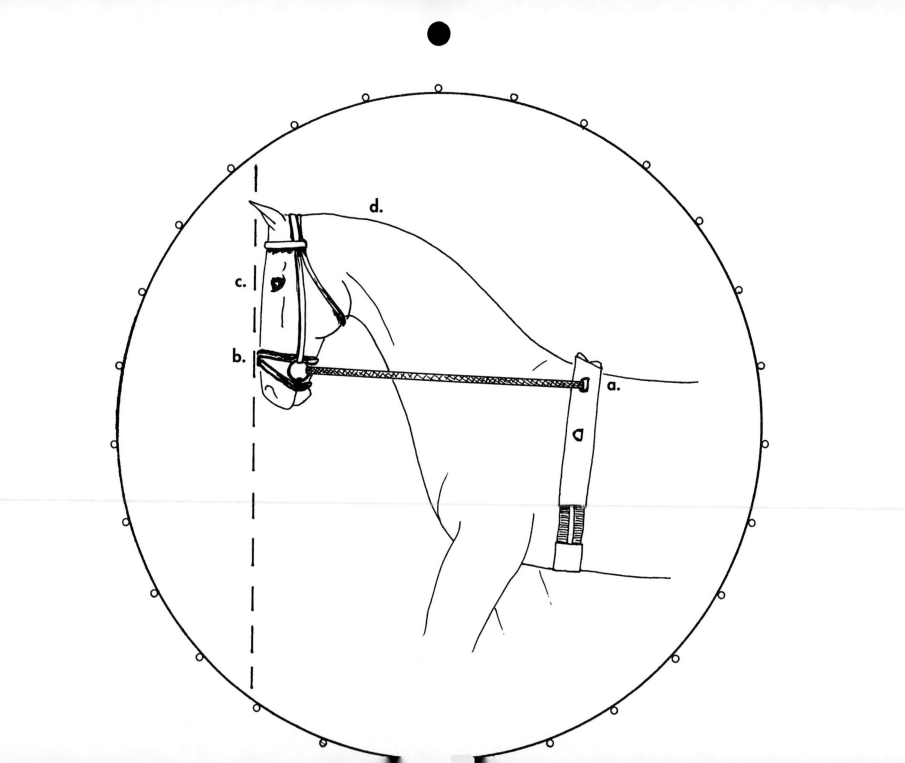

Exercise 55

Collected Contact

As a horse progresses physically, he begins to add muscle along the topline of his neck (**d**). This is due to the fact that he is actively elevating his neck by lifting it and his forehand with muscular activity. The impulsion comes from an engaged hindquarters. So as a horse's front end elevates, his hindquarters are positioned more under his mass. The hind legs step deeply under the horse, the croup is dropped, and all results in a rounded topline and elevated poll. The poll, the highest point of the topline, should appear flat. The horse's face line approaches the vertical (**c**).

If the muscles under the neck develop instead, it indicates that the horse is not lifting or elevating his forehand with muscular effort but is being "held in place" and is bracing against the contact from the side reins or the riding reins. This is to be avoided at all cost.

When a horse gets to the collected stage of side rein use, he should be well into his mounted training. During days when groundwork takes the place of riding, side reins substantiate the progression and development in the mounted lessons. A flash noseband (**b**) is appropriate.

The point of attachment at this stage should be at a position to approximate the rider's hands:

- The top rings of a surcingle (**a**).
- The breast collar D's of the English saddle.
- The breast collar D's of a Western saddle.
- The saddle horn of a Western saddle.

Is the horse correct?

1. Is the poll the highest point of the horse's neck?
2. Is the side rein horizontal from the bit to the point of attachment?
3. Is the horse's topline rounded and the underline relaxed?

Tack Tip: What Goes Between the Surcingle and the Horse?   You can put a surcingle:

- Directly on a clean horse.
- On a clean saddle pad.
- On a surcingle pad.
- On top of your saddle.

Tack Tip: Using a Longeing Cavesson as a Dropped Noseband   Sometimes a cavesson is positioned below the snaffle bit like a dropped noseband. This is mainly for the control of a very strong horse but should be used only by an experienced horse trainer and with discretion.

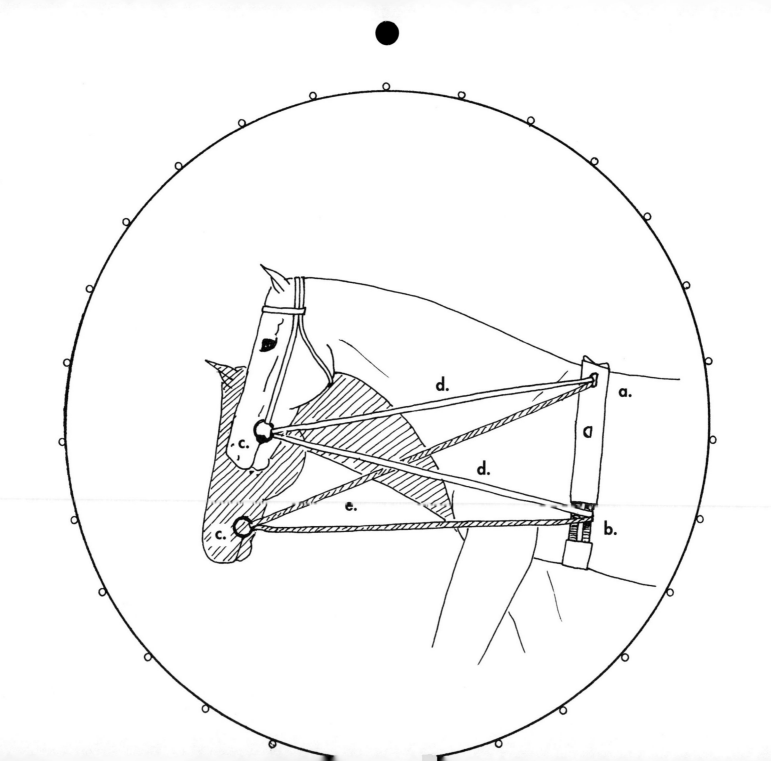

Sliding Side Reins

Sliding side reins (also called Lauffer reins) form a triangle on the horse's side. The point of the triangle (**c**) is at the bit. Each rein is one continuous piece that is twice as long as a regular side rein. The top leg of the side rein is affixed rather high on the surcingle or saddle (**a**), for example, to the breast collar D-ring. The rein is then run through the ring of the snaffle (**c**) or snapped to it, depending on the style. The lower leg of the triangle is affixed in a relatively low position to the surcingle (**b**) or saddle at the girth.

Sliding side reins allow a horse to "give to himself" as he searches for a balanced way to carry his head and neck for each gait and extension or collection within each gait. Since the rein flows without resistance through the snaffle bit ring, the shape of the triangle can change quite easily. This means that at one moment the top leg of the triangle can be long and the bottom leg short, as when a horse stretches low and forward (**e**). At the next moment, as the horse raises his head, the top leg of the triangle can shorten and thereby the lower leg of the triangle can become longer (**d**).

Sliding side reins have a number of advantages over regular side reins:

- They allow a horse to maintain contact with the bit as he changes the level of his head and neck.
- Less adjustment is required between gaits during a training session, as the horse can compensate.
- The reins do not tighten or loosen the contact on the bit as the horse changes his head position, and therefore contact is steadier.
- They encourage horses with a high head carriage to stretch down and forward.

HOW TO ADJUST SLIDING SIDE REINS

For a less experienced horse: When a horse is at a working trot, his neck has a slight convex arc, his face line is about 10 to 15 degrees in front of the vertical, and he should have contact with the bit. *For a more experienced horse:* When a horse is working, the neck will be slightly more arched, the face might be 5 to 10 degrees in front of the vertical, and the horse will have contact with the bit.

Tack Tip: Sliding side reins are a great training aid. Most horses are not intimidated by them. Problems and accidents are minimal. A horse could possibly step over the lower portion if it were positioned very low.

Noseband? At this stage, unless the horse shows the development of undesirable habits (tongue over bit, gaping mouth, chewing bit with teeth), don't use a noseband. This will make a relaxed association with the bit and will allow the horse to mouth the bit. Mouthing is a soft working of the bit with the tongue. It enhances salivation and sensitivity and leads to relaxation.

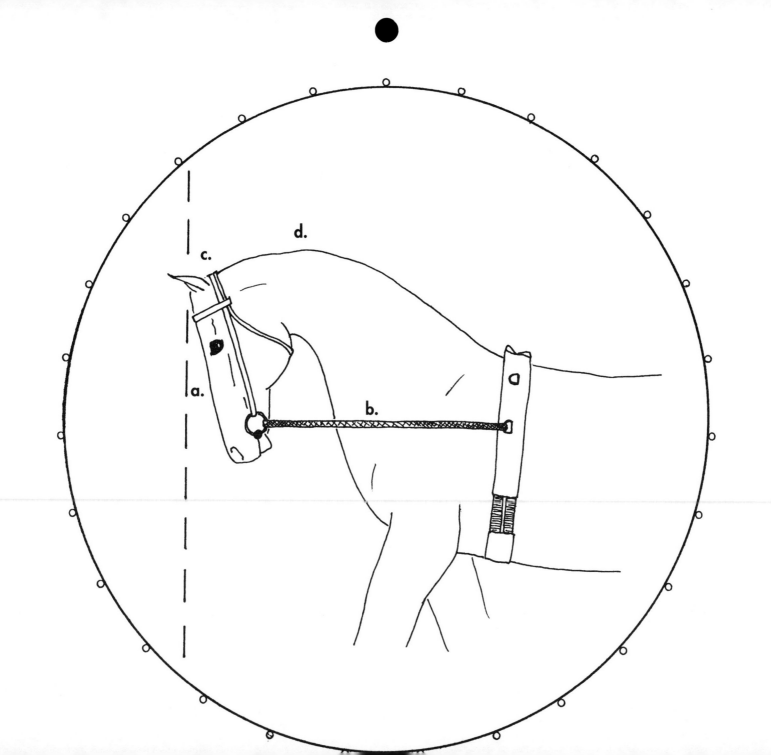

The Good, the Bad, and the Ugly

Caution! Do not try to emulate this illustration.

Instead, follow the rescue procedure outlined later in this exercise!

I include this hideous configuration because it astonishes me how many horses are worked or ridden this way! I purposely designed this drawing to be typical but not as awful as the situation can be. The configuration is called:

- False collection.
- Behind the vertical (**a**).
- Swan neck (low poll (**c**) with flexion at mid neck (**d**) rather than at poll).

I could go on with some very unglamorous descriptions. But let's not waste time. Let's fix it.

First, here are the good points. The reins are horizontal (**b**) and the horse's neck has a convex curve to the topline.

The bad news is that the neck is flexed several vertebrae behind (**d**) where it should be, the poll is too low (**c**), the face is 15 degrees behind the vertical (**a**), and the musculature on the underside of the neck is developing that ungodly bulge from bracing. The bad greatly outweighs the potential good. What is more important to know is that even if there were only one bad point, the composite does not "work."

But there is hope. The key fact that the rein (**b.**) is taut tells us that the horse still appears to be taking contact with the bit, albeit a forced contact. This means that if this horse were rescued this instant, he might be salvaged. If his trainer were to continue to work him this way, however, very soon the horse would back off the bit entirely, the side reins would go slack, and the horse would be touching his chest with his nose. If you have ever been on a horse like this, you know it is a helpless feeling because there is no contact or communication with the reins. It is a classic case of the chronic "behind the bit" horse—something no trainer or rider looks forward to dealing with.

HORSE RESCUE PROCEDURE

1. Remove the side reins.
2. Evaluate the bit. If the mouthpiece is too thin or in some way too severe, replace it with a milder snaffle.
3. Longe the horse for several weeks with no side reins. Let the horse just carry the snaffle. Use active driving aids. Work the horse in working and extended gaits, not collected gaits.
4. If the horse misbehaves, use the cavesson to help you regain control.
5. When you reintroduce the side reins, use them long and low. Attach them to the girth (Exercise 53) or use sliding side reins (refer to Exercise 56). Encourage the horse to stretch forward and relax his topline.
6. Gradually reintroduce contact with the side reins over a long period of time.
7. Keep driving aids active and postpone collected work for as long as you can.

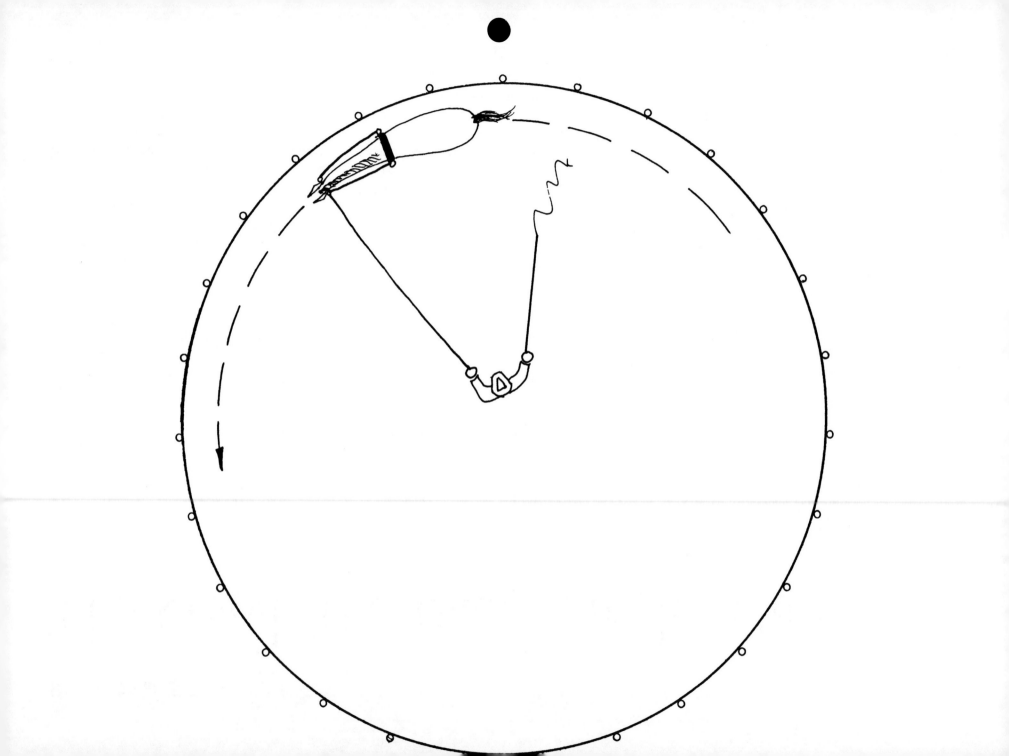

Correct Bend

Correct bend occurs when the horse tracks "straight." His hind legs follow in the tracks of his front legs, even when he is working on a circle.

Even side rein length and even bit contact should be used in these instances:

- On all large circle work.
- On young horses to introduce side reins.
- On new horses for purposes of evaluation.

To ensure that side reins are the same length, hold them side by side, stretch them taut, and measure! Often a manufacturing error or long-term use will reveal that one rein is longer than the other.

The horse that takes absolutely even contact with both reins:

- Tracks straight.
- Has an aligned neck and spine.
- Is balanced—doesn't lean in.
- Has low incidence of interference.
- Is a dream to work with!

Tack Tips: the Snaffle   Much of the reason behind an even acceptance of the bit can be attributed to proper bit selection, fit, and bridle adjustment.

Mouthpiece Shape   The shape and design of the mouthpiece can instantly affect a horse's response. Curved arms fit the contour of the horse's tongue better than straight arms or a straight bar bit. Three-piece bits are often more acceptable than bits with two-piece mouths. Due to the variation in mouth structure, some horses need more room for their tongues; a horse with a shallow palate needs less material in his mouth.

Mouthing the Bit   The movement of the arms, both at the joint and at the rings, encourages a horse to "mouth" the bit or "play" with it, that is, to roll it and lift it with his tongue (but not bite it). This leads to a suppleness and relaxation of the jaw. That's why jointed mouthpieces are preferred over solid mouthpieces for suppling and for lateral work, such as bending and turning.

Salivation   A moist mouth is potentially a more responsive mouth. The salivary reflex is triggered by the presence of food in the horse's mouth. When bridled, the mouthing of the bit, the construction of the bit, and the vertical position of the horse's head may activate the glands. The more supple and vertically flexed a horse works, whether in a bosal, cavesson, halter, or bit, the more he will salivate! A horse that actively works the bit in his mouth with the tongue while keeping the mouth closed tends to have a moist, soft mouth.

Bit Metal   The metal you put in a horse's mouth can either encourage or dry up the flow of saliva. Snaffle mouthpieces of cold-rolled steel, and nickel and copper alloys tend to keep the mouth moist.

Bit Severity   A trainer's methods have the capability to turn the mildest bit into an instrument of abuse or the most severe bit into a delicate tool of communication. Above all, good sense and good horsemanship are the keys to your horse's acceptance of the bridle.

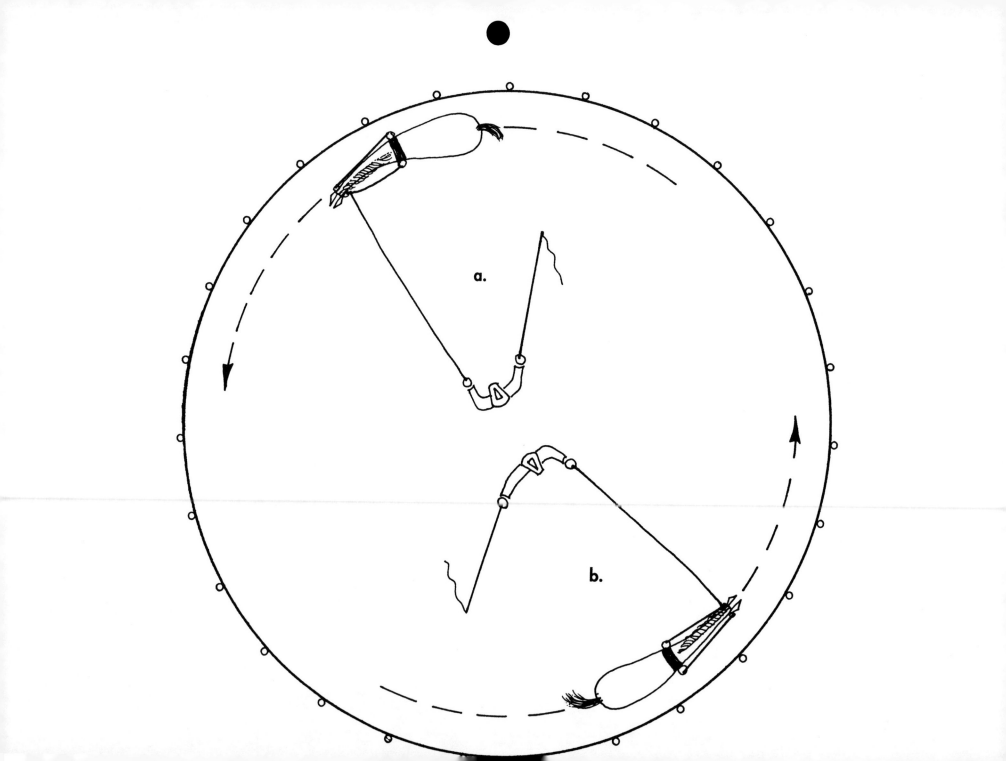

a.

b.

Exercise 59

Checking the Inside Bend and Rein

a. Overbending to the inside is most commonly seen when a horse is tracking to the left. The strong left side of the horse's body makes the horse want to curl inward and overbend to the left. The horse does not take even contact with the reins, although they are adjusted evenly. There is no contact on the inside (left) rein and excess contact on the outside (right) rein. The horse usually moves with stiffness, carries the hindquarters out off the track, might rubberneck, and the outside shoulder often bulges outward.

b. Solution? Shorten the outside (right) rein. Be sure you are working the horse on a 20-meter circle. Smaller circles exaggerate lateral imbalances. Drive the horse actively forward. This "straightens out" a lot of problems. You might want to wait until you can use long lines to address this problem, as you will have the ability to give and take instantly.

Often, making an adjustment in side rein length is designed to be a temporary remedial measure aimed at a breakthrough. Once the light bulb goes on and the horse learns he can carry himself "straighter," the side reins should be adjusted normally.

When would you want to adjust the reins so that the inside rein is shorter than the outside rein? To straighten a horse that counterflexes (see Exercise 60). If a horse overbends to the outside of the circle or is stiff and flat to the outside, the inside rein should be shortened.

Preventive medicine! Important reminder! From day one, whether you have a foal or a new older horse, work from the off side as often as you do the near side. This will help you and your horse overcome your natural one-sidedness.

Caution: Narrow Bit   If the bit is too narrow for a horse it can cause the ring/mouthpiece junction to press and rub against the corners of the lips. If a bit is extremely narrow, the mouthpiece is totally enveloped by the horse's lips, causing the rings of the bit to angle outward away from the sides of the horse's face.

With a too-narrow bit, the skin at the corners of the mouth often becomes raw or can be pinched by the mechanical action of the ring attachment. Also, if a bit is too narrow, it can cause the rings of the bit to put pressure on the skin over the first premolars. All of these factors can cause a horse to brace against the bit, toss his head, come above the bit, or resist with a variety of lateral imbalances.

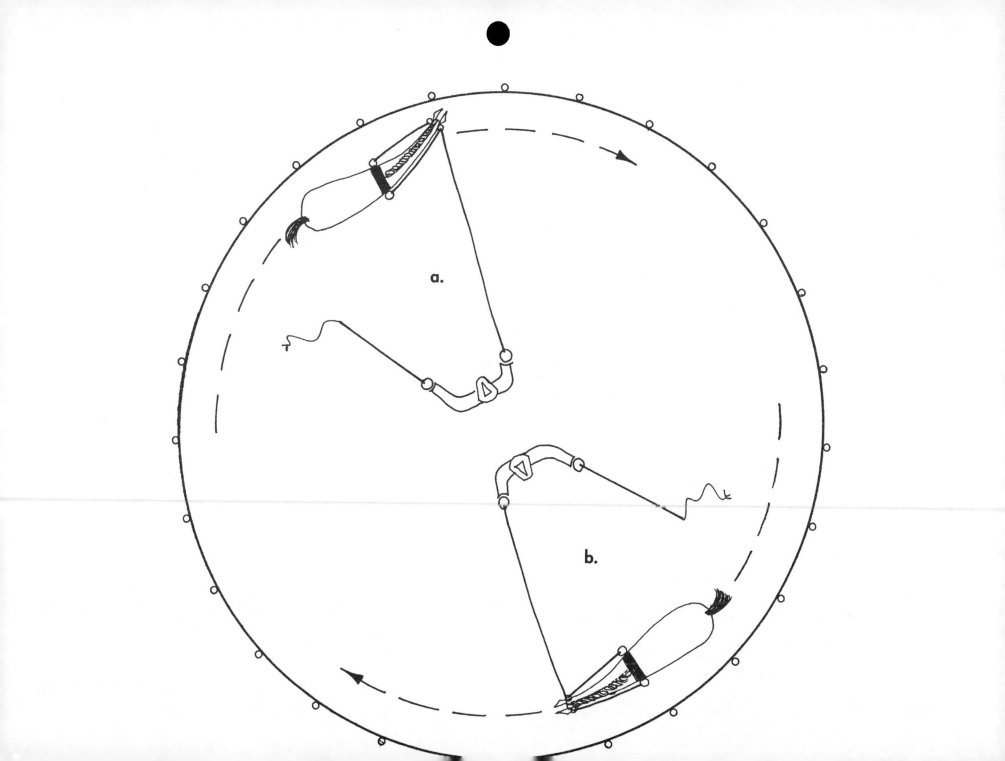

a.

b.

Exercise 60

Checking the Outside Rein

a. Is he counterflexed or is the outside rein too tight? Most often seen when a horse is tracking to the right. The strong left side of the horse's body tends to straighten his head and neck and pull it off to the left instead of allowing it to bend to the right. This happens even when the side reins are equal in length. The result is uneven contact on the reins even though the reins are adjusted evenly. There is excess contact on the right (inside) rein and no contact on the outside (left) rein. This diagnosis fits like a perfect puzzle piece when the same horse tracks left (refer to Exercise 59). The horse basically does not take contact with the left rein, no matter which direction he travels.

b. The solution is to shorten the inside (right) rein so that the horse takes contact with the left rein. Be sure you are working the horse on a 20-meter circle. Smaller circles exaggerate lateral imbalances. Drive the horse actively forward. This "straightens out" a lot of problems. You might want to wait until you can use long lines to address this problem, as then you will have the ability to give and take instantly.

Making an adjustment in side rein length is designed to be a temporary remedial measure aimed at a breakthrough. Once the light bulb goes on and the horse learns he can carry himself "straighter," the side reins should be adjusted normally.

When would you want to adjust the reins so that the outside rein is shorter than the inside rein? To straighten a horse that overbends to the inside (refer to Exercise 59). If a horse overbends to the inside of a circle or bulges his shoulder to the outside of the circle, the outside rein should be shortened.

Caution: Bit Too Wide When a bit is too wide and the bit is a jointed one, the joint in the mouthpiece can fold downward on the tongue if the bit is adjusted low and loose in the horse's mouth. If the bit is too wide and is adjusted high and tight in the horse's mouth, it can cause the horse to become obsessed with carrying the joint of the bit backward with the tongue so he can bite the bit. If a bit is very wide for a horse's mouth, the constant sliding back and forth disturbs the quietness of the communication with the horse's mouth and precludes finesse.

Tack Tip: Bit Thickness In general, the thicker the mouthpiece, the gentler the action because the pressure is distributed over a greater surface area. A thin mouthpiece (1/16 inch in diameter) presses sharply into the nerves that lie just below the skin of the tongue and bars. A moderate mouthpiece (3/8 inch in diameter) is appropriate for most uses, is comfortable for the horse, and provides you with adequate control. A too-thick mouthpiece, like some hotdog–sized rubber bits 3/4 inch or thicker, is just too much material for a horse's mouth and can cause a horse to almost gag.

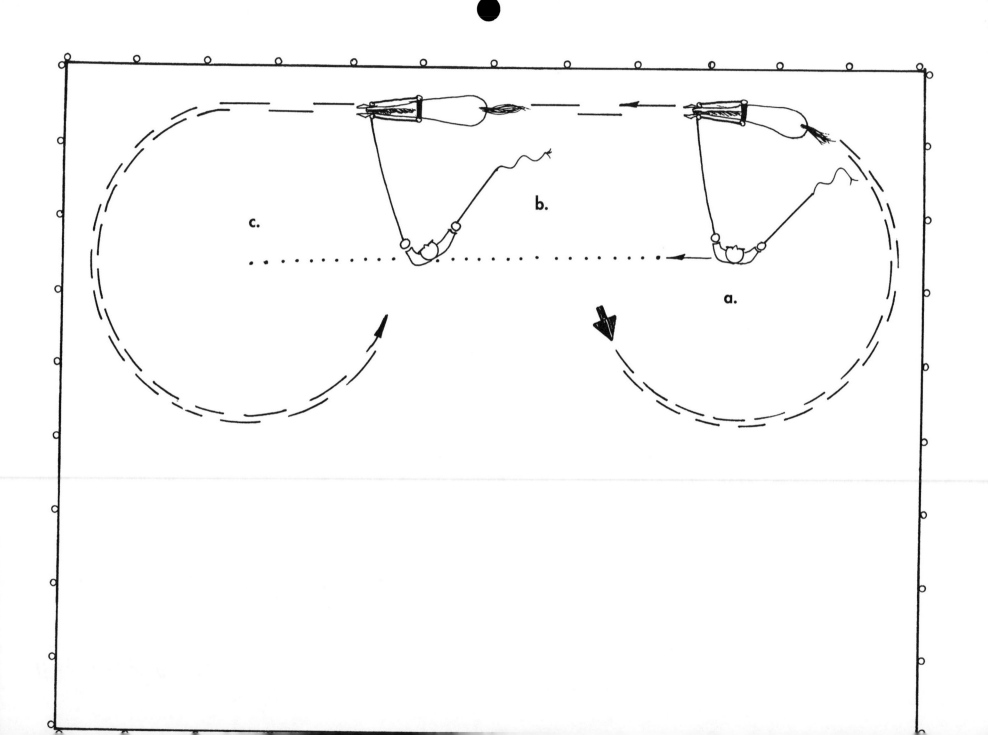

Trot-Lengthen-Trot

This exercise goes particularly well with sliding side reins because the horse is free to stretch forward for the lengthening. If you use regular side reins, adjust them a bit looser than normal so the horse will not be hesitant to extend the trot.

a. If you perform the collected trot, the circles should be about 10 meters in diameter. At a working trot, they can be 15 to 20 meters, depending on the horse.

b. Extend the trot on the straight as long as you can keep up.

c. Collect the trot and immediately go into a circle.

Problem: Bored   The horse is tuned out, listless. Causes: longeing overdone, worked too long, too many times per week; the horse is sore; the session is tedious and has no variety. Perform frequent transitions, changes in direction, and various maneuvers. Keep your horse watching you. If he ignores commands, performs upward or downward transitions when he feels like it, or is basically tuned out, you might need to go back to free longeing to get his attention. Assess your use of the aids: voice commands, body language, and the whip. Are they appropriate, consistent, and used with enough intensity?

Change where you longe; introduce a new or more advanced aspect to the lessons, such as a gait extension, collection, longeing over a few ground rails, working on irregular terrain, longeing with side reins and a surcingle or a saddle.

No response? Ask nicely once and if you are ignored, back up your request with an appropriately forceful aid. Do not use a command over and over again once the horse is doing what is asked. It is not necessary to continue saying, "Trot, trot," once the horse is trotting. This may dull him to your transition commands. Keep cues sparse and effective.

Winter Work   Especially if a horse has a short coat in winter, it's best to use a quarter sheet when working during cold weather. A quarter sheet is a wool or synthetic fleece blanket that covers the horse's loin and quarters and is fastened under the saddle or surcingle.

Extended Trot: An extended trot is a trot performed at the same tempo as the working trot but with longer strides. The horse really reaches with his front legs, while pushing and driving with the hindquarters with great impulsion. This trot has the longest moment of suspension and therefore covers the most ground with each stride as the horse glides through the air. The hind feet should markedly overstep the prints of the front feet. There is a distinct lengthening of the frame, with the nose stretching forward and somewhat downward. It is okay to have a horse perform the extended trot for a few circles as long as the round pen is 66 feet in diameter. A smaller circle than that is not appropriate for an extended trot.

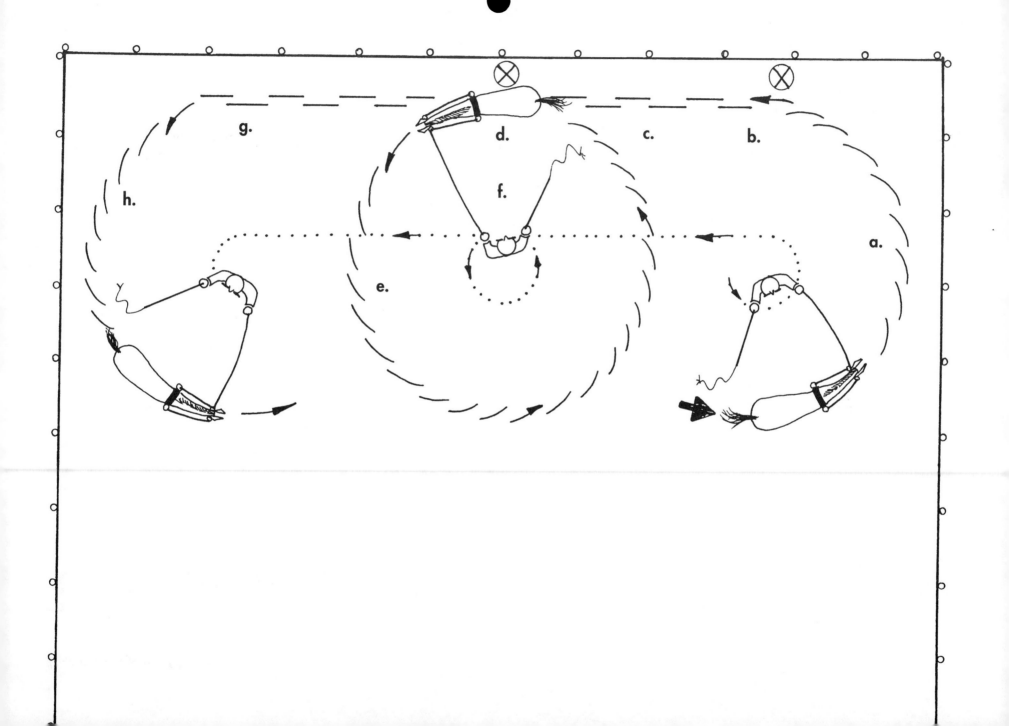

a.

b.

c.

d.

e.

f.

g.

h.

Canter-Trot-Canter

Two of the most important transitions to focus on with side reins are the canter-trot and the trot-canter transitions.

SIDE REINS

- Help stabilize your horse.
- Keep head tossing to a minimum on the upward transition.
- Decrease the "falling" or rushing that can occur during the downward transition.
- Allow the horse to find a compromise between energy and change of movement—and hopefully his answer will be balance.

a. Collected canter on a 15-meter circle.

b. The downward transition to trot occurs just where the circle touches the straight line that parallels the arena fence.

c. Trot straight 10 to 15 meters.

d. At X, transition to canter and begin another circle. Develop a sense of timing and keen observation. For example, when going to the left at the trot, just at the moment when the horse's weight is fully descended on the left hind and right front is the time to give a half halt and cue for the depart. The right hind will be the first beat of the canter.

e. Collected canter, 10- to 15-meter circle.

f. Downward transition to trot.

g. Trot straight 10 to 15 meters.

h. Collected canter and begin another circle.

Problem: Fast Trot Instead of Canter The horse rushes on at the trot instead of cantering. Half halt, half halt, collect the trot. Complete a circle and then ask him again when he is facing the arena wall.

Problem: Downward Transition to Trot Results in Front-heavy Quick Trot Before you ask for the trot transition, give the horse a few half halts while he is cantering to get him thinking about keeping his weight shifted rearward on the transition. Do not let a horse make the wrong association—that a downward transition means a rest break—or the downward transition will be lazy and unbalanced.

Problem: Bucking Some horses, on their own, will break into a canter from the trot, and add bucking. Discourage bucking. A jerk on the longe line often causes the bucking horse to load the forehand and kick out with the hind legs, which can be worse than the bucking. A better way to deal with the bucking is to strongly drive the horse forward. This encourages the horse to stretch out rather than curl up. One philosophy is that a horse should be "bucked out," which is to allow him to buck until he gets it out of his system. That tells the horse that bucking is okay, however, and does not really help him overcome the reaction to the odd sensation. A series of transitions is better. Check the cinches periodically throughout the work to ensure that they are safely adjusted.

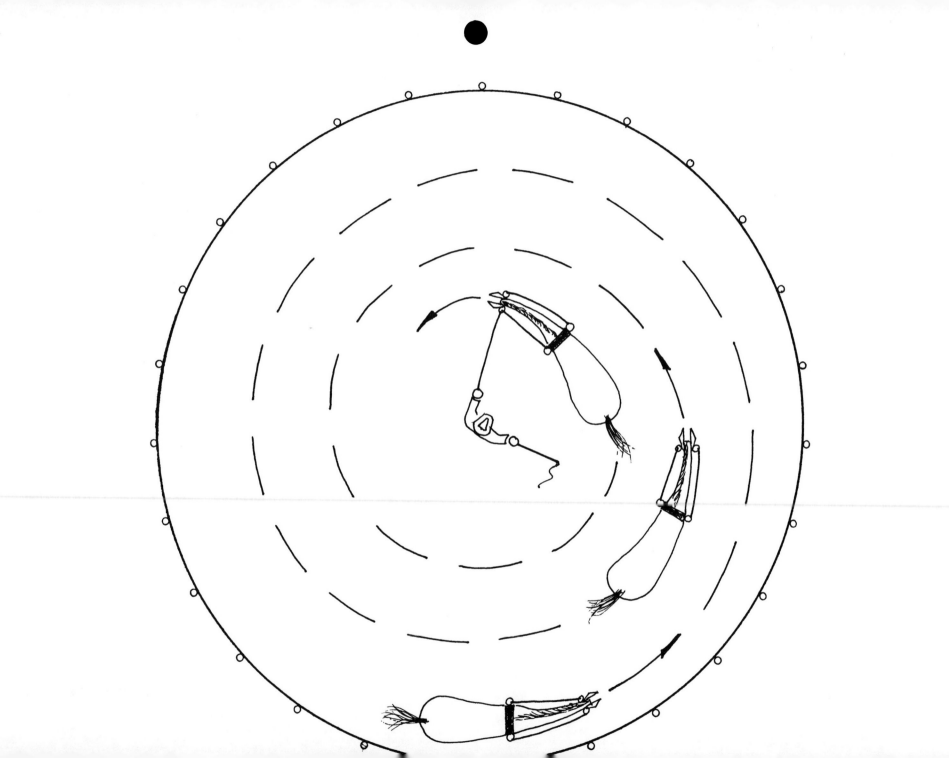

Exercise 63

Spiral In

At first, perform this exercise at the walk to get an idea of the procedure. The walk often does not have enough impulsion for the small circles, however. Spiraling in at the trot is okay up to about 10 meters, but then the diagonal support of the gait makes it more difficult for an actively trotting horse to stay balanced. Spiraling in at a jog works better. Spiral work at the canter is of tremendous benefit for collection and preparation for canter pirouette. It is an advanced exercise and is covered in more detail in Exercise 84.

Before you begin spiraling, be sure the side reins are of the proper length for the gait, the horse's stride length, and the size of the circles you plan to work. The inside side rein might be adjusted one or two holes shorter than the outside rein if you are planning collected work and small circles.

As you bring the horse in, you want to be sure the whip drives the horse forward but does not say "out."

Gather up the lines gradually (refer to Exercise 4).

It is okay to perform many rounds at 20 meters and 15 meters, but only require the horse to perform two revolutions at 10 meters. You must gradually work up to asking for two full revolutions at 10 meters. The advanced horse should only be asked to perform one circle at 6 meters before he begins spiraling out.

The closer the horse comes in, the more chance there is for imbalance and interference, so be sure the horse is conditioned, prepared, and that his legs are protected.

Tack Tip: Breast Collar A breast collar will keep the surcingle from shifting rearward or slipping sideways. It should be fastened snugly.

Tack Tip: Crupper A crupper helps stabilize the saddle or surcingle. The crupper consists of a forked strap that attaches to the surcingle, and a loop that lies under the horse's tail and fastens to both forks of the strap. Many horses will kick or buck when they first feel a crupper under their tail. But you have done a thorough job of desensitizing your horse to ropes under his tail, right?

Tack Tip: Using a Longeing Cavesson with a Bridle If a cavesson is used with a bridle, the noseband of the bridle is usually removed. The noseband of the cavesson goes under the cheek pieces of the bridle's headstall but the crown of the cavesson goes over the crown of the bridle. If the noseband were buckled over the cheek pieces of the bridle, it would interfere with the action of side reins or long lines and could affect the comfort of the bit.

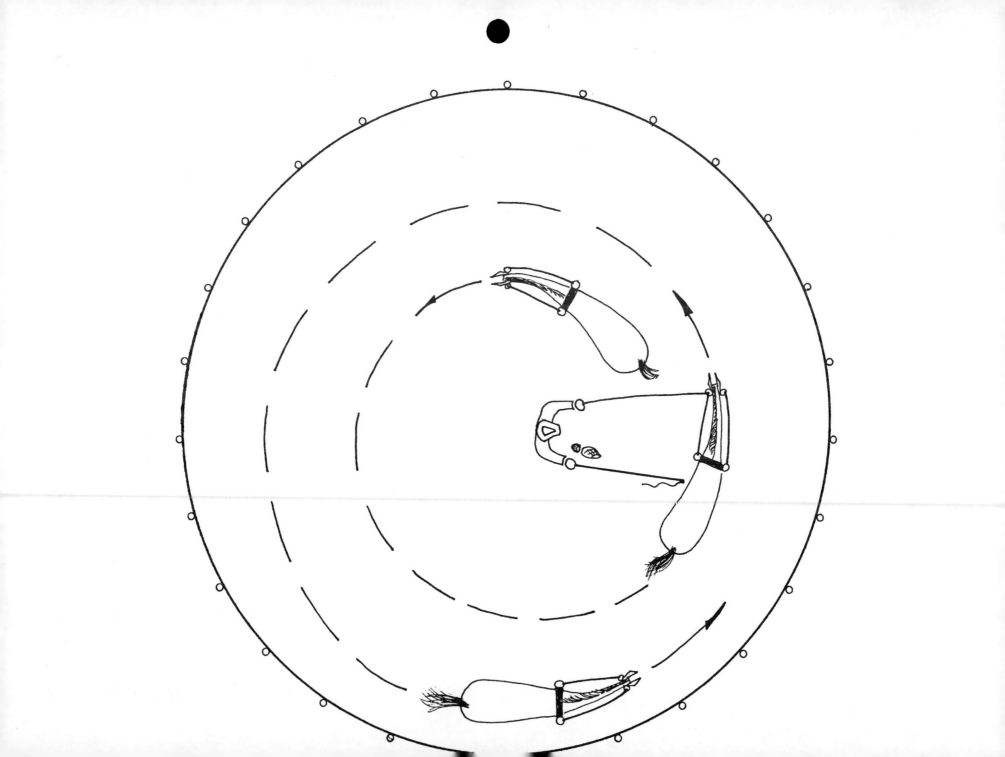

Exercise 64

Spiral Out

Refer to all the information in Exercise 63 related to appropriate gaits and side rein adjustment.

As you start to let your horse out, realize that you are in a vulnerable position. With the horse working close to you at the center of the spiral, you are in a position in which you could get kicked. Also, you will be adding aids that drive the horse forward and outward, which can elicit an irritated reaction from improperly trained horses. So be careful.

Maintain contact on the longe line so that you can always bring the horse's head closer to you if necessary. This is your safeguard because as long as you can bring the head toward you, the hindquarters will swing away.

Give periodically with the longe line contact to invite the horse to fill up the circle and make it larger. But as you give, don't lose the contact. The yields should be brief, and contact should be reestablished immediately.

Use your right foot (when the horse is spiraling to the left) to step toward the horse's hindquarters or rib cage to push him out onto a larger circle.

Point the whip at the horse's ribs to maintain overall bend and to assist you in moving the horse outward. Your whip may have to serve a double role: pushing the ribs outward and driving the hindquarters forward.

Caution: Tongue over Bit   If you see a horse trying to put his tongue over a bit, do something quick! Do not let this habit form, as it is very difficult to break. A tongue over the bit, rather than under it, makes for no communication with the snaffle. And a horse whose tongue is lolling out the corner of his mouth while he is performing is very unsightly. Be sure the bit is the correct thickness and size, and the bridle is adjusted properly. Often, the headstall needs to be shortened. In other cases, the horse may need a bit that allows him more room for his tongue.

Tack Tip: Bridle Reins   If the horse is going to be ridden after longeing, you can leave the riding reins attached:

- *English bridle:* With the riding reins over horse's neck, twist the reins together under the horse's neck and buckle one rein into the throatlatch.
- *Western bridle:* Run the reins through the gullet of the Western saddle and then half-hitch them to the saddle horn.

Problem: Playfulness   The horse runs, bucks, and does not pay attention, or he throws his head and plays instead of paying attention. This can be dangerous to the horse's legs and back and to the handler, especially when you're working in close confines such as a spiral. The horse needs to be turned out for exercise before longeing. Never take a horse who has been cooped up in a stall or small pen and expect him to pay attention and learn a new lesson. Be sure you have all equipment adjusted so that it is effective. A too long, too stretchy side rein invites a horse to play. Give a playful horse something else to think about—drive him actively forward.

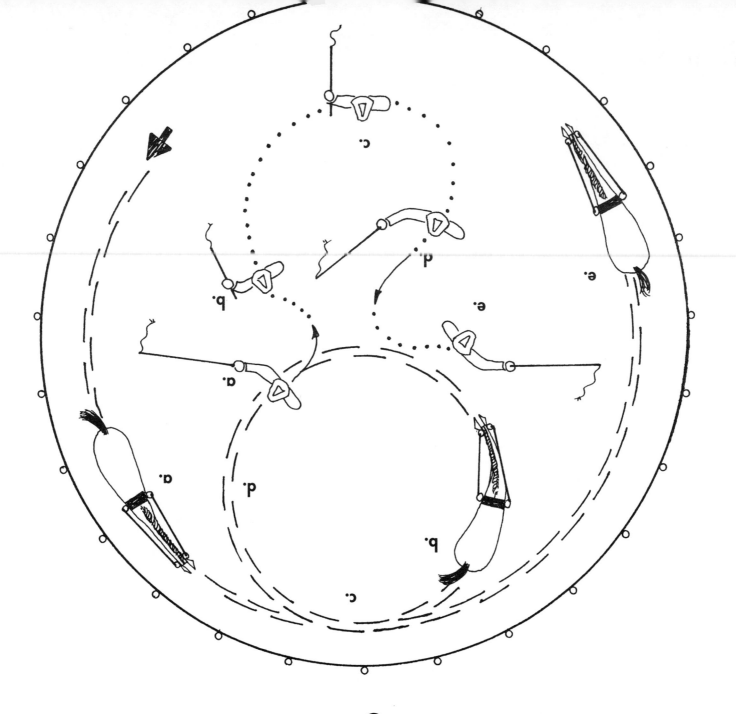

Trot-Circle-Trot

This is a free longeing exercise with side reins. If you don't have a round pen, you might be able to hold this exercise in a small arena, provided the horse is fairly solid in his training. You can't perform this exercise with a longe line because when the horse makes the full circle, the longe line would have to pass over his back and that doesn't work.

Since the entire exercise is designed to be held at a collected trot, the side reins should be adjusted appropriately and the inside rein (in this example, the left) could be one or two holes shorter, depending on the horse.

a. Trot a 20-meter circle as many times around as necessary to establish correct cadence and bend.

b. Step back and to your right as you ask the horse to come in off the rail to the left. Hold your whip in a neutral position behind you.

c. Step almost to the other side of the round pen to give the horse room to work the size circle you want. A 10-meter circle is appropriate.

d. As the horse is heading back toward the rail of the round pen, step toward him and raise your whip to assure him that you want a continuous circle to the left, not a turn to the right.

e. Rotate around the pen from your middle position, driving the horse forward for several rounds before you ask for the exercise again. After 2 to 4 repetitions of this exercise, stop the horse, and adjust the side reins for the next exercise.

Problem: Balking The horse will not go forward. Since the cause of freezing is usually fear or uncertainty, evaluate the thoroughness of the training progression. Has there been a sudden addition of side reins or a new bit? Remove and review. Are the side reins adjusted too short? This is one of the most common causes of lock-up. Lock-up could occur when you ask the horse to perform the 10-meter collected trot circle in this exercise.

If the balking is bona-fide sullen behavior, an experienced trainer should handle the horse. A sullen horse has gone into an emotional and physiological "pout" that requires careful individual assessment and therapy.

Caution: Headstall Too Short When the headstall is adjusted too short, the bit rides too high in the horse's mouth and is too tight against the corners of the lips and possibly the premolars. This type of fit is often characterized by a series of wrinkles at the corners of the horse's mouth.

When a bit is consistently adjusted too tightly, the tissues of the corners of the mouth may become thickened and hardened (i.e., "hard mouthed") and subsequently dull, due to the constant pressure of the too-tight bit. Even if the trainer releases pressure on the reins, there is no release of pressure on the horse's mouth! It is easy to understand why a horse so bridled does not relax. What's the point, when there's no reward? The surface of the tongue may also become similarly desensitized when a bit is fit too tightly in a horse's mouth.

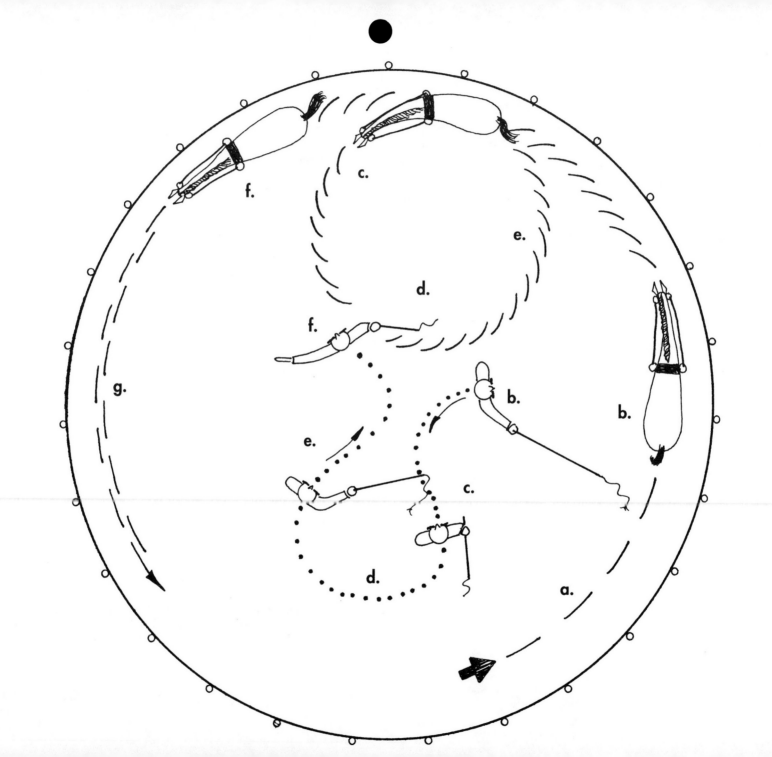

a.

b.

b.

c.

c.

d.

d.

e.

e.

f.

f.

g.

Walk-Canter-Circle-Trot

This is another free longeing exercise with side reins. (See Exercise 65.)

Since the entire exercise is designed to be held at collected gaits, the side reins should be adjusted appropriately and the inside rein (in this example, the left) could be one or two holes shorter depending on the horse.

a. The horse is walked for just a few strides. The collected canter depart is best produced from a collected but relaxed walk.

b. Walk to canter, as described in Exercise 45.

c. Invite the horse off the rail as described in Exercise 65.

d. Give the horse enough room to perform the smaller circle at the collected canter. In this case, a 6- to 8-meter circle might be your goal.

e. Step toward the horse to assure him that you want a full circle, although at this stage of training and with the use of side reins, not many horses would try to turn right.

f. Downward transition from collected canter to collected trot, as described in Exercise 43.

g. Collected trot. You can add Exercise 65 here.

A *collected* gait is performed at the same tempo as the working gait, but it has a shorter, more elevated stride with a longer support phase. Therefore it covers less ground than a working gait. Collection is brought about by a shift of the center of gravity rearward and is usually accompanied by an overall body elevation and an increase in joint flexion.

LENGTH OF SESSIONS

Early in the training progression, the sessions should be 10 minutes or less , with no canter work. As the horse progresses, work up to a 40-minute session with canter work if the horse is ready. Most work should be at the trot, with lots of transitions and turns. There can be four or more canter episodes of two to three minutes each.

Problem: Rearing The horse stands up on his hind legs. Rearing is a loss of forward motion coupled with an avoidance behavior. The horse is trying to avoid the effect of the aids. Rearing while being longed is almost always caused by too much restriction on the horse's mouth, usually from side reins. This is a situation to avoid because it seems that once a horse rears and perhaps falls over and breaks a piece of equipment, the behavior is more easily repeated. That is why side rein use is an art. Side reins are to be introduced gradually and carefully monitored. If side reins are used too short or are attached before the horse is sufficiently warmed up, the horse's topline cannot round into the contact. Rather, the back will hollow and the horse's head will come up, which leads to rearing.

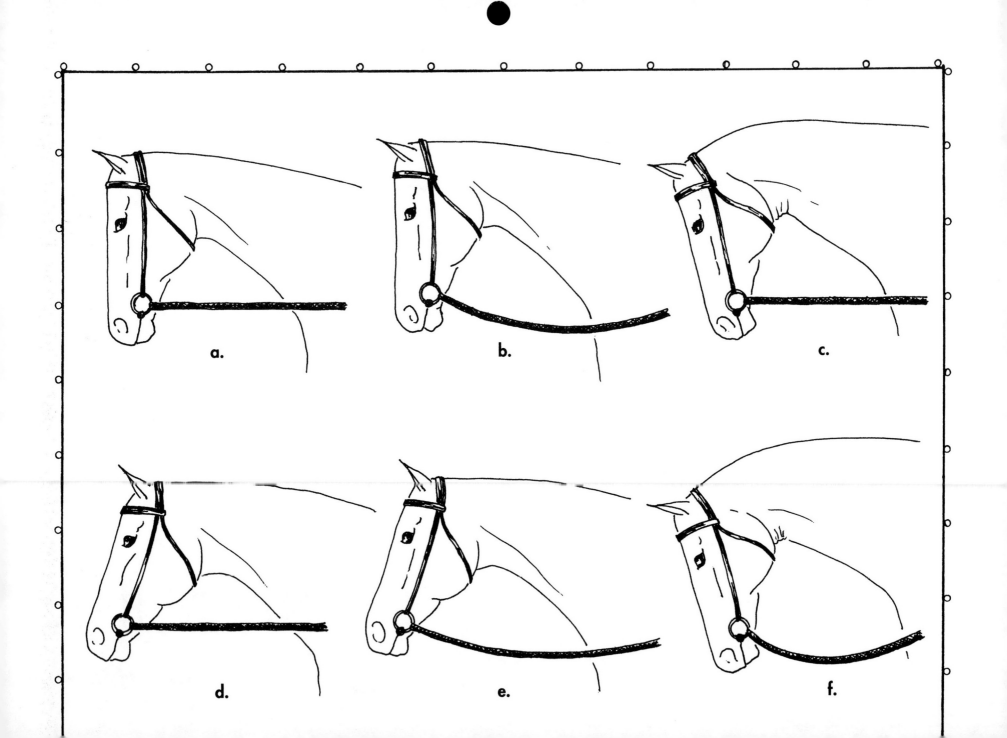

a.

b.

c.

d.

e.

f.

Exercise 67

Contact Check

Throughout side reins and long line work, you must be ever-vigilant about your horse's working form. When a horse is "on the bit," he is in an advantageous posture to allow him to change gait, speed, or direction smoothly. His body also is likely in an effective form that encourages the development of a good physique.

A HORSE THAT IS ON THE BIT

- Has well-established energy from the hindquarters.
- Has a rounded topline.
- Has a poll that is the highest point of his neck.
- Holds faceline 5 to 20 degrees in front of the vertical.
- Bends uniformly at the jaw, poll, and body as he turns.
- Keeps even rein contact.
- Usually has a moist mouth.

Although you must look at the engagement of the hindquarters and the form of the entire body to determine whether a horse is on the bit, the relationship of head and neck to the reins gives clues. The diagram depicts a horse being worked with side reins or long lines.

a. On the vertical, contact apparent. If all other criteria were met, this horse would be on the bit. This would be appropriate for side rein use with an intermediate English horse and for long line use with an advanced horse.

b. On the vertical, this horse may or may not be on the bit. If the horse is very light and sensitive, he might be backing away from the bit. If side reins, the reins should be lengthened and the horse should be encouraged to stretch. If long lining, it would be appropriate for an intermediate Western horse.

c. Behind the vertical, contact apparent. This horse might still be on the bit in spite of the side reins being too short. The reins should be loosened or removed immediately (see Exercise 57), otherwise, the horse could progress quickly to **f**, which is very undesirable. If is long lining, the trainer does not real-

ize the amount of leverage he has and must be pulling straight back with both lines. Something to be avoided.

d. In front of the vertical, contact apparent. This horse is probably on the bit. This is an appropriate configuration for beginning horses in side reins in any discipline, provided the horse still maintains forward impulsion. If long lining, it's okay for beginning horses.

e. In front of the vertical, no contact apparent. If side reins, they may need to be shortened slightly to establish contact. If long lining, it's appropriate for beginning lessons for any horse.

f. Behind the vertical, no contact. This is the most serious error to avoid. The horse has learned to back away from bit pressure. This is probably caused by too strong a bit, side reins that are too short, or improperly used long lines. The side reins should be removed and the horse should go into a major review program (refer to Exercise 57).

163

PART FIVE

Long Lining

Long lining is the logical progression of groundwork after longeing and before riding. It is the first association the horse will have with bit *action*. During longeing with side reins, the horse was introduced to bit presence and contact. Long lining will ready the horse for rein aids that will be used by the rider. It excels at teaching the horse changes in flexion, bend, and direction.

Long lining requires some specific tack. Side reins are not used in conjunction with long lining. Long lines for big figures (20-meter circles and arena work) must be 35 feet long in order to go around the horse's hindquarters. Cotton web lines are the best in terms of weight and feel. The last 10 feet should be stitched round so the line will slide more freely through surcingle rings. The snaps should be small enough to pass easily through surcingle rings.

For advanced work on the long line, close to the horse, much shorter lines are required. Depending on the exercise, lines 12 to 20 feet long can be used.

The basic long lining lessons should be first taught with a cavesson. Once the horse is familiar with the procedure and is relaxed, work can commence with the lines attached to the bit rings of the bridle.

A surcingle is ideal for long lining because the rings at various heights allow for a greater choice for running the lines. In lieu of a surcingle, an English or Western saddle can be used for the basic long lining lessons.

When working on advanced maneuvers, there are quite a number of ways to run the lines. You will want to set up the two long lines in whatever configuration it takes to equalize pressure and resistance between the two sides of the horse. The configuration will likely be different with each horse and could be different in each direction with the same horse.

When working behind the horse, or "plow driving," the lines should run from the bit through a surcingle ring at the height appropriate for the horse's conformation and level of training.

When working at the side of the horse on long lines, generally the inside line runs through a surcingle ring and to the trainer's hand. The outside line runs through a surcingle ring, around the horse's hindquarters and to the trainer's hand.

An alternative is to have the inside line come directly from the bit to the trainer's hand.

When working at the side of the horse on short lines, generally both lines run through terrets located on top of the surcingle. The lines run directly to the trainer's hands and cross the horse's back and croup when the horse changes bend.

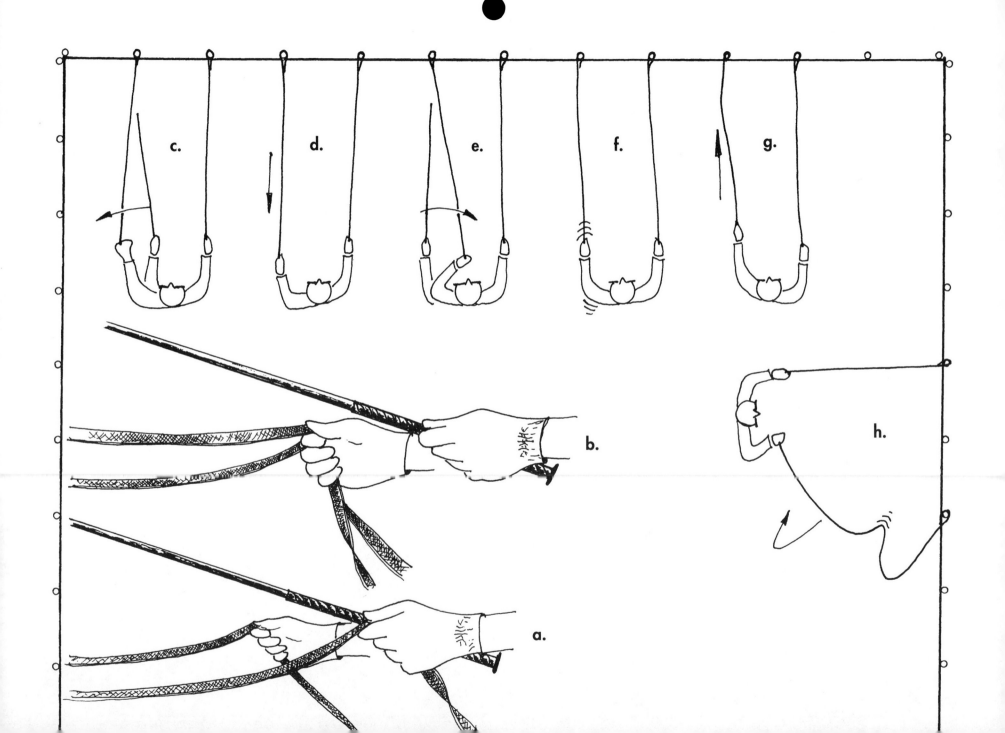

c.

d.

e.

f.

g.

b.

a.

h.

Exercise 68

Long Line Lingo

HOLDING LONG LINES
Depending on the length of the long lines, the experience of the trainer, and the type of movement being performed by the horse, the lines can be held in the following ways:

- One in each hand with loops that release from the top (handy but could trap the hand).
- One in each hand with figure-8s (the safest method but not handy).
- One in each hand with end of lines on ground. (Okay with short lines, experienced horse and trainer, quiet work, and if they are separate lines, not one continuous line.)

a. One line in each hand with a whip in the appropriate hand. In this drawing, the driving line and whip are in the left hand and the leading line is in the right hand, so the horse is tracking right.

b. Both lines in one hand with a whip in the other hand. The horse is tracking right.

REIN AIDS WITH LONG LINES
The following rein effects occur when the lines run directly to the trainer's hand or when the trainer is in a plow-driving position. When the lines run through surcingle rings or stirrups, the individual rein effects will be changed or diluted, depending on the circumstances.

During any exercise, if you have trouble getting the effect you want, you can bypass the surcingle rings and communicate directly with the horse's mouth via these aids.

In the following examples, the horse is tracking left. The left line is the leading line and the right line is the driving line:

c. An opening or leading line that invites the horse to stretch his neck, move forward, and bend to the inside, in this case, to the left. The

trainer's hand rotates 90 degrees to free up the arm. The other line must allow the movement to take place.

d. A direct line is a pull toward your body. This brings the horse in or asks for more bend. Ordinarily, it is only used unilaterally, that is, by itself. Bilateral direct line pressure (pulling both back at the same time) usually causes lock-up and resistance. Alternating direct line aids is effective for breaking up resistance. Often, when you apply a direct line aid with one hand, you give with the other line (**g**).

e. An indirect line can ask for a slow down, a bend, and/or a degree of collection. Your hand moves diagonally rearward toward your other elbow. The other line usually maintains contact to prevent overbending. Indirect rein aids are particularly suited to advanced terret driving.

f. The line tremor is a tiny wave (refer to Exercise 4) designed to get a horse's attention, break up minor resistance, and initiate bending. It is a basic line aid that is used early and throughout the horse's training.

g. The yield is a giving without losing what has been gained. Just like the yield following a half halt when riding, the yield on the long line is meant to reward the horse but not let him fall apart. Often a yield is used to encourage a horse to move out on a larger circle.

h. The driving line can be used to pop a lazy horse forward. It's handy to master for times when you don't have a whip and you need to "make" a horse obey your forward driving voice command. If the horse is tracking left, the driving line you will pop is the right line. Draw the line out to the side to the right and then quickly snap it forward. This sends a sharp wave that travels along the line to the horse's inside hip. Pop! Wake up!

Practice Time!   It is no accident that these line aids are drawn attached to a fence. Tie your regular lines to the fence, using a length of bungee cord so you can develop a bit of feel as you perfect your techniques.

Jungle Sounds   You use specific voice commands to tell a horse which gait to perform and when. You might also want to develop a set of kisses, clicks, or clucks that ask a horse to move on, and a few grunts or warnings to tell him to stop or rethink. They will come in handy for long lining.

Tack Tips: Bits Suitable for Long Lining   Never use a curb bit. A bit with shanks creates leverage, which would be very dangerous on long lines.

O-Ring Snaffle   The O-ring is the most common type of snaffle used on young horses because of its loose action. The rings moving through the holes in the mouthpiece set up a "loose action" in the horse's mouth that keeps the horse mouthing the bit, attentive, and responsive. If a horse tends to have a rigid mouth, an O-ring snaffle is the best.

Eggbutt Snaffle   Most eggbutt, or D-ring, snaffles are constructed to avoid pinching skin in the corners of the mouth. The swivel action of the rings is located in a place that does not contact lip skin. This type of bit has a little more lateral effect on the corners of the horse's mouth than an O-ring but not as much action. This means that they are quieter bits that result in quieter mouths.

Full-Cheek Snaffle   A full-cheek snaffle has a cheekpiece extension on the side of the bit both above and below the mouthpiece of the bit. Cheekpieces should not be confused with shanks. The reins do not attach to cheekpieces. A full-cheek snaffle provides the most "lateral persuasion" of any snaffle bit. When a left line is pulled, the full-cheek prongs are pulled onto the right side of the horse's face and cause him to turn left. Full-cheek snaffles are designed to be used with keepers. Keepers are small leather tabs added to the sidepieces of the bridle. The top of the bit's cheekpiece is inserted in the tab and the bit is held upright. When keepers are not used, the bit rotates forward and the prongs point forward and backward, not up and down. This changes the action of the mouthpiece of the bit.

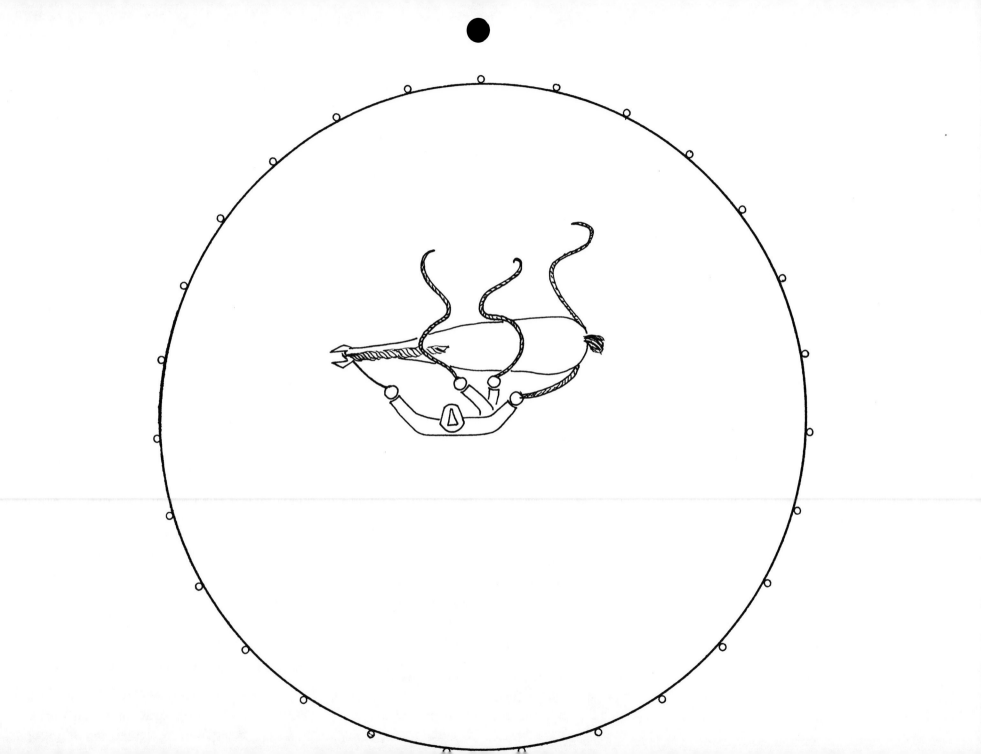

Sacking to Ropes

For the previous discussions of sacking out, refer to exercises 8 and 51.

During long lining, you will have two 35-foot lines that could tangle your horse, you, or you and your horse together. You do not want this to happen. The more you can accustom your horse to the long lines all over his body, the less chance he will react with panic if he should get tangled.

Holding the horse in-hand, familiarize him with the presence of ropes all over his body. Use a 10- to 15-foot rope. Throw the rope over his neck, shoulder, back and hindquarters.

Loop the rope around each of his four legs. Move the rope up and down on each leg until the horse gets used to the sensation.

With the rope looped around a leg, give a gentle tug. Do this with all four legs.

Let the rope slip down to the ground, especially around the pastern. Be ready to let go of one end of the rope if the horse becomes afraid.

Do this from both sides.

Drag the rope on the ground so that he can see and feel the rope from all angles.

Put the rope under the horse's tail, being careful not to be in a dangerous position if he should kick. He will probably clamp his tail on the rope and tuck his croup. Let him learn that if he relaxes, the rope will fall away from his tail.

The more you familiarize your horse to ropes, the less chance you will have of a wreck during longeing or ground driving. Usually 2 or 3 sessions is all it takes.

The Horse's Dilemma During most training, a touch from the trainer is a request for the horse to react, to move over or move forward. The trainer bases these requests on the horse's natural reflexes. During desensitization (sacking out), the request is for the horse to be still when touched with unfamiliar objects. Be sure you understand the impact here and the horse's potential dilemma. It will make you a better and more compassionate trainer.

Problem: The Spaghetti Twirl The horse wraps up in the lines. The horse turns and faces the trainer, becomes frightened and continues to spin, getting unmercifully tangled in the lines. This can be a real setback, complete with friction burns and/or broken tack, so it must be avoided at all costs. Thoroughly familiarize the horse with the equipment and use progressive stages of driving styles. Keep even contact on the lines, paying special attention to the inside line. Take care not to exert tense, unyielding pressure on it. Rather, use the inside line occasionally to push the horse (with a pop to the hip) over to the outside line. Assert the driving aids (lines and voice) early.

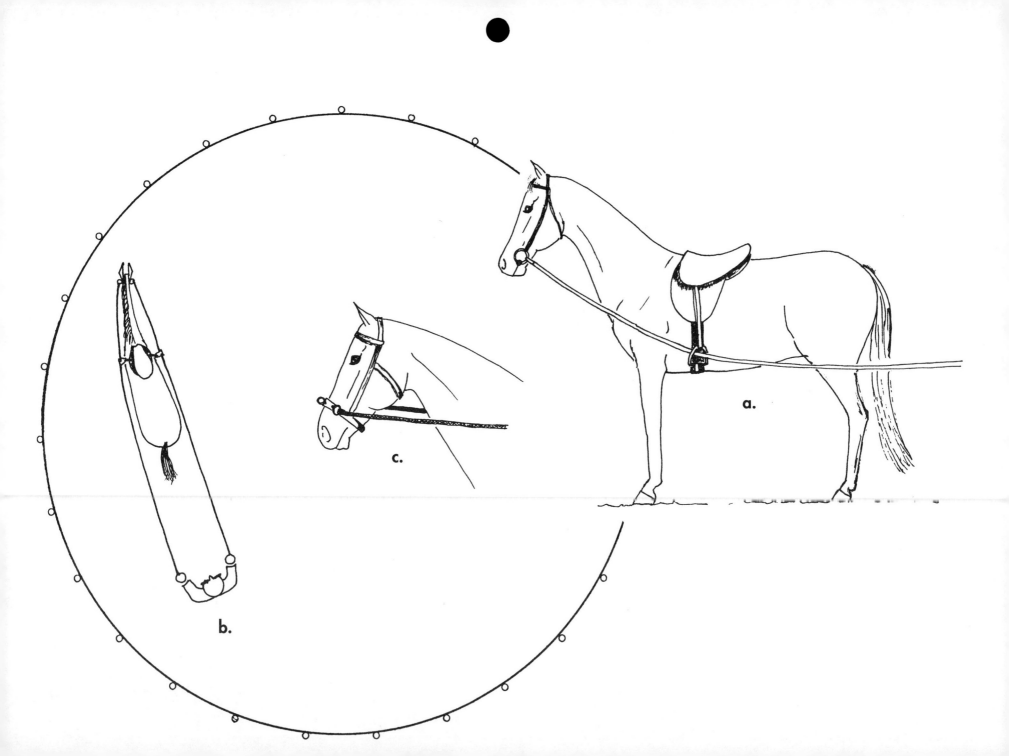

a.

b.

c.

Exercise 70

Plow Driving

The use of the earthy term "plow driving" is meant to be descriptive, not demeaning. Although you use the same position you would use if you were asking your horse to help you till the garden plot, you are looking for something other than plodding.

b. The long lines run low and along either side of the horse, thereby helping you to stabilize the horse's first wobbly movements. You will want to stay close enough to the horse so that you can easily control him but far enough away so that you are out of kicking range.

You can use a surcingle or a saddle for the early lessons. If you choose a surcingle, run the lines through the lowest rings. If it's a saddle from a harness, run the lines through the shaft loops.

a. If you use a riding saddle, lower the stirrups and hobble them together under the horse's belly. "Hobbling" here means tying the stirrup irons together with a rope or strap. Fasten them so the stirrup opening allows clear, unobstructed flow of the long lines.

c. Important note: All basic long lining lessons should first be performed using a cavesson with the long lines attached to the side rings on the cavesson noseband. Once you feel the horse has accepted the idea of long lining, you should then review all of the basic long lining lessons, using a snaffle bridle.

The horse depicted in this drawing is typical but not necessarily what you want. He demonstrates a typical reaction to the sensations of new tack and your position behind him. He has hollowed his topline and is in a braced stance with his head up and his hind legs planted behind his body. Rather than start driving a horse in this state, I suggest removing the long lines and longeing him to relax him and then starting the long lining lesson again.

All you want to do for the first lesson is to familiarize your horse with the tack and the idea of long lining. You might just tack up, stand, move the lines around a little as you walk from the side to the rear position. Or you might read your horse's readiness and proceed to a walk, turn, and halt all in the first lesson. In any event, it is absolutely essential that the horse has had adequate sacking out and lessons in "Whoa" and "Stand."

Should You Use an Assistant? Using an assistant is often recommended.

Advantages: Two heads can be better than one; there is safety in numbers; the horse is used to someone working in the in-hand position.

Disadvantages: The assistant must be experienced and confident; you must rehearse, and for some things you can't; two people can confuse a horse and he may not know who he should listen to; an assistant can get in the way or get hurt.

173

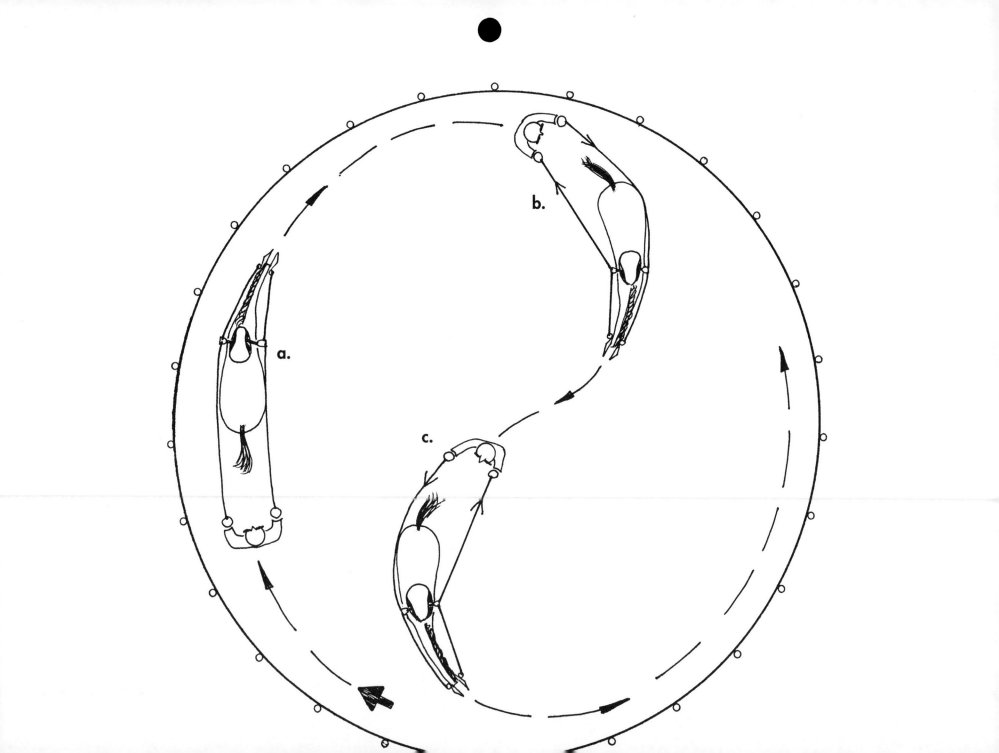

Exercise 71

Yin Yang 1

This change of rein in the circle is the most basic change of direction because you work from behind the horse during the entire exercise.

I like to hold first long lining lessons in a small pen. A round pen has the big advantage of not having any corners where the horse might get "trapped" or "stuck." If you must drive in a pen with corners, place some hay or straw bales across the corners to keep the horse out of them. If not, a horse could end up facing into a corner and the only way out, if you were working alone, would be to work your way up to him and lead him out (risky) or back him out (way too advanced a maneuver to suddenly require). A 66-foot-diameter round pen has enough room to allow you to walk the horse several strides straight before you have to think about turning him.

The early lessons are conducted from the plow driving position. The horse is worked only at the walk. The lines run through low surcingle rings or through the stirrups of an English or Western saddle. It is less confusing if a trainer does not carry a whip at first, so you will be relying on the good association you made with voice commands during longeing.

STAND AND FIDDLE
Always start every session with a prolonged session of "Stand." It is even more important here than in longeing. In fact, you should fiddle with the lines at the horse's side, gradually assume the position behind the horse, stand there for a few moments, and then return to the position at the horse's side for more fiddling. You are preventing the annoying and dangerous habits that develop from anticipation and you are trying to make a lasting impression that the horse does not go until you say so. You will greatly appreciate this when it comes time to mount up and take the first ride.

a. **Walk on.** When it is time to move on, say "Walk on" and give slightly with both lines. If necessary, repeat with a more encouraging tone. Some horses even respond better if you say something like, "It's OK. Walk on!" because they have been standing so long they want to be sure that it is now okay to move. If a horse is particularly stuck, flutter the lines on his sides a little bit.

Plan to walk the horse continuously in a large circle for several minutes before you ask for a change of direction. This will give you both the opportunity to become accustomed to the long lining procedure and equipment. Each horse will require a slightly different blend of give and take for turning, and what works in one direction often doesn't in the other.

b. When tracking right, to turn in from the circle: take with the right line, give with the left.

c. Make a large sweeping turn and when you are in the center of the pen, straighten momentarily and reverse the aids to effect a change of bend, going into a left turn. Take with the left line and give with the right line. Blend back to the large circle perimeter, now tracking left.

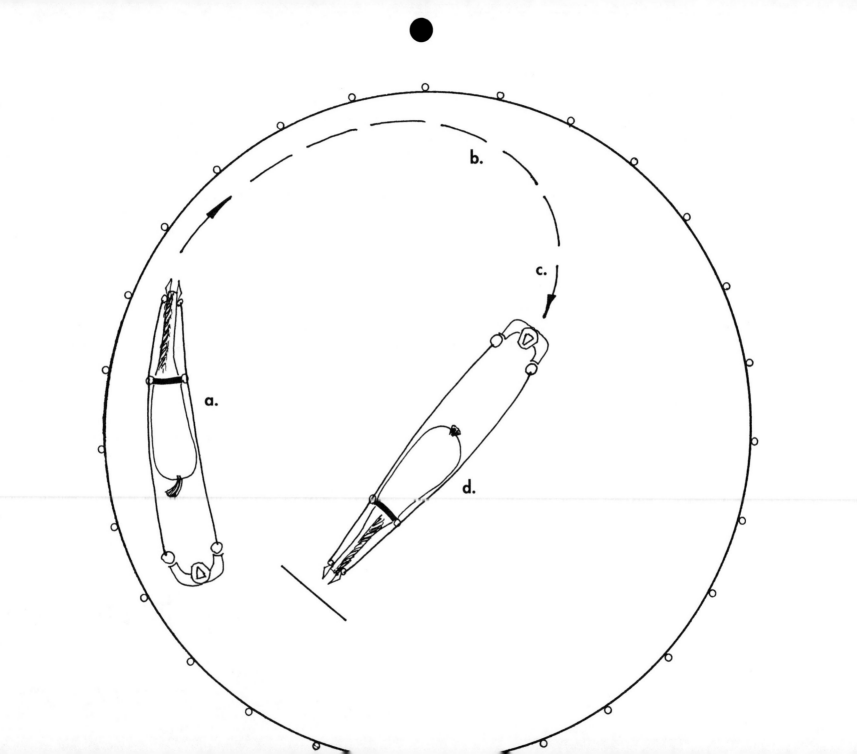

Halt and Stand

A fter you have sashayed back and forth for several minutes or more and you feel you and your horse are somewhat relaxed and confident about turning, it is time to introduce the halt.

When you stop your horse, you want to be sure it is on an absolute straightaway. The importance of this cannot be overemphasized. The reason is that you will have the best chance of exerting even rein pressure on the cavesson or bit if you are directly behind the horse and you both are on a straight line.

In addition, the long lines will be straight along the horse's sides and will further aid you in keeping him straight in the driving channel you have formed.

a. Begin in the plow-driving position along the rail of the round pen.

b. Make the turn back toward the center of the training pen.

c. Prepare to stop. Always make sure that you ask for a stop when the horse is relaxed, moving forward, with head relatively low. This will result in a forward, downward transition. If a horse's head is up and he is tense, the request will be met with rigidity, not willing compliance.

d. Stop the horse.

  1. Say "Okaaay," drawing out this pre-command to give the horse plenty of warning. But keep the tone soothing so as not to alarm him, just notify him.
  2. Say "Wo," using a low woof sound. Stop walking and let the horse meet the contact from the lines on the bit or cavesson.
  3. Be ready to either give with your arms or walk forward a step or two, if the horse doesn't power down instantly.
  4. Repeat all if the horse continues to walk forward.

5. Once you lose your "straight" position (because you will be running into the rail and must turn), you have two options: let the horse face the rail to help you stop him or turn the horse, walk on, and try the halt again on the next straightaway.

d. Once the horse has stopped, tell him "goood boy" and let him stand.

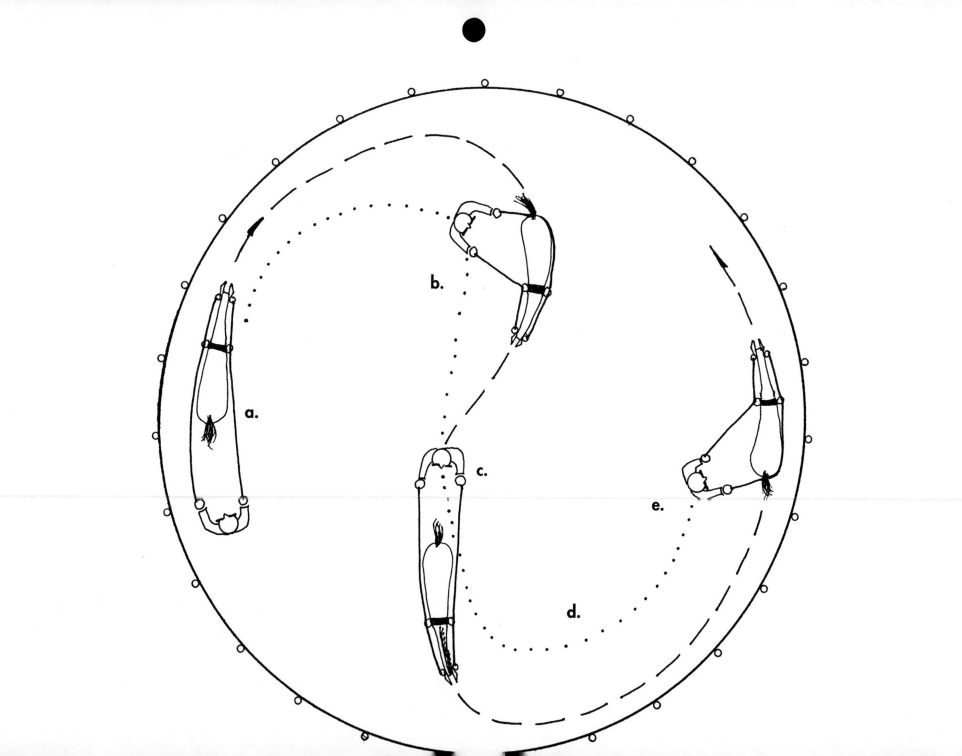

Yin Yang 2

Now it is time to begin stepping to the horse's side as you long line.

When you taught your horse to longe, the concentric-circle technique was helpful to get the horse going and keep him going, but your goal was to stand in one spot and work the horse around you.

Similarly, with long lining, the plow-driving position is somewhat a means to an end. Gradually you will want to introduce the horse to being worked from the side. This exercise is the next step after Exercise 71.

Here is how to go about it:

a. You are plow-driving your horse to the right on the perimeter of the circle at a walk.

b. At the point where you leave the circle to turn in to the right, step off to your horse's hindquarters on the off side for a stride or two as he makes the turn.

c. As he approaches the diagonal straightaway, step back behind him for a few strides.

d. As you ask for the turn left, you can step to his near side hindquarters for a few strides.

e. You might feel you can just stay on the near side and walk a concentric circle quietly alongside your horse. Be sure you have long-enough lines so you won't get kicked.

This familiarizes the horse with the idea of you being off to his side during long lining and with the feel of the lines contacting the sides of his hindquarters.

What Is "Behind the Bit"? The horse overflexes and doesn't take contact with the bit. Causes: side reins adjusted improperly, side reins too heavy, long lines too heavy, trainer's hands too heavy during long lining, bit not correctly chosen or fitted, not enough impulsion being generated. Evaluate these things and make corrections. You want the horse to be light and reaching forward! See Exercise 67 for more information.

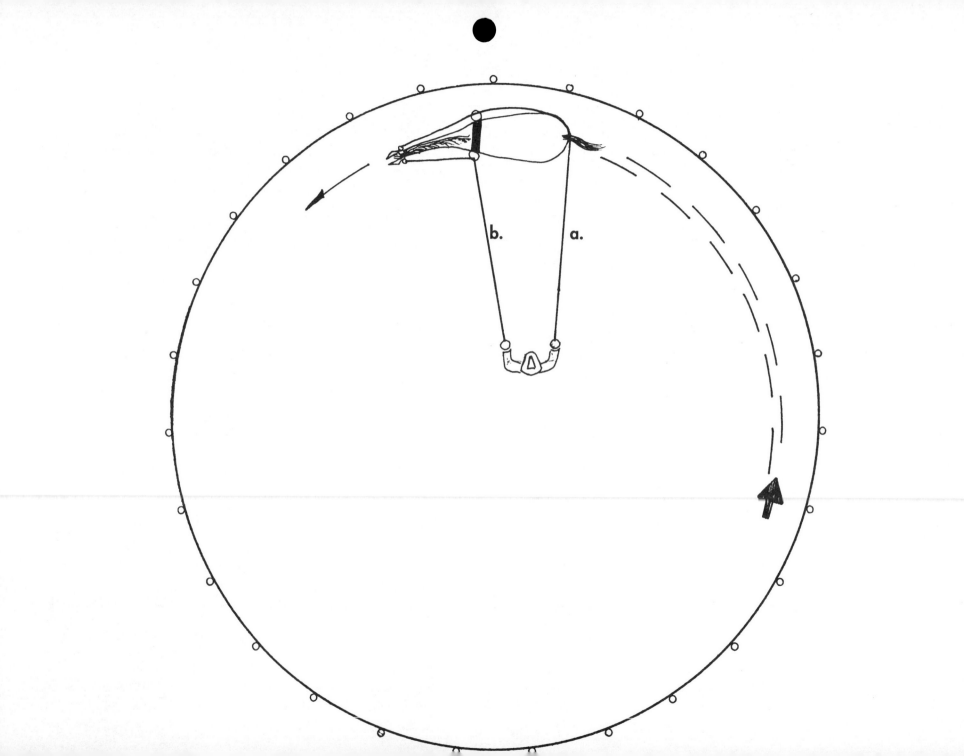

Trot From the Side

You should see something very familiar about this long lining configuration. It closely resembles the piece of pie longeing configuration. The differences are that instead of holding a whip in your driving arm, you are now holding the outside long line. This line can be used to "drive," as shown in Exercise 68.

The biggest difference, though, is your slightly more rearward position. In driving, your position is even more crucial than in longeing.

If you get ahead of the desired position that is depicted:

1. The inside line makes an acute angle from the surcingle ring to your hand.
2. The inside line doesn't flow as freely through the surcingle ring.
3. The lack of free flow often overflexes the horse to the inside, causing him to curl up and face you.

If you get behind the desired position that is depicted here:

a. You lose a good contact and feel of the outside line.

b. You lose the ability to bend and balance the horse.

Caution: Line under Tail The horse gets the outside line under his tail and panics. Don't pull on the outside line; leave it slack or even drop it. Use your inside line to bring the horse into the circle. When the horse relaxes, his tail will unclamp and the line will drop. Review sacking out to ropes as described in Exercise 69.

Letting a Horse Carry the Bit An intermediate to advanced horse, one that flexes at the poll and is somewhat collected, might do better "carrying" the bit rather than having the bit adjusted into position. Some horses hold the bit in position with the suction created by the tongue against the roof of the mouth. With such a horse, the bit can be positioned lower in the mouth and the horse will lift it up and hold it in the most comfortable position for his anatomy. Horses that "carry" a bit are usually obedient and light because the bit acts on the sensitive tongue and bars rather than on the corners of the lips.

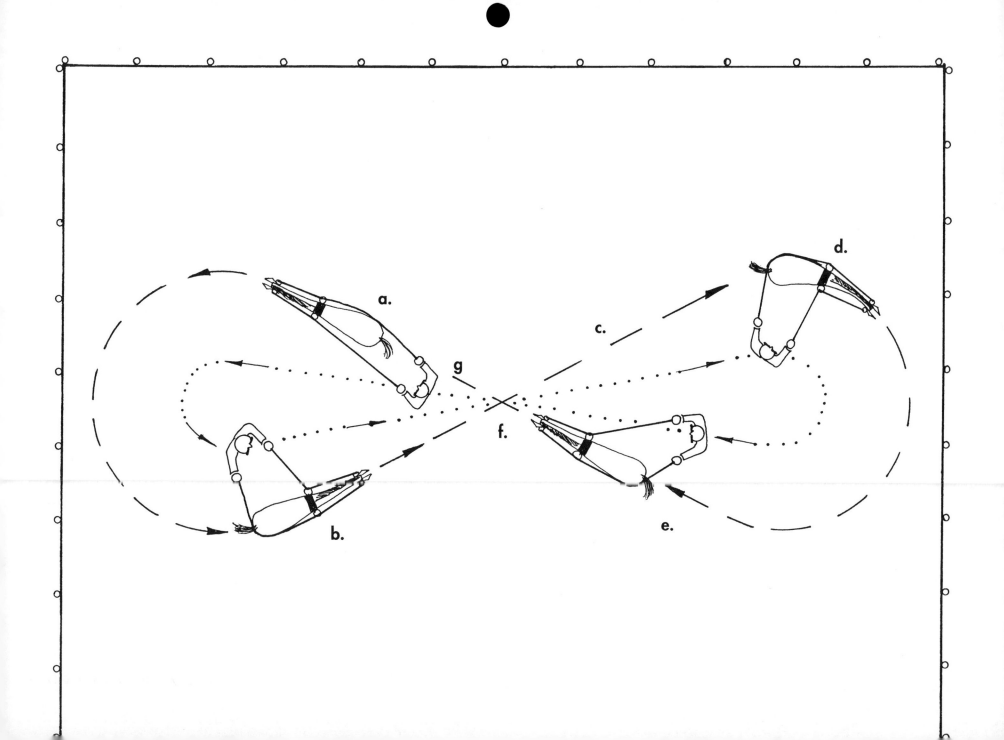

Lazy-8

Work in the round pen until you feel the horse is safely on the long line aids. Rehearse mentally what you will do to control any mishaps. When you are both confident about your roles, hold at least half of the long lining lessons in a large arena. You can switch back and forth between a small pen (to make a point and have better control) and the arena (to allow for more freedom of movement and as a test of the horse being on the aids). An arena will allow you to practice a greater variety of exercises and you can work the horse on longer lines.

One of the first things you should master in the arena is the change of rein. There are many ways to effect a change of rein, just as in riding. Here is a simple change of rein from one half circle to another half circle, with long diagonals in between. It utilizes both driving from the side and from the rear.

a. As you drive your horse from behind, begin from a point in the center of the arena and head to one end where you will drift to your horse's near side and have him make a 20-meter half circle to the left. (A 20-meter half circle is half of a 20-meter circle.) As your horse describes the larger half circle, you will walk a 5-meter concentric half circle on his near side.

b. When you are on the last part of the half circle start to drift back behind your horse, as you will now be heading across a long diagonal.

c. As you head across the long diagonal toward the other end of the arena, focus on straightness. Pick a point on the arena rail and head toward it. The long diagonal will give you plenty of time to finish the left bend, straighten your horse, and initiate the right bend.

d. At the point where the new circle begins to the right, you should step to the horse's off side. Simultaneously, you will take with the right line and give with the left line to negotiate the half circle to the right.

e. Straighten the horse at the end of the half circle and begin stepping behind him. Try to keep the feel of the lines even in your hands as you pass behind him.

f. Very soon after you cross the X at the center of the Lazy-8 you will begin drifting again to the near side to prepare for the half circle left.

g. This exercise can continue until you have developed a harmonious dance.

The Lazy-8 is suitable for work at the walk, trot, and canter.

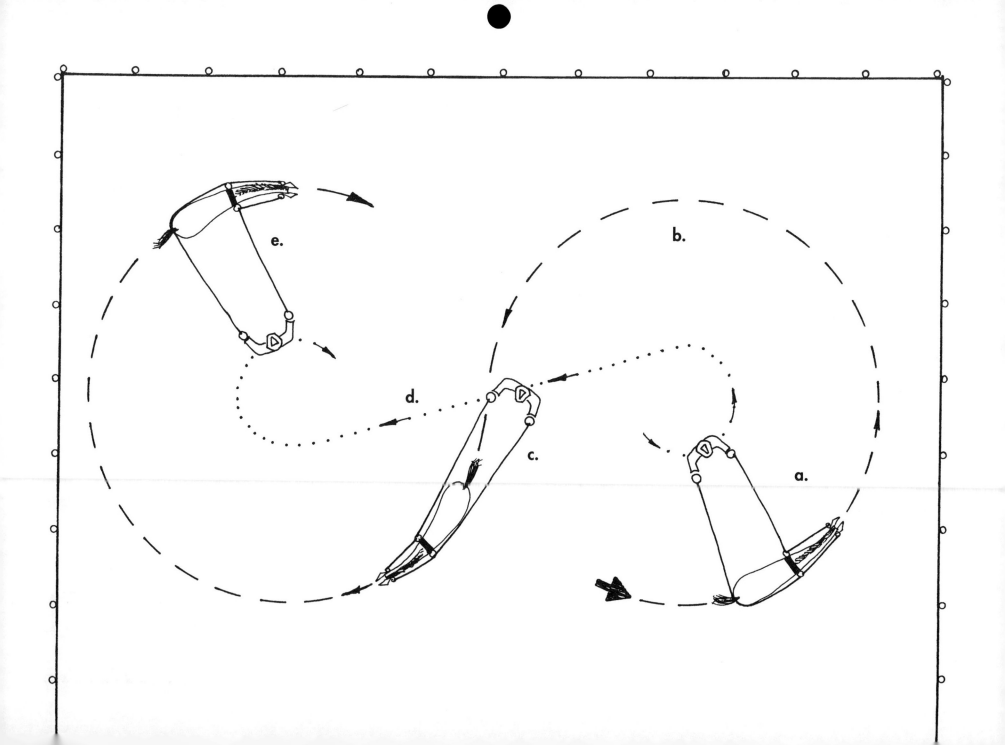

a.

b.

c.

d.

e.

Figure-8

The figure-8 is a simple change of rein from one circle to another circle, during which you drive both from the side and from the rear.

a. Begin tracking to the left, making a 20-meter circle. You will be walking a 5-meter concentric circle on the horse's near side.

b. When you are on the last quarter of the old circle (the part of the circle at the center of the arena), begin drifting behind your horse. You will have to walk quickly so that you are in position when you start the new circle.

c. Drive him ahead of you across the small diagonal between the circles.

d. At the point where he begins the new circle in the new direction, to the right, begin stepping to his off side.

e. Work the new 20-meter circle to the right. You will be walking a 5-meter concentric circle on his off side.

This exercise is suitable for work at the walk and trot. At the canter it requires a lead change at the center of the figure-8.

The goal here is to make a perfect figure-8 such as is required in Equitation and Horsemanship classes. With this type of figure-8 (in contrast to the long diagonals of the Lazy-8 in the previous exercise) there are few, if any, strides where the horse is on a straight line.

The circles can just "kiss" in one spot—about a horse-length long. Another variation is a very formal figure-8, where the circles are flattened and join, making a rather long straight line for the horse to work between the bends. This one would be more difficult to do properly, so it should be the last one perfected.

Problem: Trainer Drops a Line   This can happen if the lines are too short, if the pen is too large, or just as a mishap. The horse's reaction to this may be inconsequential if he has been properly "sacked out" and knows "Whoa." The best thing to do is let the horse continue if you think you can reach down and pick up the line. If it is an outside line and it has moved too far away from you, say "Whoa" and hope the horse remembers his lessons. If he doesn't stop, use the inside line to bring him in to the center of the circle and stop him. If you drop the inside line, take care not to pull on the outside line. Otherwise you may turn the horse to the outside of the circle since there is no inside line to counteract and keep him on the track.

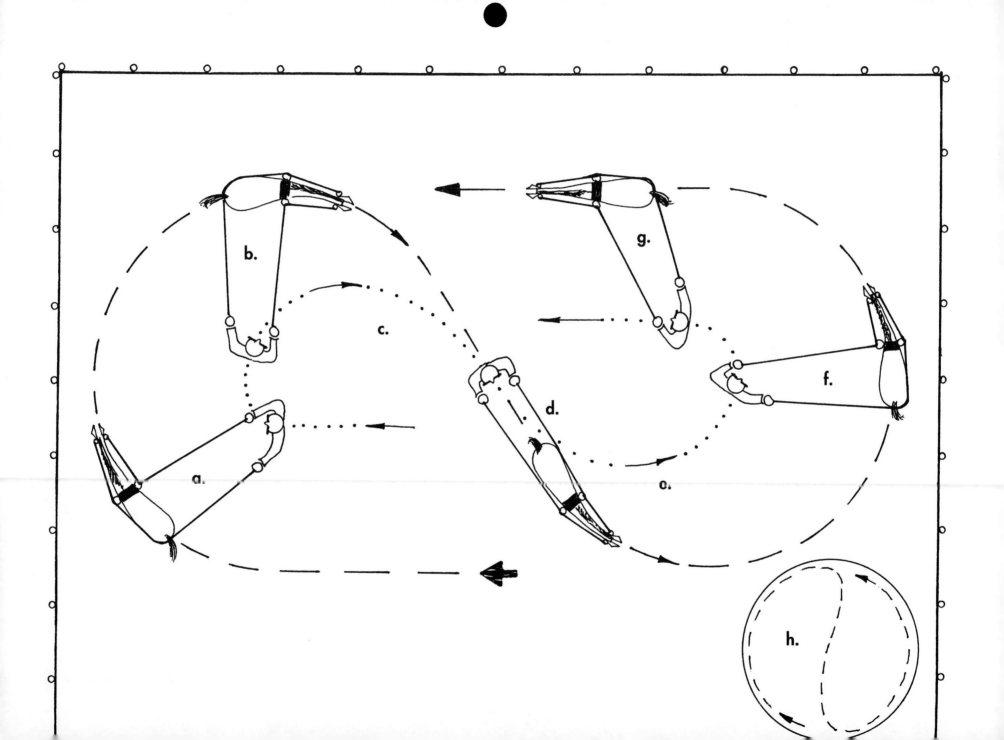

Exercise 77

Change of Rein in the Oval

The end goal for this exercise is a yin-yang change of rein like that in Exercise 71. This change of rein is stretched to fill the arena, however, so it is really a change of rein in the oval. Practice the oval and gradually compress and round it into a circle as shown in the inset h. This change of rein also employs driving from both the side and the rear. When performed within a circle, it is a very compact change of rein. It requires that the horse be sufficiently on the aids to accomplish the change of bend in the small space.

a. Begin tracking to the right, working the horse from the off side. Make a 20-meter half circle. You will be walking a 5-meter concentric circle on the horse's off side.

b. As you finish the half circle, begin drifting behind your horse.

c. You may have to pick up your pace here to keep up with the horse.

d. Drive the horse ahead of you across the "very small diagonal" between the circles. In this oval, the diagonal is much longer than it would be within a circle. When you eventually perform this exercise in the form of Exercise 71, the diagonal will not exist. In a change of bend within the circle, the horse will go immediately from one bend to the other. Again, you might need to hustle your pace a bit here.

e. Move to the horse's near side.

f. Make a half circle to the left. Remember, lengthen the outside line enough for the horse to bend into the new direction; otherwise, he might stall or go in the wrong direction.

g. As you finish, proceed ahead. Do not head back to the center of the exercise. On this diagram, straight ahead appears to be the long side of an oval shape. But if this were taking place within a circle, straight ahead would be on the perimeter of the circle, tracking left (see inset **h**).

During a change of rein, the trainer must pass behind the horse in one of his blind spots—an area directly behind the horse's hindquarters. This should not cause the horse or the trainer concern if adequate lessons in sacking and "Whoa" have been accomplished.

Tack Tip   A full-cheek snaffle adds lateral persuasion. As the right line is pulled, the left cheekpieces of the bit push on the left side of the horse's face, which causes the horse to turn right.

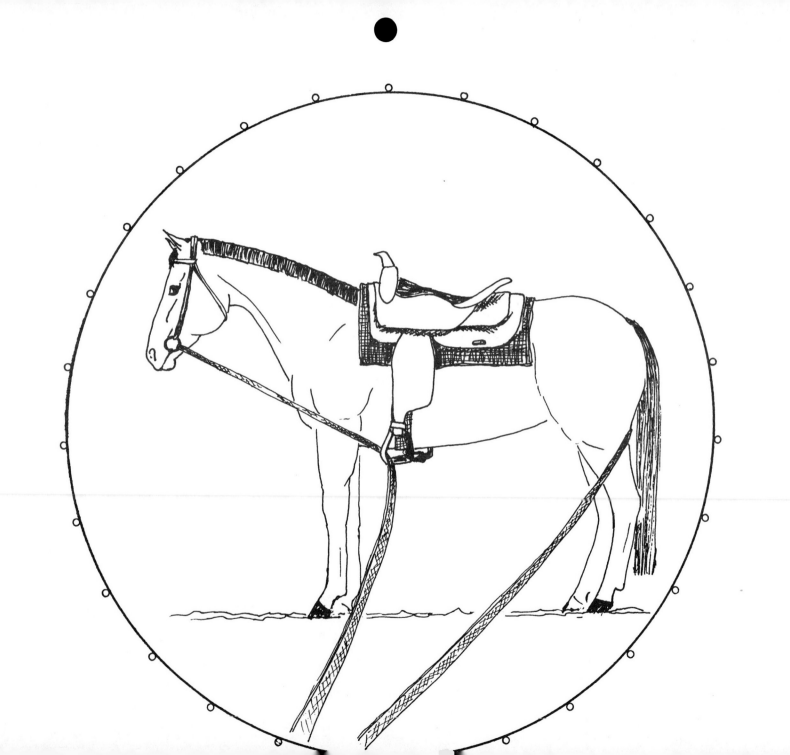

Using a Western Saddle for Ground Driving

Most basic long lining lessons can be carried out using a Western saddle with as much success as with an English saddle.

The stirrups are hobbled together under the horse's belly to stabilize them. The stirrups are set in a position so the lines can slide through them.

Caution: Due to the way stirrups are hung on Western saddles, there is a chance that the long line can become caught in the crevice where the stirrup attaches to the stirrup leather. If a line gets caught there, it can lock a horse in a turn and prevent him from straightening out. This could result in quite a scare and setback. Examine closely the junction between the stirrup and stirrup leather. If it looks as though the line could get caught there, just wrap a few layers of Vetrap™ over the crevice.

Lines run through the stirrups create an extremely low pull with a good deal of leverage. You certainly can show a horse the "way to the ground," which means you can get a horse to stretch long and low. You can also teach a horse a lifelong habit of traveling heavy on the forehand, however, if you drive too long with the lines through such a low point. Drive through stirrups for only a limited number of introductory lessons.

You can raise the stirrups up to their highest adjustment to help decrease a negative effect.

Western Stirrups The flapping and bouncing of Western stirrups during longeing should have been accepted by the horse. They provide a good way of getting the horse used to movement on his sides while he works. During long lining, the stirrups are hobbled and so are relatively stationary.

Rear Cinch A rear cinch will stabilize a Western saddle. It helps keep the saddle from bouncing up and down on the horse's back and also helps to keep it from rolling. A rear cinch might also cause some horses to buck, however.

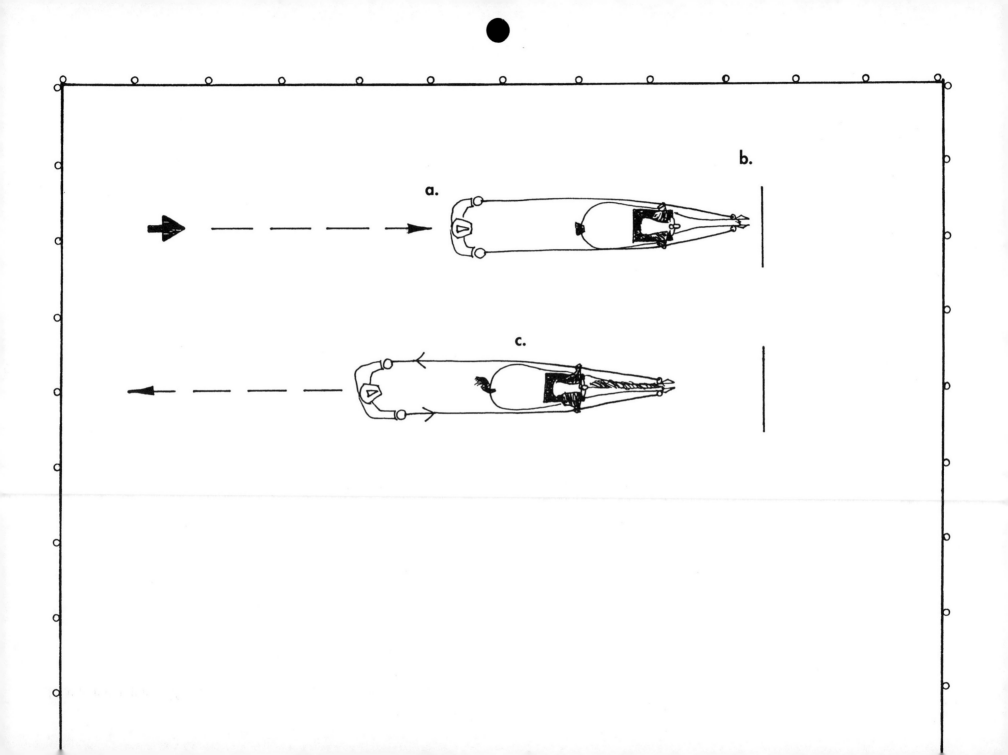

a.

b.

c.

Exercise 79

Walk-Halt-Back

Although early in the long lining sequence you taught your horse to stop, backing should be postponed until the horse is thoroughly comfortable with all tack and procedures. He must move forward readily into all transitions—including the downward transitions and halt.

If you have consistently observed that the horse rounds down into downward transitions rather than hollowing and popping his head up, then he is probably ready to learn the back.

It's good to know you can stop and back your horse in the arena before you begin any lope or canter work.

The back is a diagonal gait in reverse. The left hind and right front should lift up and set down in unison. They alternate with the right hind and left front. The legs should lift up crisply with flexed joints so that when moving backward, the toe of the hoof does not drag in the dirt. A lazy horse shuffles backward, hardly picking up his feet and just dragging the soles of his hooves through the dirt.

Caution: I have seen a few horses back up so fast and unexpectedly that you could literally get trampled. This is rare, but be on the lookout for it.

Also, some horses who have proceeded through all phases without mishap might at this point find a reason to rear, so take care to read the horse and use your aids wisely.

Backing is best performed from the plow-driving position. The lines should run low, such as through the stirrups of a saddle. This will help keep the horse's topline rounded and his head low, and it will help ensure straightness in the maneuver.

All rein cues should involve intermittent or vibrating pressure on the bit. With backing, this lesson is paramount. Steady pressure seems to encourage resistance.

a. Before you ask for the halt, be sure the horse is walking actively forward.

b. Drive the horse up into a forward halt (Exercise 72).

c. Standing a safe distance behind your horse in the plow-driving position, hold the lines evenly in your hands. Then with the voice command you used with in-hand work ("Baaaaack") gently take with the left line and give with the right. Alternate. Take with the right and give with the left. This is a slow, gentle squeezing motion, not a rough seesaw action.

Since the back is a two-beat diagonal gait in reverse, using one rein and then the other will tend to untrack one diagonal pair of legs at a time. Pulling straight back on both reins at one time usually results in resistance and no backward movement.

The first time, be satisfied if the horse shifts his body weight rearward. Release after every such response. Eventually, the horse will respond by taking a few steps back.

Always drive the horse forward immediately into an energetic walk. If you end the backing exercise with a halt, the horse tends to die in the middle of the exercise. I would much rather have a horse jet forward than lose all impulsion and stall in a back.

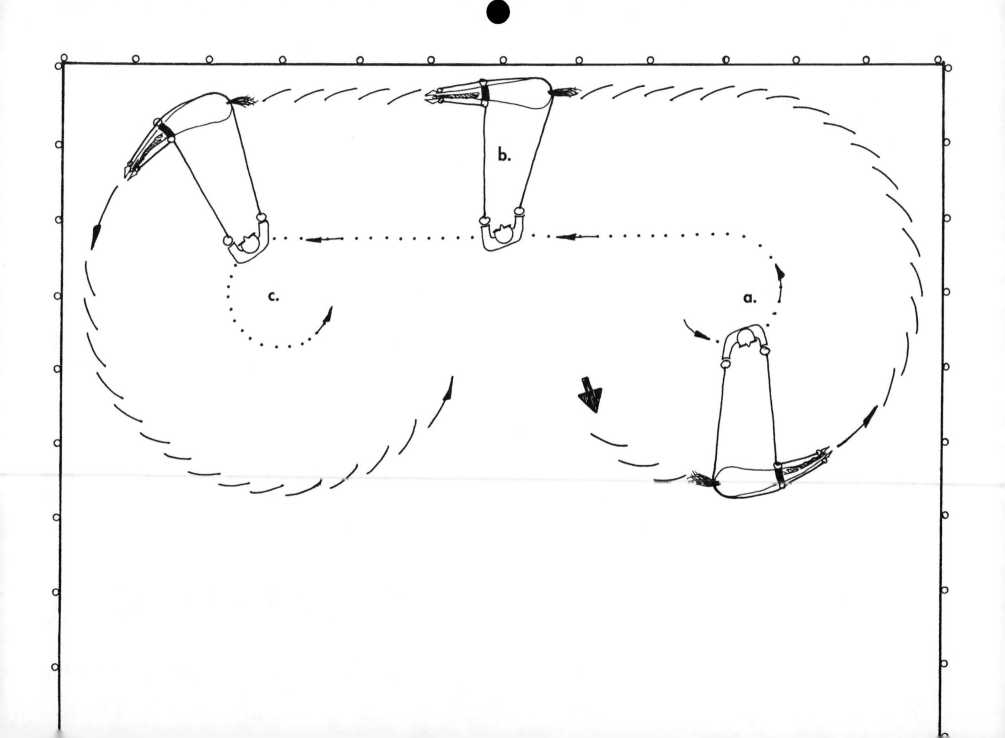

Exercise 80

Canter-Circle-Straight

This exercise is best performed with the outside line running along the outside and behind the horse's hindquarters rather than through top terret rings and over the horse's back because it will help you keep the horse straight on the straightaway.

a. Canter a 20-meter circle to the left. You will be driving from the horse's near side through the middle or lower surcingle rings. The right line comes around the horse's hindquarters. The more collected the horse canters, the more success you will have with this exercise.

b. Leave the circle and have the horse canter straight down the long side of the arena along the rail. Do it for as long as you can keep up. The more collected your horse is, the easier it will be for you to keep up. You might have to do some quick hoof work yourself.

c. When you have run out of room or breath, make a 20-meter circle to the left. Continue this circle until you catch your breath. Then make a straight line down the short end of the arena followed by another circle and so on.

OPTIONS FOLLOWING THIS EXERCISE

• You could perform the same exercise, but with the straight work occurring on the arena centerline instead of along the rail. This is more difficult, as your horse would have to be solid on the line aids.
• You could effect a downward transition to a trot or a walk and change rein, using one of the methods described in exercises 75, 76, or 77.

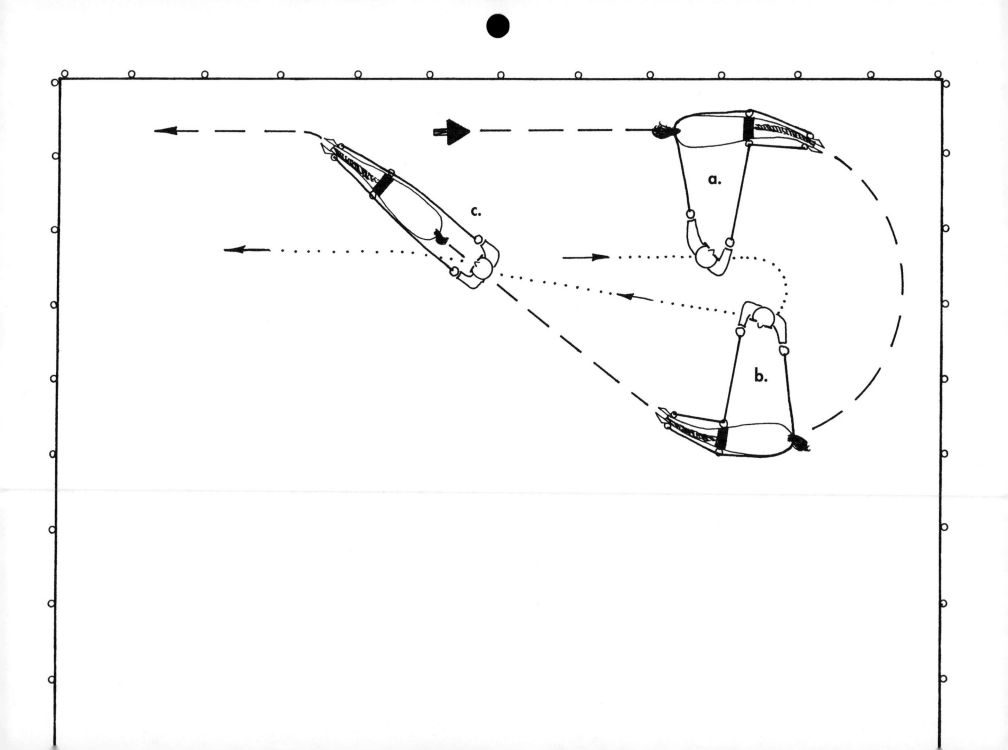

a.

b.

c.

Half Turn

A half turn provides a concise and immediate way to change direction. A half turn should look more like an ice cream cone than a teardrop or a light bulb.

Caution: Because the half turn occurs in a small space, a horse might slow down his rhythm. A change in rhythm is not desirable. This usually occurs for one of two reasons:

- The young horse decreases his tempo because he interprets increased bit pressure and working in confinement as a signal to slow down or stop. The young horse hasn't learned to differentiate between various pressures on the bit.
- The lazy or out-of-condition horse might slow down because it requires more energy to perform a half turn in balance and at the correct tempo than it does to perform one sloppily. It is important to keep the forward motion in the turn so the horse does not lose rhythm.

a. In a half turn to the right, you would leave the rail and perform a small half circle to the right, working from the off side of the horse.

b. At the widest part of the half circle, turn toward the rail on a diagonal line straight back to the rail. At this point, you might need to hustle to keep up with the horse. You will be changing to the plow-driving position for at least a few steps of the diagonal.

c. When you are near the rail, blend the horse back into the track on the rail rather than turning sharply into it. As you initiate left bend for the upcoming corner, you will be crossing over from behind the horse to his near side.

You can cruise on the curved portions but you usually must hustle on the straightaway!

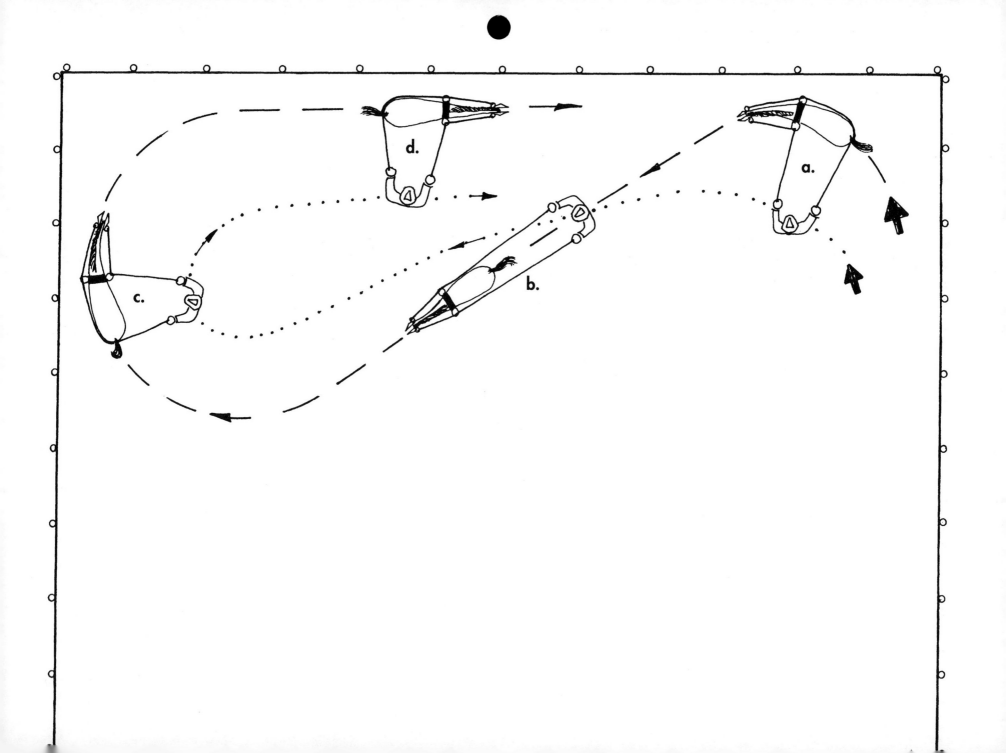

a.

b.

c.

d.

Exercise 82

Half Turn in Reverse

The half turn in reverse is a turn that can occur in a relatively small space. It has been drawn large here to show detail.

a. If you were tracking to the left, you would leave the rail initiating a slight left bend. You work the horse from the near side.

b. Straighten and follow a diagonal line, moving to the plow-driving position. You will need to quicken your pace so you can cross behind the horse and get to his off side. As you do this you will need to make compensations in the driving lines. Continue on the straight diagonal until you are about 20 feet from the arena rail.

c. Initiate a right bend, step to the horse's off side, and describe a half circle to the right.

d. Straighten and work the horse along the rail in the new direction, to the right. You can conduct this portion of the work from the side or from behind.

In All Kinds of Weather   If you work your horse only on perfect, sunny days, some day when you are out riding and it starts to rain, you will wish the horse had broader weather experience. Work in the rain unless the footing is unsafe. Protect yourself and your tack with raingear. Work when there is fresh snow on the ground but avoid icy days. Try to keep your horse's concentration when the wind blows, but head back to the barn when the wind blows a steady 20 mph. At that speed, your lines will be difficult to handle, your horse might not be able to hear your voice commands, and airborne debris poses a threat to both you and your horse.

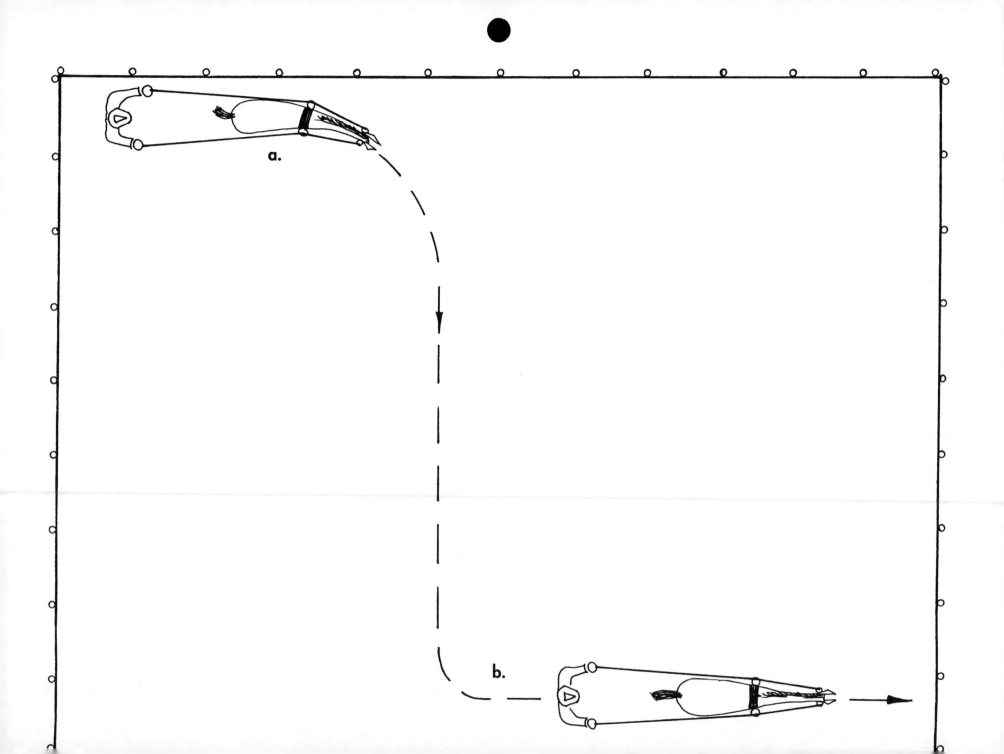

a.

b.

Exercise 83

Quasi-Quarter Turn

A true quarter turn is most appropriately performed at a collected gait. Since this exercise will be performed at the walk and trot, and not necessarily at collected gaits, it is a quasi-quarter turn. This exercise is a great preparation for the spiral and turn on the hindquarters work to come. It will teach both you and your horse what to expect when you work on more confined exercises.

Practice this exercise first at the walk from the plow-driving position. When your horse progresses to the top terret stage of long lining, you can perform this exercise at the collected trot from the side position.

Caution: Avoid Rubbernecking If you use too much left rein when turning to the left, for example, and not enough right supporting line, the horse will bulge. He will overbend his neck to the left and bulge his right shoulder and will probably just march forward with no turn!

a. As you prepare for the first turn off the rail, give your horse a half halt or check to settle his weight rearward. This will get his body thinking of a space-conservation move rather than a sweeping, arcing turn. This will give him an idea—but it is not a quarter turn.

As you head across the arena, focus straight ahead, using a fence post as a marker. Delay asking for the turn until "the last second." Your arena fence will help get the "compact" idea over to the horse.

b. To make the left quarter turn:

- Lift both lines in a half halt.
- Pull the left line back to initiate the left bend.
- Give very slightly with the right line; you need it in a supporting role.
- Keep marching yourself in small steps rather than long strides. Your cadence will be contagious.

When you are 60 degrees into the 90-degree turn, begin applying your straightening aids (release left line and maintain contact with right line) so the horse doesn't continue turning and veer off the rail.

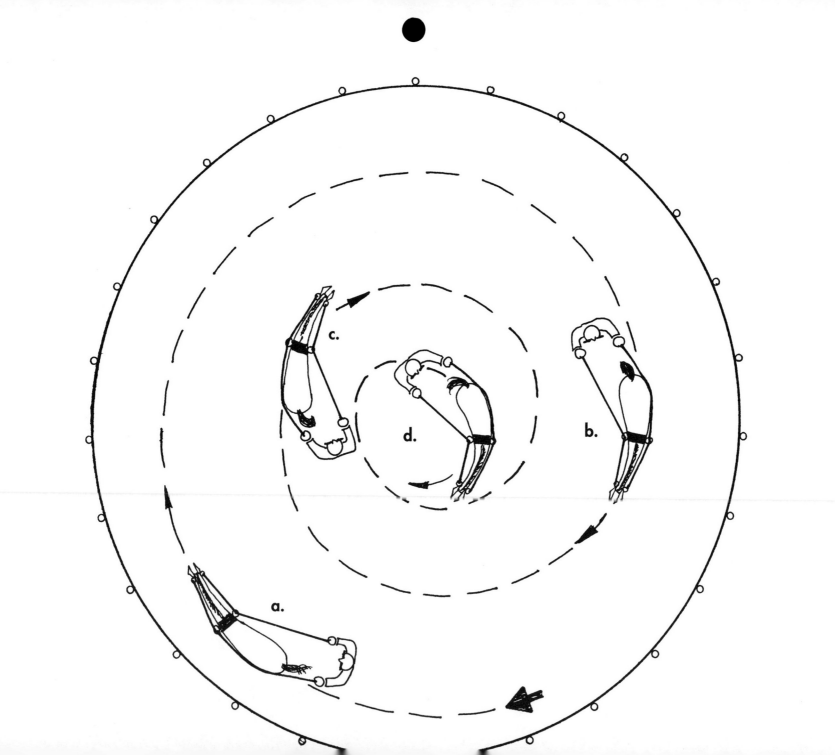

a.

b.

c.

d.

Exercise 84

Spiral

You introduced your horse to the concept of spiraling in and out on the longe line in exercises 40 and 41. This long lining spiral exercise can be conducted in a similar fashion, but now you have new options. Once you have spiraled the horse in, you can choose from a variety of ways to finish the exercise, such as:

- Spiral back out, provided you have not come into too small a circle.
- Straighten and walk forward out of the circle.
- Perform a turn on the hindquarters (see Exercise 85) and then walk straight out of it.

The spiral is best learned at the walk. Although it can be performed at the trot, the diagonal support does not work well once you get into the smaller circle and it would make a turn on the hindquarters difficult. The horse would naturally break into a walk for the turn. This exercise can also be done at a canter with a collected, advanced horse.

After the turn on the hindquarters, which actually becomes a pirouette or a turnaround, you can:

- Spiral back out.
- Perform a flying lead change and spiral back out in the opposite direction.
- Perform a downward transition to a walk or trot and go into another exercise.

To spiral in at the walk to the right:

a. Circle to the right on a 20-meter circle, working slightly to the horse's off side.

b. Maintain right bend, taking with the right and giving with the left line, while you encourage the horse to walk actively forward. This is one exercise in which you might wish to carry a whip, if only for visual help.

c. Gradually decrease the size of the circle, using the outside line to help keep the horse's body aligned.

d. Go in only as much as the horse is able to stay relaxed, in balance, and moving in proper rhythm.

When you spiral out, you will still maintain right bend, but you will release the restraining contact on the outside line.

Caution: Keep the horse's body aligned; otherwise, you might get a leg yield instead of a walk straight forward.

Note: I like to start this exercise to the right first because of the inherent straightness of most horses in this direction. It is easier to deal with a tendency for flatness in this exercise than it would be to deal with a horse that overbends to the left, as many horses do.

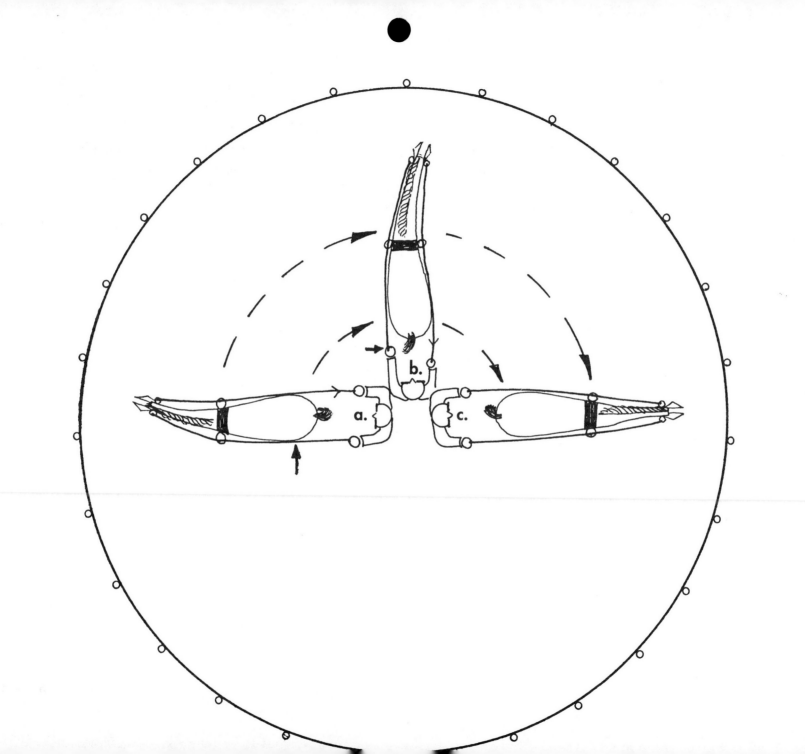

a.

b.

c.

Exercise 85

Walk-Around Turn on the Haunches

When you come to the center of a spiral you can work on the walk-around turn on the haunches. In this controlled, organized movement, the horse marches in four-beat time at the walk with the forehand rotating around the hind-quarters.

For a 180-degree right turn:

a. Just as you come to the center of the spiral, half halt the horse on both lines in a right-bend position by lifting up slightly with both lines.

b. Bend the horse more to the right by taking slightly with the right line and giving slightly with the left line. (If he would benefit from a right leading line, consider removing the lines from the surcingle rings and use a leading right line directly to your hand.) The left line controls the degree of right flexion but allows enough freedom so the horse moves his shoulders. The left line also prevents the hindquarters from stepping to the left.

c. Use your driving aids to keep the four-beat walk sequence going with impulsion and a pure rhythm. Most advanced collected horses "energize" when they are asked to perform collected movements, so they usually have plenty of impulsion. You can use a cluck, kiss, or "walk up"; a light tap on the left hindquarters with the left line while maintaining contact; or a light tap on the left hindquarters with a whip held in the left hand. Keep the horse "marching forward." If you see that your line or whip taps cause the horse to move sideways with his hindquarters instead, use the whip to lightly tap the horse's hindquarters over the tail head. You are in a very dangerous position here.

Only perform the exercise as long as the horse maintains rhythm and correct form. If at any time the movement deteriorates into an unrecognizable work, straighten the horse and drive him forward.

Note: The horse should not come to a full halt either before or after the turn. This is essential to preserve forward movement.

Note: The outside legs cross over and in front of the inside legs in a hindquarter turn. A forward step error is less serious than a backward step, which would cause the horse to possibly hit himself or cross behind.

Pirouette versus Turnaround The footfall pattern of a walk pirouette and a walk-around turn on the hindquarters are the same. To the right: left hind, left front, right hind, right front. The pivot point for both turns is the right hind. The left hind walks a tiny half circle around the right hind. The forehand moves in a half circle to the right, with the left front crossing over in front of the right front.

Pivot Point or Pivot Foot Pivot point action for dressage differs from Western. In the walk pirouette, the right hind moves up and down in place, marking time in the stride. In a Western turnaround, the right hind locks, plants, and swivels in place.

You Are the Pivot Point! Because you, the trainer, are the pivot point of the turn, the horse's hind legs are walking a small circle around you.

203

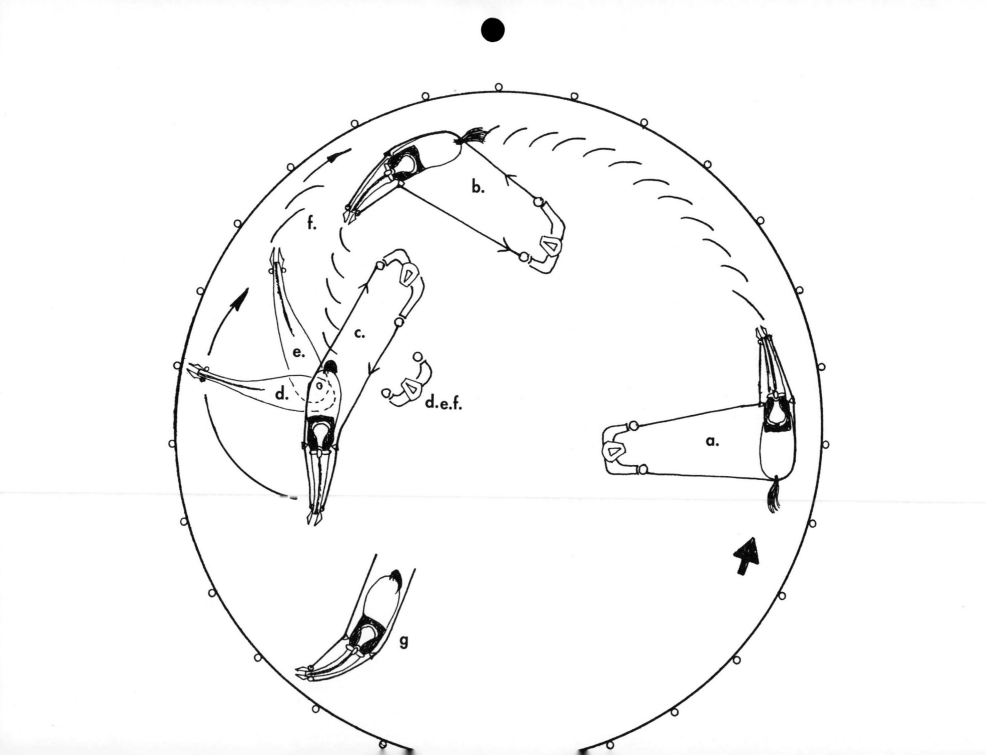

Exercise 86

Rollback

A rollback is a set and turn at a lope, in contrast to a halt and turn or a sliding stop and turn. A set is a temporary slowdown to facilitate the turn.

a. Lope your horse in a circle to the left.

b. Drift off the rail just before the turn. Keep the horse's body straight or slightly aimed to the left. This will set the horse up for a better turn to the right.

c. At the time of the turn, set the horse with a check (half halt) on both reins to settle the horse's weight rearward.

d. Instantly follow this by taking with the right rein and supporting with the left line. You have to provide some positive resistance with the left line, which keeps the horse's body straight and guides him through the turn. If you overbend the horse to the right, it will tend to make him turn on the center rather

than on his hindquarters. You want the horse to set his right hind pivot foot. A turn on the center would cause him to swing his hindquarters off to the left, making this impossible.

e. As you bring the horse around, realize that at about halfway through the turn, you need to be releasing the right line somewhat so you don't get an overturn past the 180-degree point.

f. As the horse reaches the 180-degree point, ask for a lope depart with "let's go" and a possible slap on the hindquarters with the outside line.

g. If you overbend the horse for the turn, he will rubberneck, pop his left shoulder, and swing the hindquarters off to the left, all of which result in him "swapping ends" rather than turning on his hindquarters.

Benefit: When performed properly, a rollback can show a horse what it feels like to work off his hindquarters. It can strengthen the horse's loin and back as he rounds his topline for the set, turn, and lope out of it.

Caution: This is a strenuous exercise and can strain the horse's hindquarter muscles and limbs.

Problem: Trainer Gets Tangled Some trainers prefer to carry the lines in a separate coil in each hand, others let the excess line trail behind them. The method of choice depends on how far away from you the horse is working, how much line is left in your hands, and what you are most comfortable with. Getting hands or a foot tangled in a loop is certainly dangerous!

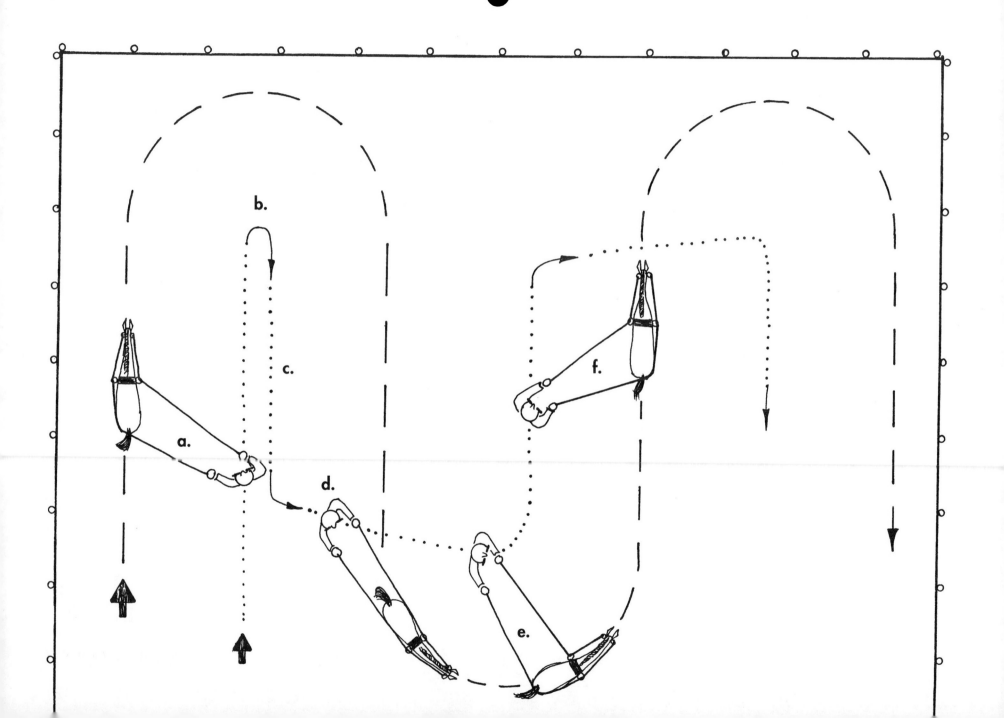

Exercise 87

Serpentine

THE CHANGING ROLE OF THE OUTSIDE LINE

At first the outside line is used mainly to control the position of the horse's hindquarters. As training advances, the outside line becomes an active aid for developing contact, bend, and collection. To achieve this, as lessons progress, be aware of any attempt by the horse to stretch into the contact with the outside line. Recognize this, respond to it, and yield when the horse softens and lowers yet retains an active contact with the outside line while maintaining active forward movement.

a. Begin on the short end of the arena, working the horse in a straight line. You are on the off side.

b. As you near the long side, stand in one position and work the horse around you in a half circle to the right.

c. You are still on the horse's off side. There has been a change of direction but no change of bend yet. Work the horse in a straight line.

d. Cross behind the horse as you initiate left bend. You will be walking an oblique line to your left.

e. At the end of the oblique line, you will be working the horse from the near side in a half circle to the left.

f. Once again, work the horse on the straight, this time from the near side. As you approach the point where you will initiate right flexion and bend, you will need to cross behind the horse, walk the oblique, and change sides.

Tack Tip: Bit Fit and Lip Length It is important to determine how much space exists between the corner of the lips and the premolars. A short-lipped (shallow-mouthed) horse usually has enough room between the corners of his lips and his premolars to carry a few wrinkles in the corner of his mouth.

But with some long-lipped (deep-mouthed) horses, whose premolars are very close to the corners of the lips, fitting a bit with two to three wrinkles might put the bit painfully close to the premolars. Skin can be trapped between the bit and the premolars and be painfully pinched.

It is common for a horse to have a slightly different tooth configuration on each side of his mouth. For example, there might be a prominent shelf of sharp upper premolars hanging over on the left side but not on the right. This would be cause for a horse to turn well to the right but with resistance in the head and neck to the left. Check your horse's mouth.

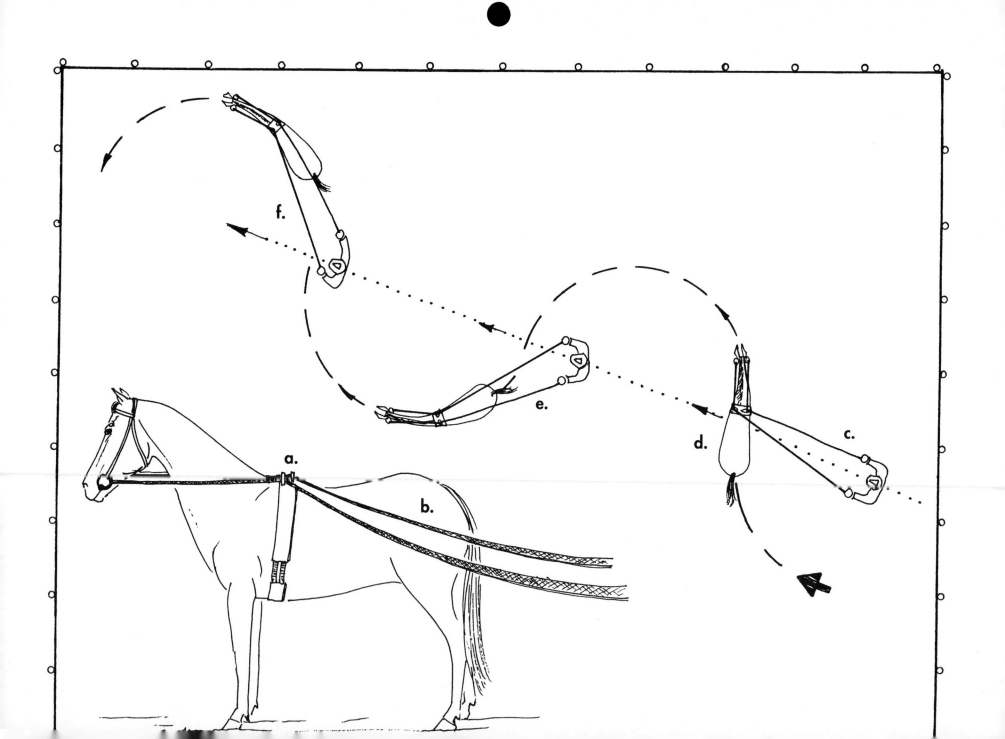

Exercise 88

Shallow Serpentine

When driving with the lines running through top terrets, it is easy to change direction. The lines are merely passed over the horse's hindquarters.

As you work a serpentine, you walk a straight line, moving the horse from side to side in front of you. The horse describes half circles on either side of your path. This is a very smooth, controlled change of bend. This exercise is suitable for work at the walk and trot. It can also be performed with the lines running through lower surcingle rings and along the horse's sides.

a. Terrets are rigid, fixed rings that are screwed into the top of the surcingle or driving harness saddle and are at the approximate position a rider's hands would be. Because terrets are fixed and do not move during long lining, they are the choice for long lining. In lieu of terrets, most surcingles have large D-rings sewn or sewn and riveted into the top of the surcingle. Some Ds stand in a rigid position—others are floppy. Rigid top rings are desirable because driving lines flow through them freely. When a D-ring flops down, it could trap a line.

b. When using terrets, the outside line comes to the trainer's hand across the horse's back.

c. On a shallow serpentine, you walk a straight line and work the horse in half circles on either side of your projected path. When you start on the off side in this exercise, you'll need to make the change from right bend to left bend. This is the point when the horse's hindquarters cross in front of you. You will momentarily be directly behind the horse as he shifts to the new bend.

d. As the horse crosses your path, the lines will cross over from the off side to the near side.

e. Each time you change the horse's bend, you will momentarily be behind the horse as the lines change sides. The right line is maintaining the right bend of the half circle and the left line is supporting and preventing overbend.

f. Here is the point where you have to hustle your own footsteps to get into the side-driving position.

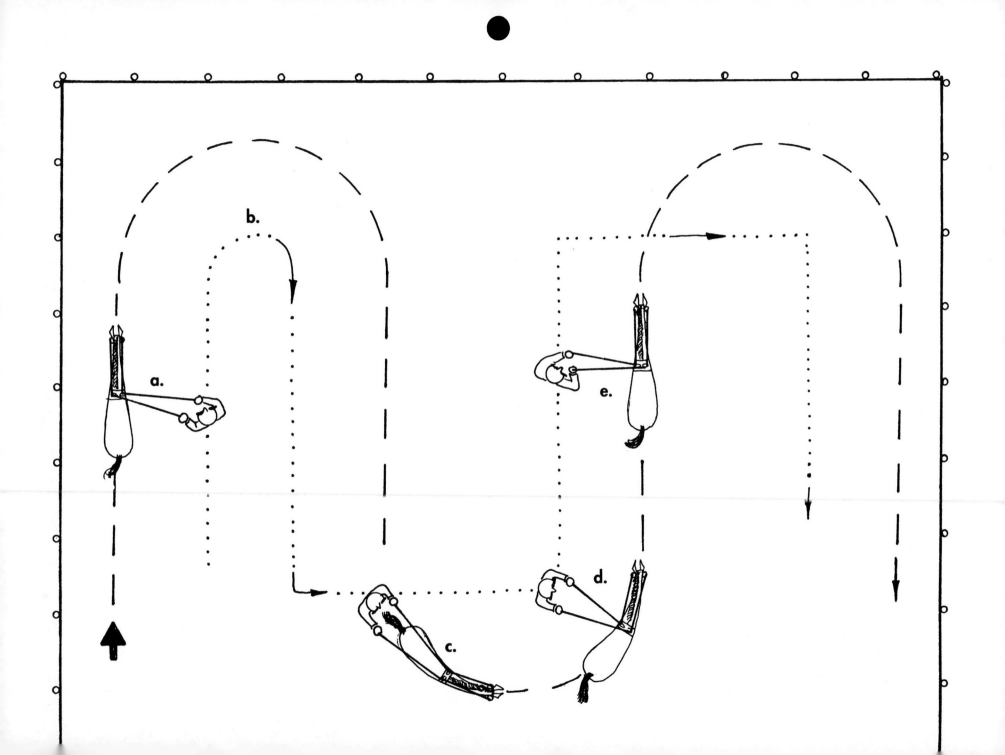

Deep Serpentine

This serpentine exercise is similar to that in Exercise 87. But because the lines are running through the top terrets of the surcingle, the horse must be collected, and both the horse and trainer must be very solid in the work on the long lines. It would be very easy for a horse to suddenly twirl and face the trainer or face away from the trainer. An even, appropriate contact must be maintained to prevent this.

To perform at the walk and trot, refer to the directions as outlined in Exercise 87.

a. Establish an even, steady contact on the straight lines.

b. The first half circle to the right will be performed from the horse's off side.

c. Because the lines pass over the horse's back when using terrets, the trainer's position in relation to the horse during a change of bend is slightly different than in Exercise 87. The trainer's path is somewhat straighter as he can step into the direction of the new bend sooner than if the lines were running around the hindquarters.

d. Straightening involves a gradual release of the left line as the horse completes the turn, coupled with added contact on the right line.

e. Now working from the near side, prepare for the bend right.

Although this exercise should be practiced at the walk and trot to ensure the horse's understanding and cooperation, there is an interesting variation for the advanced horse. Using longer lines, work the same pattern with collected canter on the half circles and simple changes through the walk on the straight lines.

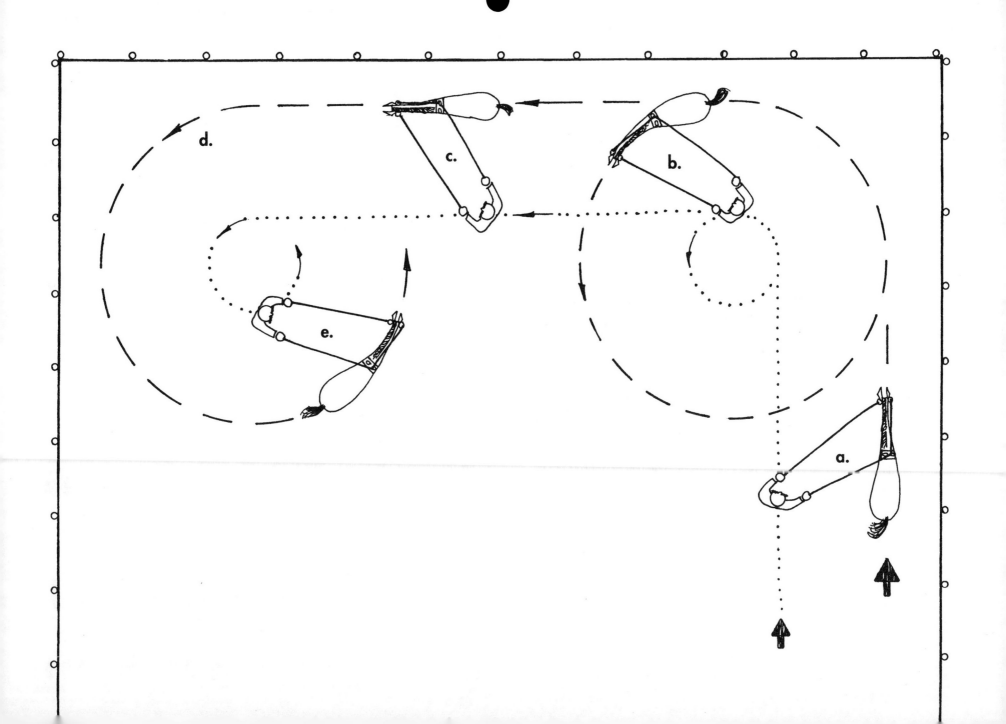

Exercise 90

Circle Variation

At one time or another in the training program of most horses, the horse tends to get bunched up and either overbends or gets behind the bit. One way to counteract this tendency or to prevent it from occurring in the first place, is to change the configuration of the inside long line.

If the inside long line is run directly to the trainer's hand, bypassing the surcingle, the line's message is translated from a compound message to a much simpler one. When a line runs through a surcingle ring, the action involves leverage and a "direct" (rearward) rein signal. When the inside line runs directly to the trainer's hand, the trainer can use the line in a wider range of actions. Most important, the trainer can ask for bend with a "leading" or "opening" line signal. A leading line is a pull on the bit directly toward the trainer. So for a horse that needs a rest, refresher, review or regrouping, this can be helpful.

The outside line can remain in its normal configuration. If you are using top terrets, the outside line can run through the terret to your hand. If you are going to ask for a good amount of inside bend

with the leading line, however, and the horse's neck is not securely anchored to his shoulder, it might cause the horse's hindquarters to swing off the track. In that case, you might want to run the outside line through the middle or lower surcingle ring and around the horse's hindquarters to encourage an even head-to-tail bend.

a. As you walk alongside the horse on his near side, be aware that contact with the outside line is essential for you to retain control and keep the horse tracking straight.

b. As you work the horse on the 20-meter circle, use soft, intermittent squeezes on the inside line to cause the horse to bend left. Maintain contact with the outside line. If the horse's hindquarters start to swing to the right, change the configuration of the outside line, as previously discussed.

c. On the straight portion along the rail, if the horse begins to wobble, it's usually due to a

loss of impulsion. Drive the horse forward, using a voice command and/or a step toward the horse. It's ok to trot here if necessary. Take care not to lose contact. If you were carrying a whip, it would be in your right hand and could be used to tap the horse on the croup.

d. Initiating left bend again for the second circle.

e. When in the center of the arena with no rails to help guide the horse, be aware that the tendency is for the horse to drift right.

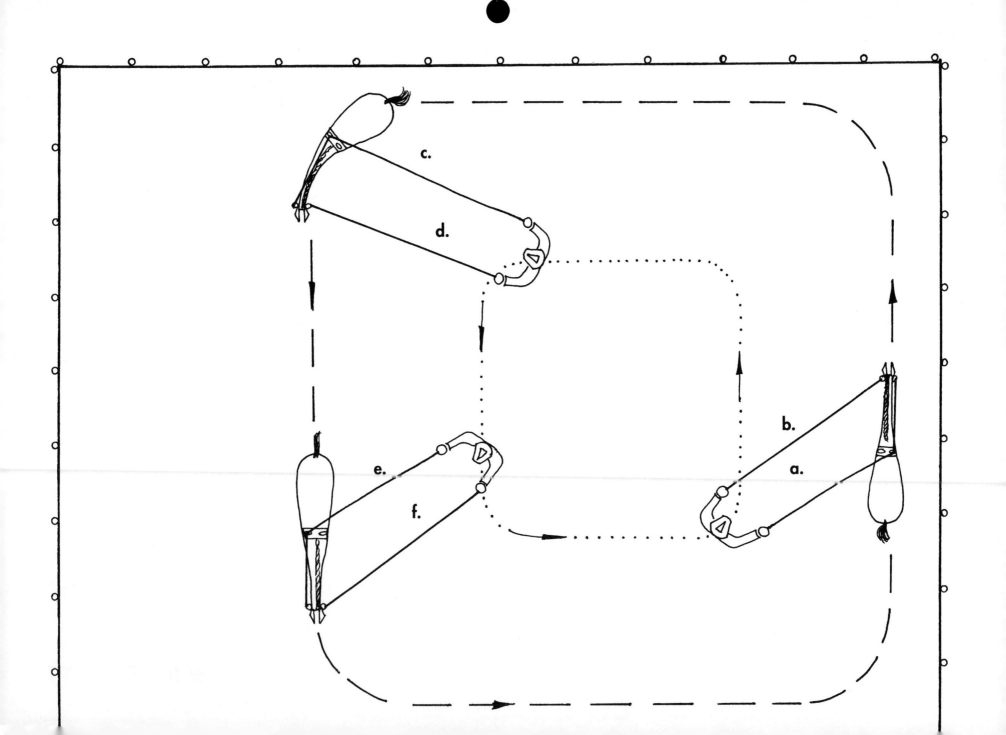

Exercise 91

Rounded Square

Here is one more exercise with the inside line running directly to your hand.

This exercise is conducted on longer lines, so it is appropriate for collected work at the walk, trot, or canter. You will be walking a large rounded square, so this figure can be quite large and you will still be able to keep up.

You will be asking for a deeper bend in the corners than the bend in the 20-meter circle asked for in the previous exercise. The bend in the corners of this large square approximates that of a 10-meter circle. Therefore the horse must be sufficiently collected and solid with his contact on the bit.

The deep bend required to negotiate the corners should last only a few strides. Most horses at this stage of training can hold such a bend correctly for that long but might tend to overcurl or get behind the bit if asked to hold it longer.

a. On the straight line you will have to pick up the pace to keep up with the horse; but you don't want to get ahead of the surcingle. If you do, you might lose your driving advantage.

b. You are using a left leading rein and a right supporting rein.

c. To work the corner, you are still on the straight track of the previous side of the square. Even so, at the moment when the horse is deepest in the corner, you are as far ahead as you should ever be when long lining through top terrets.

d. As you take with the left line, the horse's head turns to the left. If the horse's bend is secure, his neck and spine will follow. If he has stiffness or insecurity, his hindquarters will swing right. You will need to alter the outside line, as discussed in Exercise 90.

e. When approaching each corner, on the last stride the horse's body will be straight; apply a half halt with both lines, as described in Exercise 48.

f. The half halt action with the left line will be a lifting up and back toward your right elbow. The half halt is intended to be a momentary awakening before the normal bending aids are applied.

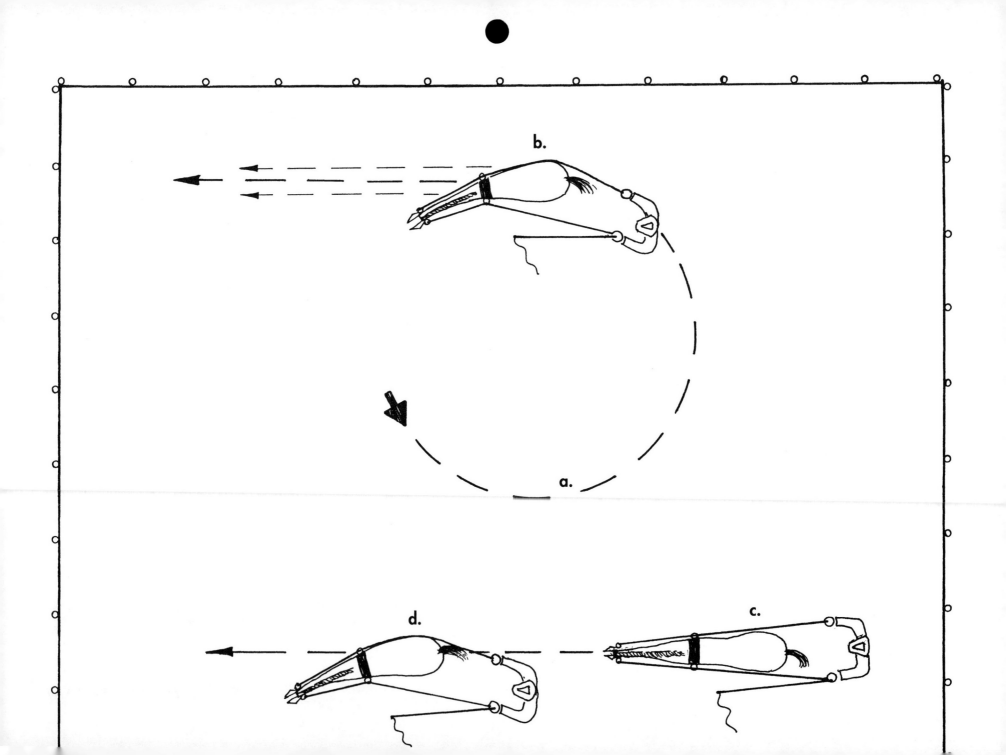

b.

a.

d.

c.

Exercise 92

Shoulder-In

The shoulder-in is *the most valuable exercise* for straightening, collection, increasing hind leg activity, and strengthening the inside hind leg. There are three tracks to a shoulder-in left:

1. Right hind.
2. Left hind and right front.
3. Left front.

The shoulder-in is easiest to achieve with the lines running through the middle rings of the surcingle. You can use short lines to focus on this type of work; however, the best remedy for lateral work problems is to move the horse forward actively, and that might be difficult if you have short lines.

The horse must be collected and able to execute prompt and accurate transitions. Become familiar with the aids for the shoulder-in at the walk first, and then the trot.

For a shoulder-in left:

a. Work the horse in a 10-meter circle to the left.

b. Just as you join the rail, the horse will be in the approximate configuration for a shoulder-in left. The horse's forehand should be in 30 to 35 degrees, maximum, so the right shoulder is in front of the left hind leg. If you carry a whip, hold it in your left hand. It can be used to point at or touch the horse's rib cage to help maintain the bend and to affect the forward and sideways movement of the left hind.

Don't depend on the wall or rail to hold the horse's hindquarters from swinging to the right. The right line controls the tempo and the degree of bend in the neck. The left line guides the horse to the left and maintains left bend. After several strides of shoulder-in, straighten the horse by bringing the forehand back to the original track. Work the shoulder-in left down the centerline and the quarter line to check if you are dependent on the rail to hold your position.

Caution: If you use the left line too strongly, you will overbend your horse in the front end. This causes him to bulge his right shoulder and makes it hard to keep his hindquarters aligned—they will want to swing off the track to the right.

If he gets behind the bit or shortens stride, straighten him and drive him actively forward.

Shoulder-Out It might be easier to start with a shoulder-out because the arena wall or rail will keep the horse from turning. Try this exercise following half turn (Exercise 81) just as you are finishing and returning to the rail. The horse will be approximating the shoulder-out position.

c. If you stand behind the horse to start, hold the whip in your left hand. Use the right line to help hold the hindquarters on the track. You will be displacing the forehand toward the arena rail. Ask for inside bend with the left line. The whip is a visual cue for bend at the ribs. The right line supports and contains the hindquarters and limits the left bend.

d. Once the horse is in the shoulder-out position, step to the left slightly, to have a better view and control of the movement.

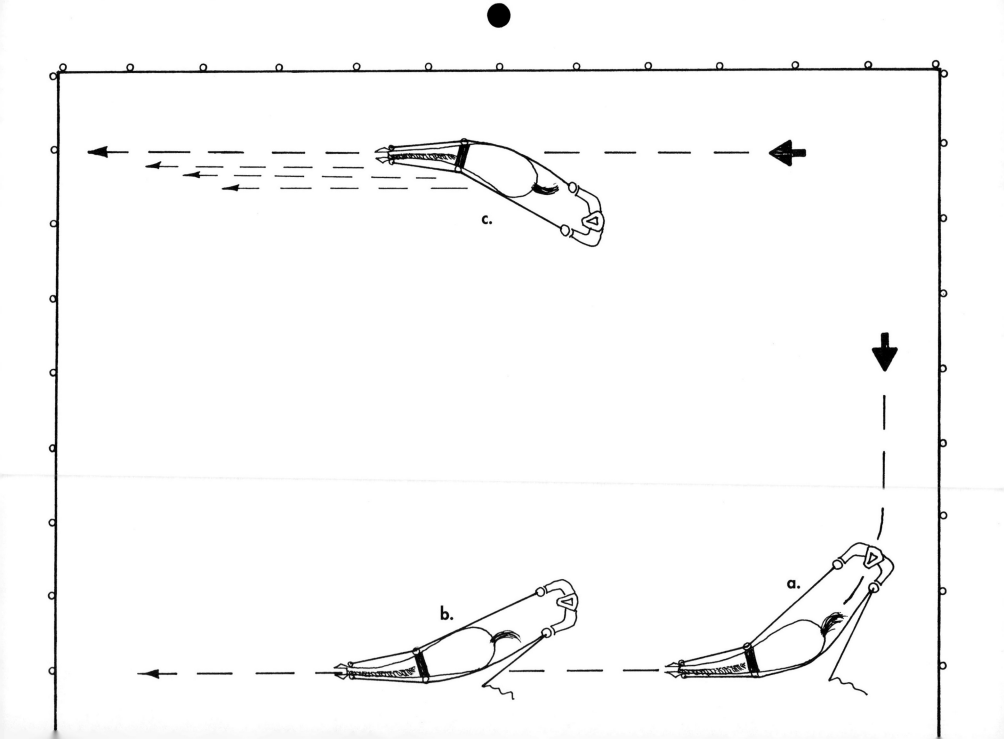

c.

b.

a.

Exercise 93

Travers

Travers is haunches-in. It should be practiced at the walk to familiarize the horse with the aids. Then it can be mastered at the trot and, in some cases, the canter.

The travers left (**c**) has four tracks; from the rail inward, they are

1. Right front.
2. Left front.
3. Right hind.
4. Left hind.

Note: The right hind travels in a path very close to that of the left front. The right legs cross over the left legs.

a. It is easiest to start travers by walking directly behind the horse coming out of a corner.

b. For a travers right, the left line is held low to contain the hindquarters and to secure the horse's neck so he doesn't "rubberneck." If a whip is carried, it is held in the left hand to tap the side of the hindquarters to maintain impulsion and keep the hindquarters in off the track. The right line initiates and maintains right flexion.

After a few strides of travers, the horse is straightened by bringing the forehand in front of the hindquarters. That means the new track will be inside the track the horse has been walking on.

BENEFITS OF THE TRAVERS

- It helps to develop the shoulder-in.
- It improves straightness, engagement of the hindquarters, and collection.
- It increases the engagement of the inside hind leg. The joints bend more and the leg carries more weight.

Caution: If the hindquarters are brought in too much to the right, the gait will lose rhythm and the horse might step sideways to the right with the right hind. This defeats the purpose of strengthening the inside hind leg to carry more weight.

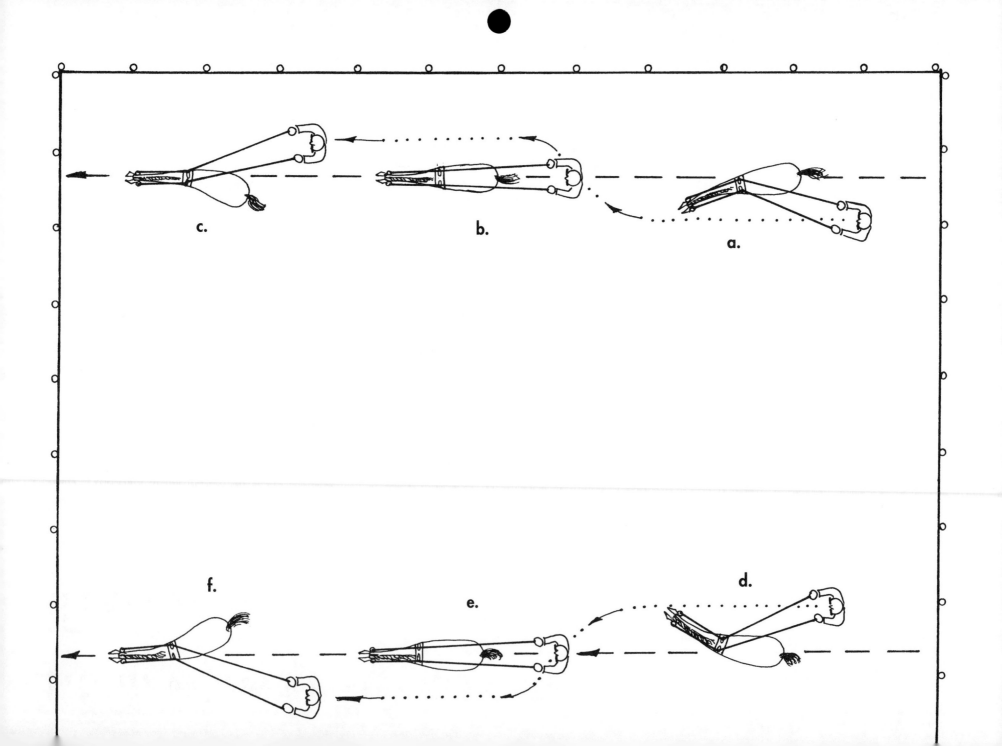

c.

b.

a.

f.

e.

d.

Shoulder-In to Travers

Once you and your horse are proficient at the shoulder-in and travers, you can combine them in this exercise. In some cases this exercise will make the shoulder-in and travers better. This exercise is best performed with the lines running through the top terrets of the surcingle. If you have trouble controlling the hindquarters, you can run the lines through the middle rings of the surcingle.

a. Perform a shoulder-in left, working from your horse's near side. If you carry a whip, it would be in your left hand.

b. Straighten by bringing the horse's forehand in front of his hindquarters as you pass behind him. You will need to move the whip to your right hand in preparation for the travers left.

c. Move the reins over the horse's back as you move to the off side and give the aids for the travers left. The left rein is the active rein in both the shoulder-in left and the travers left. If you carry a whip, it would be in your right hand.

d. Perform a shoulder-in right, working from your horse's off side.

e. Straighten by bringing the horse's forehand in front of his hindquarters as you pass behind him.

f. Move the reins over the horse's back as you move to the near side and give the aids for the travers right. The right rein is the active rein in both the shoulder-in right and the travers right.

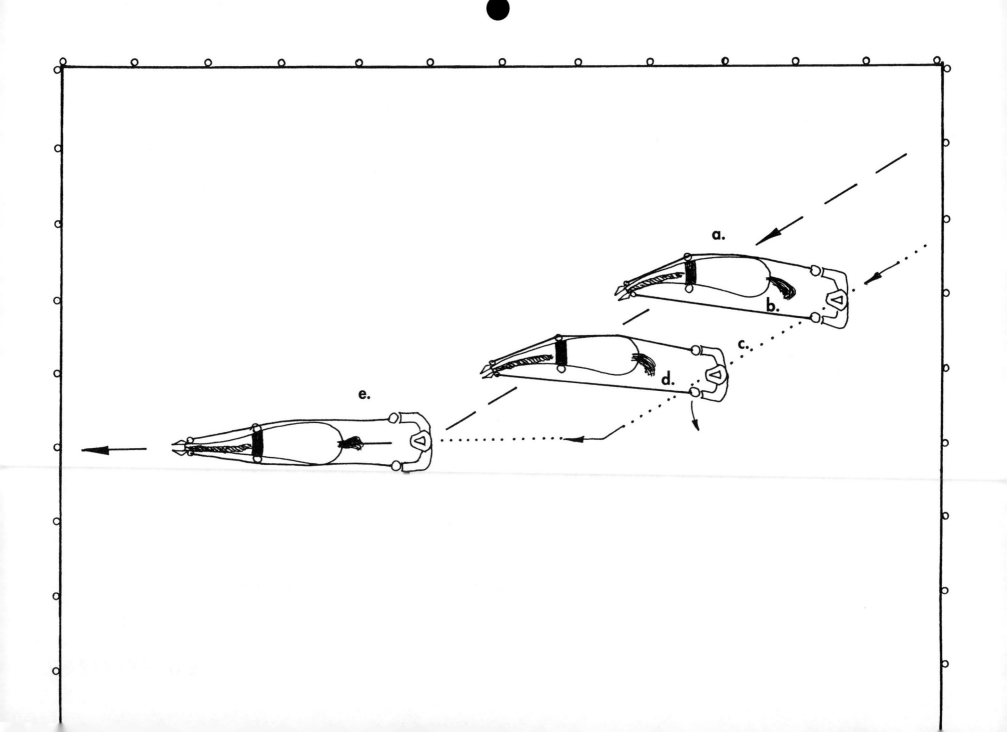

Exercise 95

Half Pass to Straight

A half pass is a forward and sideways movement. The horse is bent into the direction of movement.

In half pass left, the horse moves forward and sideways to the left. The horse is flexed and bent to the left. The horse's body is basically straight and parallel to the rail, with the shoulders slightly in advance of the hindquarters.

The half pass supples the horse evenly on both sides. It develops straightness and balance. It develops collection and strength of the inside hind leg.

To become familiar with this exercise, you can try it first with the long lines simply attached to the side rings of the cavesson. Another option (for the half pass left) is to run the right line through the middle ring of the surcingle. Leave the left line free so it comes directly to your hand and does not pass through a surcingle ring. This will allow you to position your horse the best for this movement. The right line will aid you in limiting left bend, keeping the horse's body straight, and moving it over laterally. The left line will create the left bend and, in its free position, can be used as a leading line to invite the horse to step to the left.

Once you and your horse become familiar with the half pass, as with all exercises, you will want to use the bridle and the lines running through surcingle rings.

When first practicing the half pass to the right, reverse the line set up: left line through the middle surcingle ring and right line free.

It is easiest to get the feel for the half pass position coming out of a turn, so begin after the second corner of the short end of the arena.

Trainer's position: Behind and slightly to the left for a half pass left, to control position and movement of the hindquarters with the right line and to control the bend with the left line.

Work into the half pass by asking for a half halt with both lines.

Next, shoulder-in left (Exercise 92) for a few steps to be sure the forehand is leading.

a. Right supporting rein low, to secure the horse's neck at its base, to regulate left bend, and to help keep the horse's body straight.

b. Left direct rein to create the bend.

c. You will be walking on a diagonal path forward and to the left, parallel to the diagonal line of the horse's travel.

d. You might need to use the left line in a brief opening fashion to remind the horse to move sideways. Keep the right line low and use it to secure the horse's neck at its base, to regulate the left bend, and to help keep the horse's body straight.

e. Straighten by evening the pressure on the lines and walking straight ahead.

Note: Practice at the walk to learn the aids. Then the exercise can be performed at the collected trot, and in some cases, the collected canter.

Caution: If you attempt this using top terrets, it is easy to overbend the horse's neck to the left. And the right line would be too far to the left to assist you with the hindquarters.

223

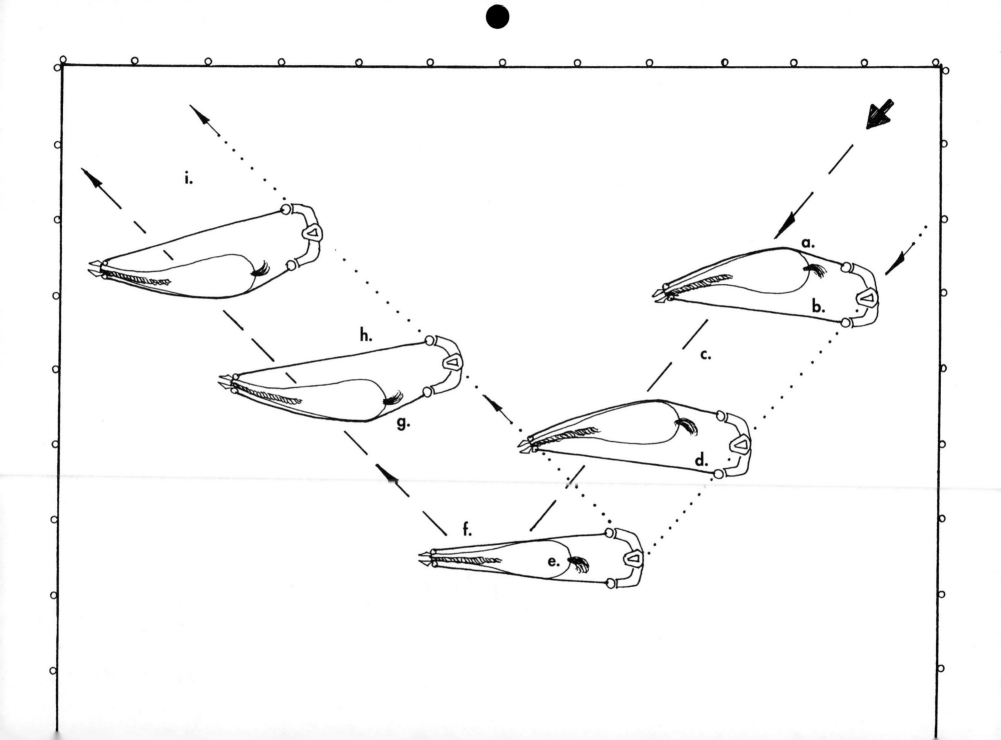

Exercise 96

Zigzag Half Pass

Since you will be changing bend and direction in the zigzag half pass, it sometimes works best to use the lines free, that is, not running through a surcingle. This will allow you to use either line momentarily as an opening line to invite the horse sideways. The outside line can be versatile: low to keep body straight; as a reminder to help the horse move laterally; as a popper to wake up the horse. If you carry a whip you can switch it in your hands when the horse is straight or you can just carry it in the hand in which it is most likely to be needed. For example, you might wish to carry it in your left hand to visually remind the horse not to overbend left and to tap the horse's hindquarters if he loses his impulsion to the right.

a. Start the half pass left by initiating a shoulder-in left after the turn in the corner. You will be working at the rear and slightly to the near side of the horse. Right rein limits, supports, and drives.

b. Left line creates bend.

c. Half pass the horse forward and sideways to the left on a diagonal line.

d. Use the left line occasionally in an opening fashion to invite the horse sideways.

e. Straighten by equalizing your aids and walking forward one or two strides.

f. Initiate right flexion and shoulder-in right.

g. Half pass right. Left line limits, supports, and drives.

h. Right line creates bend and invites sideways movement.

i. Half pass right, then straighten and ride forward.

Note: On the straight line (**e**), the horse's hindquarters must be absolutely straight with the forehand before initiating new bend. Then be sure the forehand is in a shoulder-in position before asking for the half pass movement. If the shoulder-in is not firmly established, the hindquarters are likely to lead in the half pass.

Caution: If the exercise deteriorates in rhythm or form, don't continue an attempt to half pass. Work actively forward on a straight line in shoulder-in, or move forward in a circle. Then set the horse up to try again.

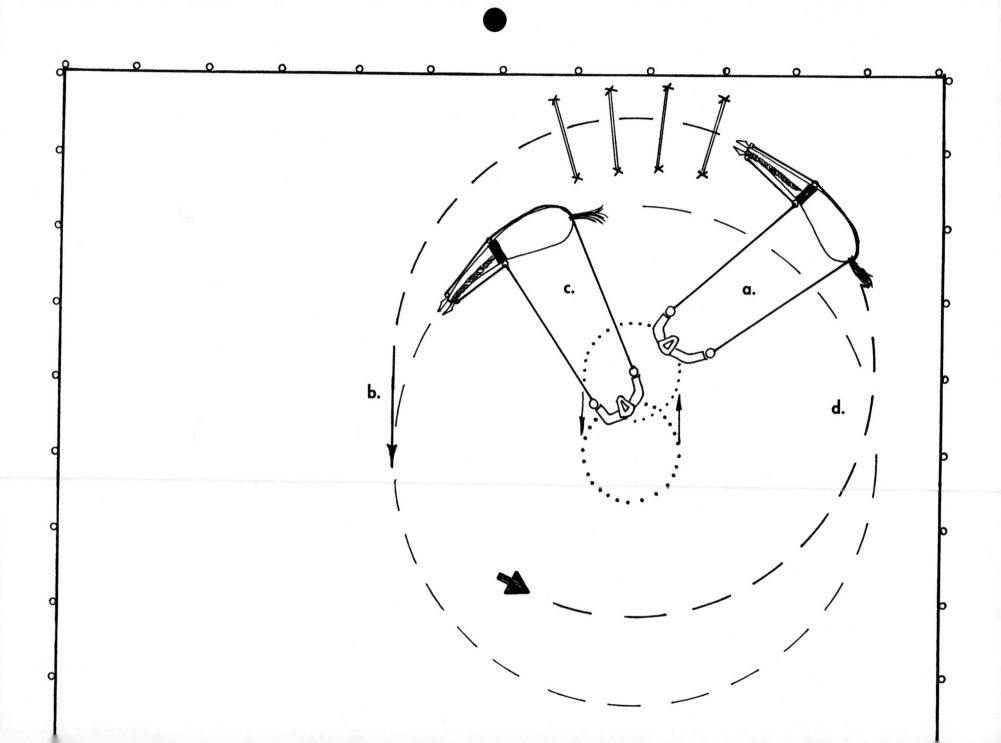

Exercise 97

Cavalletti on Circle

This exercise should not be performed in a round pen but rather in an arena. That way the cavalletti can be placed in an arc in one portion of the arena and worked only when desired. If rails are placed across the only track in a round pen, there is no way to avoid working them. You want to work a horse only once or twice over the poles before returning to regular circle work.

a. The outside line will help you keep the horse from ducking to the left to avoid working over the poles. There should only be enough contact on the inside line to prevent the horse from turning to the right. The horse should approach the center of the first pole. As you guide the horse over the cavalletti, be sure you don't get in front of his field of vision. If you need to carry a whip for impulsion, carry it in your right hand.

b. Drive the horse straight for a few strides to move him away from the circle that includes the poles and onto a new circle.

c. Work the horse on the new circle, varying his gaits until it is time to take him over the ground poles again.

d. Drive the horse straight for a few strides so he is back on the pole circle.

Cavalletti work improves stride length, balance, rhythm, sure-footedness, suppleness, and concentration on work. In addition, working over rails strengthens and develops the horse's neck and back muscles.

The work is conducted primarily at the trot, but begin at the walk until the horse is accustomed to the procedure. It is better to use cavalletti secured with X-shaped ends than to use ground poles that can easily be rolled by the horse. Cavalletti should be set at their lowest setting, about 6 inches. The footing should not be too deep; deep footing will alter the horse's movement.

Start with a single rail first. Then add two more rails, one on each side of the original rail. If you just add one, it could cause the horse to jump. As you add rails, the spacing will depend on the gait and the individual horse. Start with 2 feet 6 inches to 3 feet for the walk and 4 feet to 5 feet for the trot.

Measure the spacing accurately from the center of one pole to another.

Adjust the distance between the poles. Make them farther apart to lengthen the stride and develop the horse's extended gaits. Move them closer together to shorten the stride and develop the collected gaits.

Stride Check: If you are using four poles, remove the third pole to see whether the horse continues to regulate his stride.

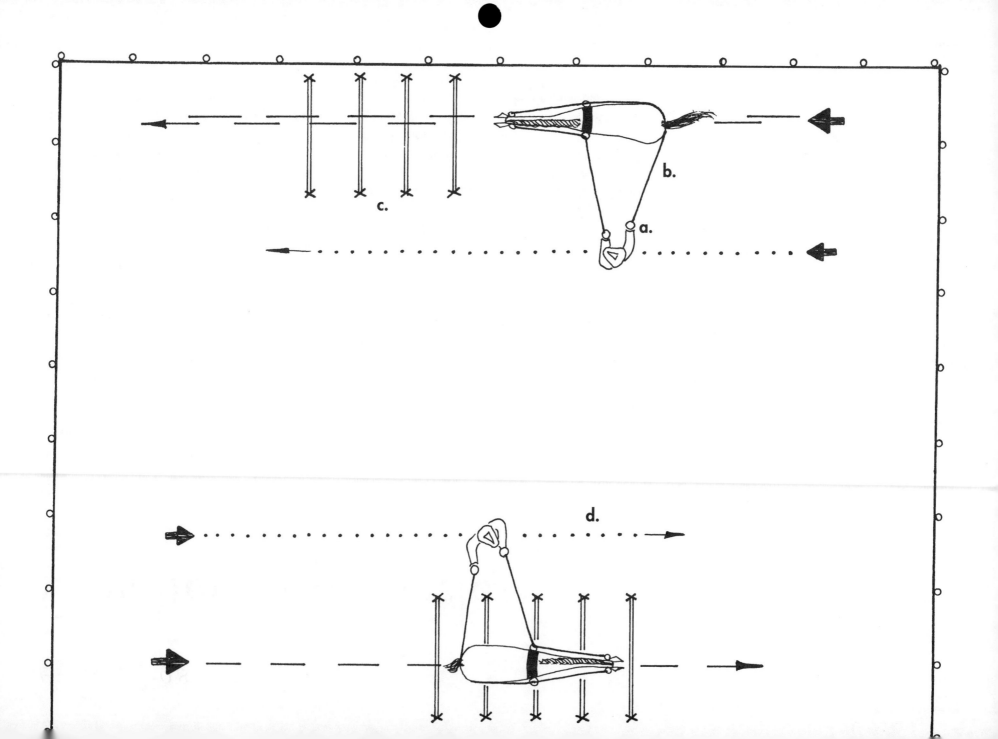

Exercise 98

Ground Poles

Negotiating ground poles is a mandatory obstacle in many horse show Trail classes. In the classes, the poles are set up as walk overs, trot overs, or lope overs. In some instances the poles are placed even distances from each other and sometimes they are radiated like spokes of a wheel.

A horse earns the most credit in the trail class if he negotiates the poles in the following manner:

- He looks where he is going, straight ahead and slightly down toward the ground.
- He approaches the exact center of the poles.
- He walks through the poles in a straight line.
- He steps in the middle of the space between the poles.
- He does not rub, tick, graze, roll, or stumble over any of the poles.
- He leaves the poles on a straight line.

To negotiate ground poles:

a. Work alongside your horse on about 6 feet of line. This will give you enough room so that you don't have to walk through the obstacle yourself, but you can walk on the outside edge of the poles.

b. The outside line will prevent the horse from ducking to the left.

c. The poles should be evenly spaced and set for the gait and the length of the horse's stride.

d. Take extra care that the horse's body remains absolutely straight as he passes through the poles. A deviation will likely cause him to rap a pole.

Approximate dimensions used in the horse show Trail class for an average-sized stock horse

Walk over Poles	20 to 24 inches between poles
Trot over Poles	3 feet to 3 feet 6 inches between poles
Lope over Poles	6 to 7 feet between poles

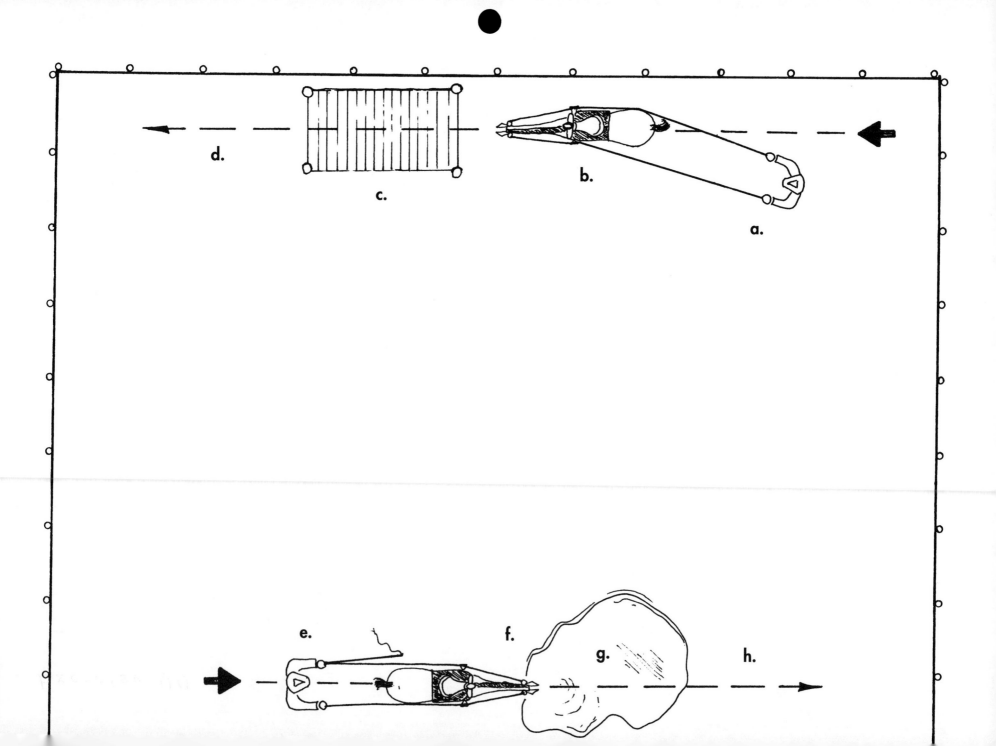

d.

c.

b.

a.

e.

f.

g.

h.

Exercise 99

Bridge and Water

To teach a horse to cross a bridge and a small body of water requires trust and confidence between trainer and horse. Uncertain footing poses a threat to a horse. He would like to see what he is stepping onto or into but just as he is about to do so, the object disappears into one of his blind spots just below his head. Before you long line a horse over a bridge or water, walk him over in-hand.

a. You can keep a horse lined up best by driving him from behind. If you can't see the front of the horse or where he is stepping, you might move a little bit off to one side or the other to get a better view.

b. When crossing a bridge, just as when negotiating poles, line up the horse so that his first step is dead center. Give the horse enough play in the lines so that he can stretch down a bit to take a look, but don't give him so much line that you lose him.

c. The bridge should be very sturdy and safe. It should be about 6 feet long (minimum) and no narrower than 36 inches. The sound that the horse will make when he steps on the bridge is likely to startle him, so be ready with soothing words and controlling aids from the lines.

d. Once across the bridge, make sure the horse tracks straight for at least a stride before you turn him. You might want to drift to his near side to turn left.

CROSSING WATER

Take advantage of the puddle that formed in your arena after the last downpour. It is a great time to teach your horse not to fear crossing water. You might want to walk the horse through the puddle in-hand at first. Be sure you wear tall rubber boots so you can splash through and show him there is nothing to fear. If you wear your good riding boots and leap over or dash through, he will be likely to model after your behavior.

A horse is unsure about the safety of stepping into water because he is incapable of visually determining the depth of the black hole before him. If he is allowed to put his head down just as he approaches the edge of the water, he can usually allay his fears. But if he is not allowed to do this, he will likely get as far as the front edge of the water, plant his feet, and balk with his head up. At that point the water is in one of his blind spots, directly below and in front of his head.

If you lead the horse over in-hand, first review some exercises in Part 1. Carry an in-hand whip to keep the horse moving forward next to you. When you are approaching the edge of the puddle, invite your horse to reach down and take a look. It's okay if he stops, as long as his nose is down and investigating. Pawing once or twice is okay. It's not okay if he starts violently pawing the water or backing or swerving sideways.

Once the horse has inspected the water, the next time you approach, just pick a point on the other side of the puddle, look at it, and go there. You want to keep the horse moving forward, using a light tap with the whip if necessary. Since you don't want him to bolt or rush through the water, you'll need to know your horse and mete out the proper incentive. If he starts to rush (which usually means he will be turning left and crossing your path), you will have to push him to the right and pull back on the lead rope.

e. When you first drive the horse through the water, walk behind him. If you carry a whip, in this example it would be in your left hand so you can keep the horse moving forward and contained to the right.

f. Let the horse lower his head to inspect the water as he approaches the edge.

g. A water obstacle should have solid, safe footing. It should not be excessively deep or mucky. Be sure you are wearing rubber boots because you will be walking through it too.

h. Be sure the horse tracks straight for at least one stride before you turn him. This will keep him from ducking out of the last part of an obstacle.

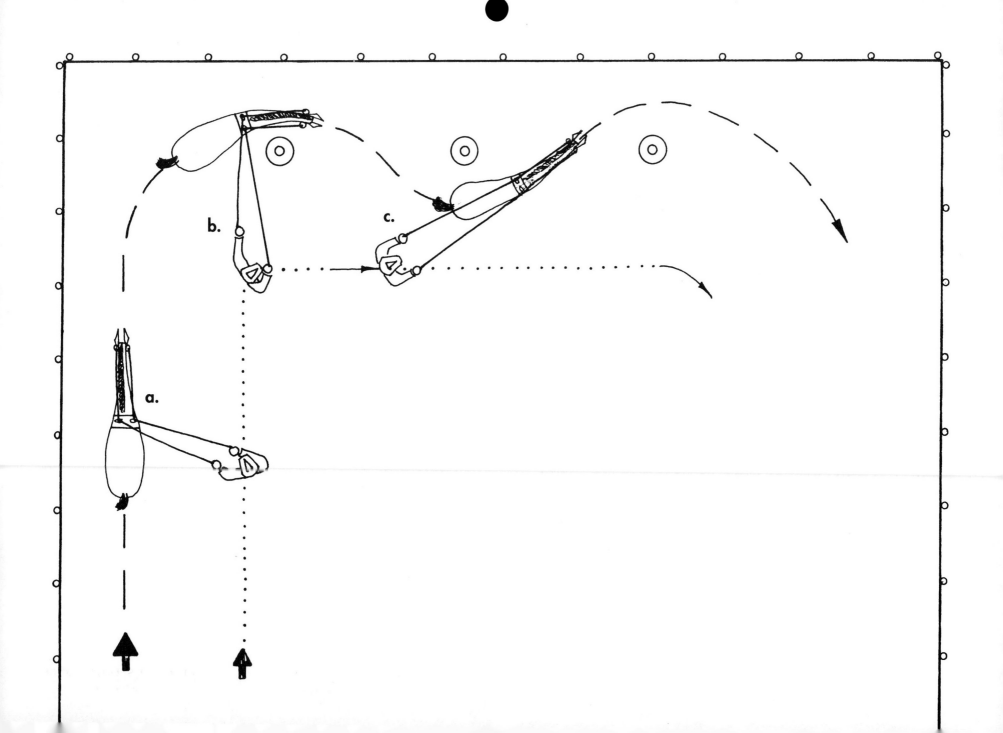

Exercise 100

Weaving Cones

Walking a horse through closely spaced cones further hones his bending and change of direction lesson that you started as shallow serpentines. I like to work this exercise strictly from the side. Using top terrets gives you the possibility of a finer, more instantaneous change of direction than running the lines longer and lower. You can also perform this exercise with the lines running through lower surcingle rings or the stirrups of a saddle, however.

Set up the cones with generous distance between them at first—maybe as much as 4 to 5 feet, depending on the size and skill of your horse. Eventually try to work the cones set 40 inches apart.

a. Work your horse from the off side on the straightaway.

b. Set up the cones so that you start them just after a corner. As you approach the corner, get ready to bend the horse to the right by taking with the right rein and giving with the left rein. Continue this set of aids around the first cone. When the horse's nose reaches the second cone it's time to reverse the aids for a left bend: a taking with the left line and a giving with the right line.

c. By the time the horse's hindquarters are even with the second cone, his body should be ending the left bend and changing to right bend. Your aids shift once again to a taking with the right line and a giving with the left line. This continues until you have negotiated all the cones. Five cones would be the maximum.

Note: In this type of very shallow serpentine, it is not necessary for you to cross behind the horse and change sides. You walk in a straight line and move the horse around the cones. With such a shallow change of bend, this is true whether the lines pass through top terrets or stirrups.

Visual goals such as cones are very beneficial for both the trainer and the horse.

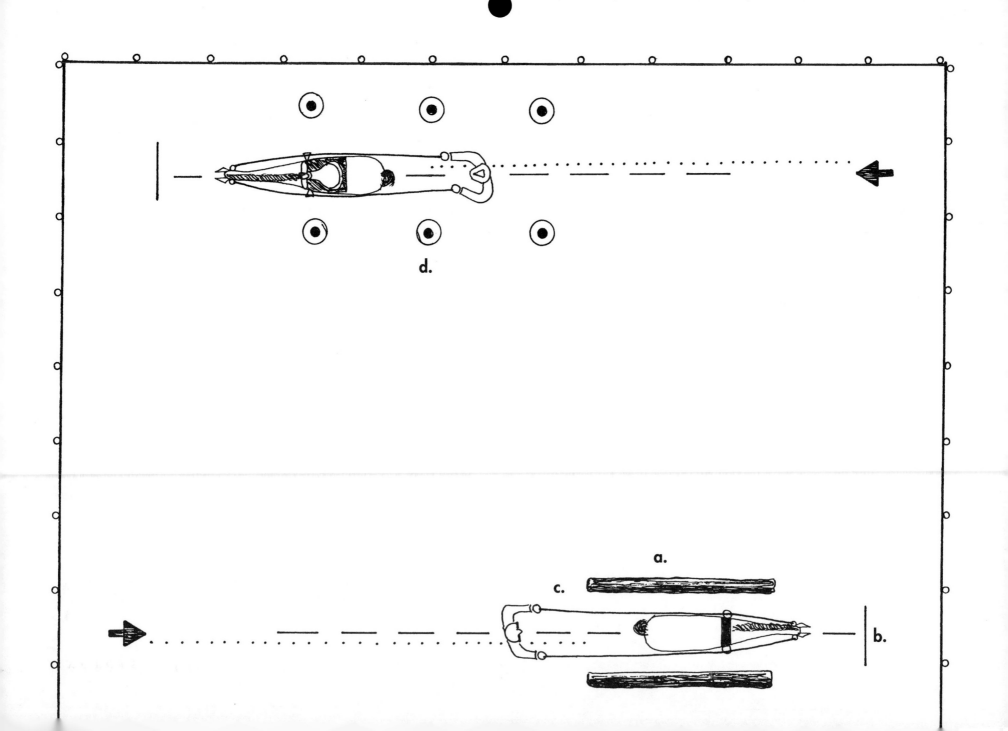

d.

a.

c.

b.

Exercise 101

Back Through

Sometimes, using obstacles will help a horse back up in a straight line. You can use cones, rails, railroad ties, straw bales, and other safe items.

Remember, the back is a two-beat diagonal gait in reverse, so the left hind and right front alternate with the right hind and left front. The diagonal pairs should flex, lift up crisply, and the toe of the hoof should not drag in the dirt.

Backing is best performed from the plow-driving position. The lines should run low, such as through the stirrups of a saddle. This will help keep the horse's topline rounded, his head low, and it will help ensure straightness in the maneuver.

Rein cues should be intermittent or vibrating pressure. Steady pressure leads to resistance.

a. Before you ask for a halt, be sure the horse is walking actively forward. Here he is being channeled between two heavy railroad ties. They should be spaced a minimum of 28 inches apart. To begin with, set them at about 3 feet.

b. Drive the horse up into a square halt (refer to Exercise 72).

c. Standing a safe distance behind your horse in the plow-driving position, hold the lines evenly in your hands. Using your voice command ("Baaaaack"), gently take with the left line and give with the right line. Alternate. Take with the right and give with the left. This is a slow, gentle motion, not a rough seesaw action.

Once the horse has backed out of the obstacle, immediately drive him forward and continue on through the obstacle.

d. Try the same exercise with small cones and see whether the horse does as well.